New Directions in Liability Law

New Directions in Liability Law

88-171

Proceedings of
The Academy of
Political Science

Volume 37
Number 1

ISSN 0065-0684

Edited by Walter Olson

The Academy of Political Science
In conjunction with the
Manhattan Institute for Policy Research

New York, 1988

We extend our thanks for financial support to Aetna Life & Casualty Foundation, the AT&T Foundation, the Broyhill Foundation, the Dana Foundation, General Dynamics Corporation, the Lounsbery Foundation, Monsanto Fund, the Moses Foundation, the Schultz Foundation, Sea-Land Corporation, Smith Richardson Foundation, the Starr Foundation, the Sunmark Foundation, and the Weyerhaeuser Company Foundation.

Contents

Preface

This volume attempts to explain the crisis in the American liability system, which took on dramatic dimensions in the late 1980s. Liability-insurance premiums for American business, when the insurance was available, multiplied in cost. Moreover, exclusions, exemptions, and increases in deductibles made insurance coverage less effective. The reaction in the business community was vocal, and all sides looked to the federal and state governments to deal with the crisis. The parties with an interest in the matter by no means agreed on the action to be taken. Indeed, the crisis has been explained in many ways by the various interested observers.

Some supporters of the current legal system have charged that the crisis is the result of collusive actions of the insurance industry. Their perspective is perhaps best exemplified in the action of eight state attorneys general who filed an antitrust suit in March 1988 against the leading insurance companies and trade associations in the liability-insurance business. Such critics think the crisis reflects problems within the insurance industry. They view the large increases in premiums and the simultaneous refusal to insure as the kinds of collusive behavior that the antitrust laws are meant to prohibit. Many critics of the industry also charge the insurance companies with poor management and investment strategies that have led to losses that the public is now being asked to cover.

Others have seen the problem as a part of the substantial growth that has taken place in the scope of liability under American tort law. For these critics of the system, the problem is that the widespread expansion of liability has driven up the cost of defending, settling, and paying tort claims. According to these observers, there have been too many cases of excessive jury awards, too much expansion of liability, and too much uncertainty in the exposure of American business. The liability crisis, for them, calls for fundamental changes in the way courts operate. Many of them think that the matter goes far beyond the liability-insurance crisis and adversely affects the United States's ability to compete in world markets. They have waged battles on many fronts — in legislatures, courts, and executive departments — to challenge some fundamental assumptions about the civil-justice system and to reverse the trend toward huge monetary judgments.

This volume represents an effort of the Academy of Political Science and the Manhattan Institute for Policy Research to contribute to the dialogue on liability law. The two organizations sponsored an all-day conference on 10 November 1987 at Columbia University, and many of the papers in this volume were presented at that conference. The volume was edited by Walter Olson of the Manhattan Institute, and we are grateful for his hard and able work in directing the project.

The Academy of Political Science was fortunate to have had the association of the Manhattan Institute and its president, William M.H. Hammett, in this effort. The Institute, founded in 1977 as a not-for-profit research foundation, underwrites books, conducts conferences, and holds forums in an effort to raise the level of public discourse on current policy issues. The Academy could not have had better associates in this or any other venture.

The views expressed in this volume are those of the authors and not necessarily those of any organizations with which they are associated. The Academy of Political Science, founded in 1880, serves as a forum for the development and dissemination of opinion on public-policy questions. A nonpartisan, not-for-profit organization, it does not make recommendations on political and social issues.

Finally, the Academy is grateful to William V. Farr for his editorial direction of this project and to Eric C. Banks and Ingrid Sterner for their editorial assistance.

FRANK J. MACCHIAROLA
President

Contributors

RICHARD L. ABEL, professor of law, University of California at Los Angeles, is the author of *American Lawyers* (forthcoming).

KENNETH S. ABRAHAM is professor of law, University of Virginia School of Law. He is the author of *Distributing Risk: Insurance, Legal Theory, and Public Policy.*

DOUGLAS J. BESHAROV is resident scholar, American Enterprise Institute for Public Policy Research, and adjunct professor of law, Georgetown University Law School and American University Law School. He is the author of *The Vulnerable Social Worker: Liability for Serving Children and Families.*

ROBERT COOTER is professor of law, University of California at Berkeley. He is the coauthor, with Tom Ulen, of *Law and Economics.*

MARC GALANTER, Evjue-Bascom Professor of Law and South Asian Studies, University of Wisconsin — Madison, is president, Law and Society Association. His most recent book is *Law and Society in Modern India.*

PETER HUBER, senior fellow, Manhattan Institute for Policy Research, is the author of *Liability: The Legal Revolution and Its Consequences.*

EDMUND W. KITCH is Joseph M. Hartfield Professor of Law, University of Virginia. He is the coauthor, with Paul Goldstein and Harvey Perlman, of *Selected Statutes and International Agreements on Unfair Competition, Trademarks, Copyrights and Patents.*

FRANK J. MACCHIAROLA, formerly chancellor of the New York City school system, is president and executive director, the Academy of Political Science, and professor of business law and taxation, Columbia University.

MICHAEL W. MCCONNELL is assistant professor of law, University of Chicago Law School, and formerly assistant to the solicitor general, U.S. Department of Justice.

JEFFREY O'CONNELL is John Allan Love Professor of Law, University of Virginia Law School. He is the coauthor, with C. Brian Kelly, of *The Blame Game: Injuries, Insurance & Injustice.*

WALTER OLSON, senior fellow, Manhattan Institute for Policy Research, is formerly associate editor, *Regulation.*

GEORGE L. PRIEST is John M. Olin Professor of Law and Economics, Yale Law School.

JEREMY RABKIN is assistant professor of government, Cornell University. He is the author of *Judicial Compulsions: How Public Law Distorts Public Policy* (forthcoming).

ROBERTA ROMANO is professor of law, Yale Law School and Yale School of Organization and Management.

AUSTIN SARAT, the William Nelson Cromwell Professor of Jurisprudence and Political Science, Amherst College, is coauthor, with Malcolm Feeley, of *The Policy Dilemma: Federal Crime Policy and the Law Enforcement Assistance Administration, 1968–1978.*

PETER H. SCHUCK, formerly deputy assistant for planning and evaluation, U.S. Department of Health, Education, and Welfare, is Simeon E. Baldwin Professor of Law, Yale University Law School. He is the author of *Agent Orange on Trial: Mass Toxic Disasters in the Courts.*

STEPHEN D. SUGARMAN is professor of law, University of California at Berkeley. He is coauthor, with Robert H. Mnookin et al., of *In the Interest of Children.*

W. KIP VISCUSI, George G. Allen Professor of Economics, Duke University, is the author of *Learning about Risk.*

The Liability Revolution

WALTER OLSON

Through most of American history, liability law has been an obscure legal byway, mostly involving traffic accidents and other local mishaps, with little discernible effect on the wider society or economy. That is no longer the case. "On almost all fronts and in almost all jurisdictions," as Peter H. Schuck writes in his essay in this volume, "liability has dramatically expanded." And the targets are mainly producers and service providers--manufacturers sued for product-related injuries, physicians and hospitals sued for malpractice, towns and counties sued for injuries in parks and playgrounds.

Why this rapid and unprecedented shift? At bottom is what Schuck calls "a change in the ideology that courts bring to tort law." Formerly, they searched for corrective justice between the two litigants; now they pursue broad social goals, such as "advancing public control of large-scale activities and altering the distribution of power."

These goals have enjoyed wide support in the legal academy. Some commentators dispute whether the shift in court goals has led to a "litigation explosion," or that such an explosion if it happened would necessarily be a bad thing. In his essay, Marc Galanter observes that today's rates of lawsuit-filing per capita may not exceed those in other times and places — colonial America, for example, or present-day Canada or Denmark. He notes that most potentially actionable injuries and troubles still do not give rise to litigation. Richard L. Abel and Austin Sarat build on similar themes in their essays, and Abel argues forcefully that the litigation revolution has not gone nearly far enough. Many victims remain unaware of their legal rights or are afraid of retaliation. They should be urged to press claims, not just so that they may gain compensation but also so that unsafe conduct may be deterred and producers punished for predatory behavior.

Accident data assembled by George L. Priest, on the other hand, indicate that the rise in litigation probably does not reflect a major rise in the underlying rate of physical injuries. And ultrastringent producer liability may not be a reliable way to reduce those injuries, the present writer argues in his essay. Overdeterrence of risks can drive away producers who do more good than harm. The resulting dangers of inaction are usually graver than the incidental hazards of productive action.

The other major goal of the expanded tort law, the provision of surrogate social insurance for injury victims, requires a smoothly working market for liability coverage. In 1985 and 1986 that market went through massive disruptions, and some critics demanded more regulation of the insurance industry. Kenneth S. Abraham's essay suggests that such measures are unlikely to counter the basic legal trends that drive up insurance costs — trends that, as Priest warns, may at some point prove inconsistent with the provision of insurance at any price.

Just as courts expand tort law to find liability where none was expected, so they stretch their reading of insurance policies to find coverage where none was contemplated. Roberta Romano shows how these efforts have backfired, reducing the availability of new coverage for the very groups of customers it was intended to help. A good example is the case of directors' and officers' (D&O) insurance, which protects managers from liability claims. Among the groups hardest hit by the D&O shortage and by the liability revolution in general are not-for-profits. The irony, as Frank J. Macchiarola points out, is that such groups, far from being "deep pockets," typically live from hand to mouth; the liability burden can impair their charitable or educational missions.

For readers interested in political science, liability law offers a dramatic, many-sided clash between governments — between state and federal authorities, between individual states, between judicial and executive branches, and even between nations. Most tort matters in the United States have historically been left to the states, and Edmund W. Kitch argues that the tradition is sound; federal intervention should be reserved for special cases. One such area may be product suits, which usually pit an in-state plaintiff against an out-of-state manufacturer. As Michael W. McConnell relates, trends in "choice-of-law" doctrine have tended to magnify the problem by allowing proplaintiff states to export their law to other states, whose own prodefendant laws may become a dead letter. When liability suits cross national boundaries, Douglas J. Besharov reports, the results are even more problematic. Foreign consumers have won large liability verdicts from United States manufacturers by suing in American courts. Yet American consumers injured by foreign products sometimes find no recourse under either domestic or foreign laws — while American businesses are doubly handicapped.

The federal government's own tort obligations might be expected to grow rapidly, writes Jeremy Rabkin, since it is "in a sense the deepest pocket of all" and well situated to prevent accidents through regulation. But the courts have been reluctant to breach long-standing limits on federal liability, Rabkin says, because of certain political realities that shed light on matters of private liability as well.

Injuries on the job account for much of the new litigation, and here the courts are venturing into areas long occupied by other branches of government: workers' compensation systems that provide financial sustenance to injured workers and agencies like the Occupational Safety and Health Administration (OSHA) that regulate workplace safety. The courts try to combine and extend the compensatory and the regulatory functions, argues W. Kip Viscusi, but as a result do both badly.

Liability law sometimes openly conflicts with safety regulation, as Peter Huber observes. Regulators may strike one balance between risks, but the next day a jury can hand down a verdict imposing a quite different balance. Courts condemn drugs as defective, for example, after federal regulators have specifically pronounced them beneficial and encouraged their use. To give local juries a veto on new technologies is to defeat the aim of a coherent public risk policy.

Some reformers propose to move away from the adversary aspects of the legal process toward mediation or arbitration of disputes. But as Austin Sarat points out, these categories can be rather vague, and ambiguities could lead to trouble in practice. Moreover, many disputants say they prefer the formal protections and "language of rights and principles" that courts provide; they would refuse "alternative dispute resolution" if given a choice.

A different way of avoiding litigation would be to settle disputes before accidents occur. Robert Cooter and Stephen D. Sugarman outline an imaginative plan under which potential victims could "presettle" claims with potential injurers, leaving both sides better off. Employers, which already provide health and disability benefits to most of the population, could help arrange such exchanges. Similar in concept but different in detail are Jeffrey O'Connell's proposals for "prompt payment for actual losses." New incentives could encourage defendants and plaintiffs to agree on early settlements covering measurable losses like hospital bills and lost wages but not intangibles like pain or fear.

As George Priest's concluding essay shows, most Americans already enjoy a good deal of economic protection against injuries, without help from liability awards. Health and disability plans now protect most Americans and grow more extensive every year. Thus, the idea of liability as a financial safety net may be fast becoming obsolete — and "new-tort" judges may have been fighting a battle that has already been won.

For all its far-reaching effects on society, the liability revolution has occurred without any real debate except among legal specialists. Legislation, regulation, and diplomacy are considered fit matters for public debate, but jurisprudence still arouses far too little discussion. Bringing these essays to a wider audience is one way to encourage informed citizens to take an interest in issues of judicial policy and to work for constructive change.

The New Judicial Ideology of Tort Law

PETER H. SCHUCK

The recent transformation of American tort law has attracted much attention, and with good reason. On almost all fronts and in almost all jurisdictions, liability has dramatically expanded. It does not seem to matter what kind of party is being sued. Doctor or public official, landlord or social host, government agency or product manufacturer – all are more likely to be held liable today.

Numerous legal doctrines reflect and reinforce this change. Courts have enlarged the concept of "action," a traditional prerequisite for liability, to encompass inaction. In this way, they have placed individuals under a legal duty to help strangers in many situations, thereby hauling new kinds of relationships (and nonrelationships) into the net of tort liability. They have accorded legal protection to new categories of interests, including emotional well-being, freedom from fear of cancer, and avoidance of unwanted children. They have extended the domain in time and space over which defendants' duties apply by imposing responsibility for risks that eventuate long after the defendant acted and, in some toxic-tort cases, for risks that were scientifically unknowable at that time. They have accepted relatively weak claims of causation, especially in drug, toxic-tort, and medical-malpractice cases, where proving cause and effect is often difficult. They have routinely ignored or overridden express contractual limitations on tort liability as well as implicit agreements by parties to allocate risk between themselves. They have abandoned or severely curtailed long-standing charitable, governmental, and familial immunities from tort liability.

Presumably, this expansion of liability will not continue indefinitely and without limit. Like other tides in human affairs, it will ebb as well as flow. Even so, one is struck by its duration. Tort scholars appear to agree that liability has expanded steadily since at least the late nineteenth century, when employers' traditional defenses to industrial-accident liability began to erode (even before the enactment of workers' compensation schemes). Some scholars argue that the trend toward wider liability may have begun much earlier in that century. Decisions like *Brown v. Kendall* (1850), which declared that, in general, liability could not be found without "fault," are an apparent exception to the trend. But Gary Schwartz and some other commentators have suggested that these decisions did not so much put new limits on liability as codify existing limits that had been concealed by earlier doctrines and practices.

Legislatures, of course, have occasionally sought to arrest this growth in certain areas; products liability and medical malpractice are obvious recent examples. But as the periodic crises in these insurance lines suggest, legislative intervention has seldom been effective in curbing the growth of liability. And at the same time, these legislatures have been busy expanding liability in other areas (as in the 1986 federal vaccine law) and in other ways (as in new laws authorizing courts to make defendants pay the attorney's fees of plaintiffs). In tort law, moreover, courts almost always have the last word, and that word has usually been *compensate*.

What accounts for this long phase of liability growth? The answer is not at all obvious. In many other areas of the law, after all, the courts oscillate between traditionalism and innovation, self-restraint and self-assertion, and other familiar antinomies. The emphasis in constitutional law, to take one example, has cycled between governmental interests and individual liberties, federal power and states' rights, broad and strict construction. In administrative law, one observes shifts from close judicial scrutiny of agency decisions to greater deference to administrative expertise, and then back to "hard looks." Even in private-law fields, such as domestic relations, legal evolution often seems to come full circle. Why has tort liability followed so straight a path, with its growth even accelerating in recent years?

Institutional developments have surely played an important role. The growth of private liability insurance, for example, has meant that more "deep pockets" are now available to satisfy judgments. But this explanation is plainly incomplete, for the expansion of insurance has also undercut the argument for compensation through the tort system. Prospective accident victims now purchase more of their own direct ("first-party") insurance against accident losses, and the government has established massive income-maintenance, disability, and health-insurance programs. Coverage is still far from complete, of course, but it is much more comprehensive today than ever before, even when compared with the far larger accident costs — wages, medical costs, pain and suffering, emotional harm, and third-party consortium claims — that the expansive tort law now makes compensable. In short, most accident victims would now be compensated for most of their economic losses even without having recourse to the extremely costly, protracted lottery known as the tort system.

Other explanations of a more sociological kind are equally unsatisfying. Community life in the United States is indeed fragmented, and strangers increasingly demand that tort law protect them from risks posed by people with whom they lack a relationship of trust or shared experience. But this development is also far from new. The anomie and individualism of American culture, deeply imprinted upon our law, impressed de Tocqueville more than a century before David Reisman dissected it in *The Lonely Crowd*. And even Reisman's lament antedated the dramatic liability expansion of recent years.

This essay will emphasize a different cause for the expansion of liability: a change in the ideology that courts bring to tort cases. The term *ideology* is not meant pejoratively here. It simply denotes a set of assumptions by contemporary judges that organize and render coherent their perceptions of legal reality. To furnish a fully satisfying account of this ideology, it would be necessary to trace the history of its principal ideas, the social forces that have shaped it, the functions it has served, and the personalities of the individual judges who have implemented it. Such a comprehensive account is well beyond the scope of this essay. For now, it is enough to identify the nature of this ideology, to examine how it leads to expanded liability, and to consider whether the tort law that it has spawned can satisfy its own normative criteria of legitimacy and effectiveness.

Although the new judicial ideology of tort law is complex and multifaceted, four elements stand out: (1) a profound skepticism about the role of markets in allocating risk; (2) a shift in the dominant paradigm of causation; (3) a tendency to broaden jury discretion; and (4) a preoccupation with achieving broad social goals instead of the narrower, more traditional purpose of corrective justice between the litigants. This last element entails a change in the conception of the judges' role that serves to link, legitimate, and effectuate the first three elements. Needless to say, some of these elements are further developed than others, and few courts have yet taken them as far as have the supreme courts of New Jersey and California (at least until the electoral defeat of several liberal justices in California in 1986). But anyone who has read a large sample of contemporary tort cases will recognize their importance.

Distrust of Markets

Judges' rulings, and occasionally their supporting rhetoric, bespeak increasing skepticism about both the efficiency and the justice of permitting the market to allocate risk. This is most apparent in cases arising from disputes over liability-insurance coverage. One might expect courts to defer to bargains explicitly concluded between insurers and their customers on what risks a policy will cover. Yet, as Kenneth Abraham has demonstrated, courts have devised numerous techniques to reshape or interpret insurance contracts so as to provide coverage of risks that the parties never agreed to shift.[1] Although this development has affected all areas of tort law, its implications are especially profound in mass-toxic-tort cases. A dramatic example occurred recently in the massive asbestos litigation pending in San Francisco. In that case, Judge Ira Brown ruled that in order to maximize the pool of funds available to compensate victims, all insurers who wrote policies over several decades would be liable for all injuries, regardless of whether any given risk came into being during any given policy period.[2]

In tort law proper, risk bargains are seldom as explicit as in insurance contracts, and judicial respect for them is correspondingly lower. The courts' skepticism is entirely warranted in many tort disputes in which it would have been prohibitively costly for the two sides to reach some agreement about risk—the classic example being the collision between total strangers on the highway. Such skepticism may even make sense in those cases, also common in tort law, in which the parties could in principle have bargained at low cost about risk but in which one of the parties is a "low-attention" decision maker, to use Howard Latin's phrase.

Courts' disregard for risk markets, however, now extends well beyond these kinds of situations. Increasingly, judges override market risk allocations even in those cases in which both parties are plainly "high-attention decision makers" who have already engaged in actual bargaining over the very sorts of risks that are at issue. Yet many of these decisions serve no evident purpose; they do not even promote a more progressive distribution of wealth.

The traditional approach to such cases is represented by a 1927 Supreme Court decision, *Robins Dry Dock and Repair Co.* v. *Flint*. The defendant, a dry dock, had negligently damaged a ship and rendered it unusable for a time. The plaintiff was not the owner of the ship but a third party who had chartered the vessel and was deprived of its use. The terms of the chartering agreement relieved the plaintiff of any hiring charges in case of such mishap but did not indemnify him for his lost profits, for which he proceeded to sue the dry dock in tort. Justice Oliver Wendell Holmes, Jr., rejected the claim, holding that even if the plaintiff might recover against the owner of the vessel, who might in turn recover against the dry dock, the dry dock owed no direct obligation to its customer's customer. Such an obligation, the Court reasoned, could arise only through contract.

Contrast this decision with the 1979 case of *J'Aire Corp.* v. *Gregory*, in which the California Supreme Court, confronted with roughly analogous facts, had no trouble imposing tort liability. A commercial tenant sued its landlord's contractor in tort for the profits it lost when the contractor negligently delayed completing repairs to the tenant's premises. Both parties had negotiated commercial contracts with the landlord; these contracts presumably took into account the risk to all sides of business interruption. The tenant was hardly without remedy, since he could have sued the landlord under the lease and may well have even had a direct contract remedy against the defendant as a third-party beneficiary of its promise to repair. For aught that appears, the parties were equally rich or poor and equally well- or ill-provided with insurance. Moreover, shifting the tenant's loss to the contractor in this situation might well be economically inefficient for two reasons. It may fail to establish incentives that minimize the costs of repair errors, since the landlord and tenant are best situated to allocate that risk between them, and it may require needless administrative outlays in the course of establishing tort liability.

The examples could easily be multiplied. In *Sprecher* v. *Adamson Cos.*, another California case, the court upheld a tort claim by the owner of an ocean-front home in Malibu against his uphill neighbor for failing to install a fence that might have prevented damage from a naturally occurring mud slide. The defendant did not cause the mud slide, the plaintiff could as readily and perhaps more cheaply have erected the fence, the prices of Malibu lots are bound to reflect such a common, notorious risk, and Malibu neighbors are remarkably well situated to allocate it among themselves justly and efficiently. Still, the court—rushing to the rescue of downhill members of the upper class—imposed liability. In yet another revealing group of cases, courts have overruled or seriously qualified the long-standing doctrine that prevented third-party investors from suing accountants for negligently preparing financial statements for client companies on which the investors relied to their detriment.

Decisions like these reflect what Grant Gilmore called "the death of contract."[3] Gilmore was referring to the courts' growing tendency to resolve contract disputes through principles drawn from tort law, with its relatively fluid legal obligations grounded in social goals, rather than from contract law, with its more structured rules grounded in the mutual consent of the parties. Gilmore's insight must now be extended to tort cases proper, where the courts are increasingly rejecting market risk allocations that would limit responsibility for accidental injuries.

New Causal Paradigms

A plaintiff cannot establish tort liability without proving two analytically distinct propositions. He must show that a particular act or omission is what caused his injury (the "determinate plaintiff" issue) and also that a particular defendant is the one responsible for that conduct (the "determinate defendant" issue). This two-step paradigm of causation, which has governed tort law from its inception, was traditionally grounded in turn on two interrelated ideas: a moral conception of how people are responsible for actions and a phenomenonological conception of how harmful consequences come about.

The moral conception, closely linked to the norm of corrective justice, emphasized the personal responsibility of each autonomous individual for his actions. A defendant, in this conception, was liable to a plaintiff only if that particular defendant was the agent of harm to that particular plaintiff, and the extent of responsibility determined the extent of liability. The phenomenological conception was based on an essentially Newtonian understanding of how events occur; it posited a set of mechanical relationships between things and events governed by general scientific laws, so that once the defendant's action was set in motion the plaintiff's harm followed in the same way that a moving billiard ball strikes another.

These linked conceptions, of course, did not always furnish satisfactory answers to causal questions in real-world cases; indeed, perhaps no issue has bedeviled tort scholars more than that of causation. But together, the conceptions set important normative and practical limits on tort liability. Recently, however, this traditional view of causation has been challenged by a competing paradigm premised on the contingent character of all phenomena and the inevitably probabilistic nature of all causal statements. This probabilistic view of causation is most salient in cases of mass exposure to toxic hazards, where it has eroded both the determinate-defendant and the determinate-plaintiff requirements.

The effect on the determinate-defendant rule is illustrated by the well-known 1980 case of *Sindell* v. *Abbott Laboratories*. Women whose mothers had taken diethylstilbestrol (DES) during pregnancy brought a class action against eleven DES manufacturers alleging that the drug caused their vaginal cancers. The plaintiffs could not identify which particular firms had manufactured the DES that each of their mothers had taken. But the California Supreme Court nonetheless permitted their claims to go forward. Liability, the court held, could be found if the defendants' products were interchangeable and companies with a "substantial share" of the DES market were before the court as defendants. Under the court's "market share" approach, each defendant's share of liability for the plaintiff's injuries would be determined by its original share of total industry production of the drug; hence its liability would be based on the probability that its product injured a particular plaintiff, even though it might not actually have done so. This approach plainly attenuates the determinate-defendant requirement. Indeed, it may even eliminate the requirement in some cases, for it means that a manufacturer can be liable to a plaintiff who never even used its products.

In mass-exposure cases, probabilistic causation also threatens to overthrow the traditional determinate-plaintiff limit on liability. The *Agent Orange* case, a class action on behalf of 2.2 million veterans exposed to dioxin in Vietnam, demonstrates this development.[4] The causal issue in *Agent Orange* was muddied by the presence not only of indeterminate defendants (because various manufacturers' products had been mixed before being used) but also of indeterminate plaintiffs (because the veterans' symptoms could have had many causes other than exposure to the defendants' products). In approving a class-action settlement, Judge Jack Weinstein endorsed an ensemble of innovations that could vastly enlarge tort liability in indeterminate-plaintiff cases, including the use of class actions in mass-exposure cases; the use of epidemiological and other statistical evidence rather than "particularistic" evidence to establish causation; and proportional liability for defendants that create any "excess risk" above background levels, however small. (The traditional threshold for liability is creation of a risk that is more probable than not, that is, greater than 50 percent).

These innovations fit comfortably into what a leading proponent, David Rosenberg, has called a "public law vision of the tort system."[5] It is far too early, of course, to declare a full victory. The recent appellate court decision in *Agent Orange*, while essentially affirming Weinstein's rulings, casts serious doubt on future use of the class-action device in most cases of this kind, although that device would seem essential if epidemiological evidence and the concept of probabilistic causation are to be brought to bear in mass tort cases.

Still, these developments, along with some parallel changes in the legislative arena, such as (at the federal level) the National Childhood Vaccine Injury Act of 1986, place enormous pressure on the traditional view of causation. They may prefigure a fundamental shift in the ruling paradigms not only of causation but also of tort law itself. Tort law is abandoning its individualistic grounding and groping toward a more collective one. Increasingly, it treats the parties less as idiosyncratic actors than as relatively interchangeable units within large, impersonal aggregations, and their actions or injuries less as discrete occurrences than as statistical events within broadly defined classes and epidemiological populations.

The Empowerment of Juries

The American jury evokes the mythic symbols of democracy and the living law. It is viewed, especially in tort cases, as the repository of yeoman virtues, community norms, intuitive justice, and common sense. But juries are prone to certain dangers. Their natural sympathies for the unfortunates who come before them can offend the principle of a justice blind to contingencies of wealth or status. Juries, moreover, are neither learned in the law nor elected to legislate. Their proper role is to find facts and apply existing norms, not to discern or make law in a quest for a more just society.

In principle, at least, judges control juries by making procedural and evidentiary rulings and formulating the substantive law that juries are to apply. Rising judicial caseloads, along with recent concerns about the threat that juries can pose to constitutional values, have intensified pressures to fortify these controls. In the *Agent Orange* case, Judge Weinstein granted summary judgment despite conflicts in expert medical testimony on the all-important issue of causation. In three different 1986 cases — *Celotex Corp.* v. *Catrett, Anderson* v. *Liberty Lobby, Inc.*, and *Matsushita Electric Industrial Co., Ltd.* v. *Zenith Radio Corp.*— the Supreme Court urged lower courts to grant summary judgment more liberally on matters ranging from defamation to antitrust.

But in tort cases, at least, this restraint on juries is blunted, neutralized, and sometimes overborne by powerful forces working to broaden their role. Perhaps the most important of these countervailing forces is the relative ambiguity of most of the substantive rules of tort law. Standards based on "reasonableness" are common in many areas of modern law, of course, but tort law's "featureless generality" (as Holmes once described it)[6] — especially its "reasonable person" negligence standard — probably surpasses that in any other field.

This generality, moreover, is unlikely to diminish in the future. Statutes are only seldom used to define standards of care and even then are rarely binding on juries. Dogged efforts by judges and legal scholars to make tort norms more specific and outcomes more determinate will always be confounded by the factual richness and diversity of the circumstances under which tort disputes arise. In practice, then, tort juries not only find the facts but also supply the normative standards for interpreting and applying them. Juries' latitude has always been great in the United States, but it is steadily growing as judges employ it for broader social purposes. As tort law seeks to regulate relationships and interactions whose value conflicts are harder to resolve, with consequences that are harder to predict, even the most elaborate and refined doctrinal tools are useless unless the jury can answer the kinds of questions that courts now put to it. Those questions, however, often turn out to be intractable.

We can glimpse this dynamic at work in the well-known case of *Barker* v. *Lull Engineering Co.* (1978), in which the California Supreme Court tried to define the concept of "design defect" in products-liability cases through a two-part test. One part of that test requires the jury to decide whether "the risk of danger inherent in the challenged design outweighs the benefits of such design." In applying that standard, the jury is to "consider, among other relevant factors, the gravity of the danger posed by the challenged design, the likelihood that such danger would occur, the mechanical feasibility of a safer alternative design, the financial cost of an improved design, and the adverse consequences to the product and to the consumer that would result from an alternative design."

For present purposes, it is irrelevant whether these are the "right" questions for the law to ask or whether a jury could ever undertake the kind of analysis that would be necessary to address them responsibly and answer them competently. The point is that beneath most of today's innovative legal doctrines lies a broad set of ultimate, policy-laden factual issues that a jury must resolve if the doctrine is to be applied at all. *Barker* is not an isolated example; throughout contemporary tort law, especially (but not only) in toxic-tort cases, courts are busy elaborating new doctrines that pose questions of similar complexity and policy significance for the jury. By multiplying the occasions that call for jury discretion, these doctrines further empower the jury.

In *Rowland* v. *Christian* (1968), another California Supreme Court decision that has been followed in other states, the court abandoned the traditional method of evaluating the claims of people injured while on another person's land. Over the course of centuries, judges had used this method to clarify the rights and obligations of landowners and their visitors through rules that limited jury discretion and produced relatively predictable outcomes. In *Rowland*, the court jettisoned this familiar structure, substituting a new legal regime of broad jury discretion. Under this approach, landowners' obligations to persons injured on their property are now decided by juries on a case-by-case basis under a "reasonableness" standard without any meaningful guidance from the courts.

But the relation between expansive new tort doctrines and jury empowerment may run both ways. It may be that jury discretion not only follows but also *generates* the judicial innovations that expand liability. Today's judges often seem to use the jury as a kind of deus ex machina to relieve themselves of troublesome responsibilities, doubts, and anxieties. Judges themselves can feel freer to innovate, secure in the knowledge that it will be up to anonymous jurors to determine the concrete meaning and consequences of new doctrines.

Jurors thus serve as a buffer that insulates judges from full responsibility for what happens when their doctrinal creations get implemented. By tradition, the jury is expected to be a "black box": explanation of how it reached its decision is not even permitted (except informally, after the case is over). This lack of accountability encourages judicial irresponsibility (in this special sense). Consider an analogy: if it were somehow made easier for men to conceal their paternity, they would presumably father more children — at least until the children's mothers took a stand. Similarly, when the cost to judges of innovating goes down, it is not surprising that they engage in more of it — at least until legislatures catch on.

If this is so, then an interesting paradox follows. Courts often invoke the principle of cost internalization to justify their expansion of enterprise liability. But the very same courts fail to apply that principle to the judicial enterprise itself. By relying on the opacity of jury verdicts, judges can externalize the error and administrative costs of innovative, liability-expanding doctrines to the parties and the social system as a whole. Any remaining inhibitions about innovation are further reduced by judges' near-absolute immunity from liability for their errors.[7] The paternity analogy suggests that many of the judicial progeny spawned by this incentive structure will be illegitimate.

Changing Legal Purposes

From the earliest days of the common law, judges have given thought to how their decisions will affect the larger society outside the courtroom. Sometimes their decisions have invoked explicit social purposes, especially the deterrence of risky behavior. An emphasis on compensating injured persons is also nothing new; it is central to any justification of tort law. Nevertheless, liability law was traditionally and preeminently the domain of corrective justice, which required a wrongdoer to return to a victim what he had "taken." This conception encouraged courts to view tort cases as essentially isolated disputes in which the law's role was simply to allocate losses between two (or a few) injurers and victims. The court could readily adjudicate such disputes by eliciting from the parties relatively simple, comprehensible accounts of past events. And because the ultimate decision owed much to the specific facts and was not explained by the jury, it rarely constituted much of a precedent for other cases.

Today, in contrast, the law books abound with tort cases that affect not a few individuals but great aggregations of people and vast economic and social interests. The decisions in these cases are preoccupied not with meting out corrective justice between individuals based on their past interactions but with advancing public control of large-scale activities and altering the distribution of power and the nature of social values. In such cases, the parties are often little more than quaint anachronisms, mere placeholders for these larger social interests. Even in conventional tort cases, judges and juries increasingly act (and view themselves) as risk regulators, cost-benefit analysts, and social problem-solvers rather than as adjudicators of isolated, morally self-contained disputes.

This shift toward a more functional view of tort law derives in part from a heightened concern for the goal of compensating victims in an era of soaring medical costs, high litigation fees, and extended life expectancies, and from institutional changes, such as the spread of liability insurance, that appear to make compensation more feasible. But the shift goes further. As George Priest has shown, many other functional concepts — enterprise liability, risk-spreading, deterrence through cost internalization, and incentives to produce information — have moved to the center of discussions of private tort law by contemporary judges, scholars, and litigants.[8] Administrative efficiency, another functional goal, dominates analysis of the mass-exposure cases involving asbestos, dioxin, and DES. The same goals animate most of the proposals for legislative tort reform.

The new functionalism, in supplanting the old corrective-justice ideology, has not simply changed how parties litigate tort cases and how judges and juries rationalize their decisions. It has also altered the outcome of cases, systematically enlarging the scope of tort liability. Indeed, courts (and most tort scholars) cite each policy goal as a reason to expand liability; ironically, even administrative efficiency, certainly tort law's weakest suit, has been invoked in this case, to justify abandoning negligence rules in favor of strict liability.

The courts have striven to integrate the discrete elements of the new ideology — skepticism about markets, a stochastic view of causal responsibility, broad jury discretion, and a shift to functionalism — into an intelligible, morally compelling worldview in which judges play a central policy role. Most of the courts' justificatory techniques are familiar and not particularly noteworthy. In tort cases, as in others, judges continue to reshape legal doctrine through the repertoire of methods sanctioned by a millennium of the common law. They reclassify legal categories and issues, invoke "changed conditions," choose among competing analogies, select the level of generality at which to characterize facts, carve out and widen some exceptions to rules while narrowing or abolishing others, shift burdens of proof, alter procedural settings, devise new remedies, and regulate juries. Although the case names may have changed, the techniques of judicial lawmaking and law-applying have not.

What *has* changed dramatically is the courts' conception of their own place in the ongoing business of government. Traditionally, judges tended to view themselves as adjudicators who effected legal change incrementally through the slow accretion of precedents, moving in directions that were often discernible only in hindsight. Of course, there were always exceptions, judges like Colin Blackburn, Lemuel Shaw, and Benjamin Cardozo, who did not shrink from using individual tort cases to propel the law toward one policy goal or another. But even these exceptional judges felt constrained to conceal their instrumentalism by paying conspicuous obeisance to the normative premises of the common law: the rule of *stare decisis*, the discipline of particularized facts, the obligation to defer to the legislature, and the strong presumption in favor of private ordering. They invoked these pieties even as they flagrantly and creatively violated them.

Today both the pretense and the underlying reality have changed. Not only legal innovators like Roger Traynor and Jack Weinstein but also ordinary, standard-issue judges increasingly regard themselves not simply as logicians and case analysts in the small but as rationalists and systems analysts in the large. They have become less principle-oriented and more goal-oriented.

The signs of this change can be found in almost any sample of modern tort decisions. The court's opinion usually begins with a perfunctory bow to traditional legal categories and distinctions, followed by a critique of these distinctions as "wooden" or "formalistic." The court then explains why the precedents do not ordain any particular decision in this case, leaving it free to choose the "best" rule. From that point on, instrumental rationality is the mode of analysis: the court identifies the relevant social goals (the current favorites are compensation, deterrence through cost internalization, and loss-spreading), assesses how well these goals would fare under alternative legal rules, and finally selects the optimal one.

In these opinions, certain rhetorical features often recur. Plausible arguments, general assertions, and profuse footnoting take the place of hard empirical evidence. The court couples facile conclusions about the perversity of the existing rule with heroic predictions about the excellent effects of the rule being adopted. It characterizes the facts of the case abstractly enough to support broad, rulelike decisions. It further enlarges its discretion by assuming that unless the legislature has spoken to an issue with unmistakable clarity, the court is on its own. It proceeds as if private behavior were infinitely plastic, easily molded by legal rules into new, more functional forms.

Contemporary tort decisions are almost wholly benefit-oriented. Although they often read like a government agency's policy memorandums, they seldom address the kinds of questions about the costs of legal change that would preoccupy any self-respecting policy analyst. It is the rare tort decision, for example, that takes seriously such matters as the opportunity cost of adopting a particular rule; the institutional barriers to its implementation; the rule's secondary and tertiary consequences; the strategies people will use to evade it; the costs of administering it; the competence of juries to comprehend and apply it; the effects it will have on insurance markets; or its implications for more elusive, difficult-to-measure values like innovation, diversity of choice, and political accountability.

In ignoring or only casually touching on these questions, judges are no worse than most of the professors who train their law clerks and the legislators who write the statutes. Judges are often like architects who are instructed to design a splendid, state-of-the-art edifice but are also told not to worry too much about budget because the money will be found somehow. When that is the case, it is perhaps not surprising that they come up with the juridical equivalent of Washington's Rayburn Office Building.

The problem with all this is not that the new functionalism fails to advance some of its goals all of the time and all of them some of the time. It does both. Thus, it succeeds in compensating victims—at least that tiny subset who are fortunate enough to be injured by negligent, fully insured defendants and can gain access to the tort system. And it deters some risk—at least that small subset of activities that is affected by tort-law incentives. In many cases, the functional approach may well be superior to what preceded it. This is true if today's judges get the rule "righter" than their predecessors or if the rule that "defendant is almost always liable" is so much clearer than the "reasonable person" standard that people can more easily plan and bargain around it. But any gains of this kind have been purchased at an enormous price in sheer administrative cost. And the real question remains: Do functionalist courts achieve anything approaching the right mix of social goals under the present system?

Moving Beyond the New Ideology

Policy making in this complex world is problematic, regardless of how it is organized institutionally. The real choice is between better and worse ways of structuring it. But whatever the wisdom or efficacy of the court's central role in allocating the costs of accidents, its *legitimacy* cannot really be doubted. Tort law has always been preeminently a field in which judges initially devise common-law principles to which the politicians then react. All that legislators need in order to have their way is a willingness to take political responsibility for the change. They may control judicial rulings by substituting different principles or by establishing administrative regimes to supplant or supplement the common law. But if past is prologue, they will usually acquiesce in the judicial innovation; future legislative interventions will be confined to a few areas and will not much disturb the central corpus of judicially created tort law.

Even if "liability-insurance crises" did not periodically erupt, however, there would be ample reason to doubt that tort litigation is a good vehicle for deciding how to distribute risks in society. These doubts remain even (or especially) when one asks the essential question: "Compared to what?" The defects of legislatures and administrative agencies have been demonstrated in great detail. But even a brief comparison of the courts' policy-making capacities with those of legislatures and agencies indicates the severe limitations on courts' competence to perform the kind of policy making to which their new ideology of tort law commits them. The most important comparisons can be grouped under three headings: organizational expertise and rationality, success in implementation, and political responsiveness.

Judges are trained as generalist lawyers (usually as litigators), not as policy specialists. They are unlikely to acquire, or know how to exploit, the kinds of information that a competent policy analysis requires. Few litigants possess the resources needed to adduce this information, and most lack adequate motivation to do so as well, such information being in the nature of a public good and often marginal (or harmful) to their cause. Only a fraction of the many social interests affected by a legal rule are represented by the parties before the court, and the relatively few tort cases that reach trial are likely to be unrepresentative of the social reality that a policy must address.

Finally, courts lack any reliable way to obtain feedback on their policies' real-world effects. They must depend for fresh information on the particular litigants and disputes that happen to come to their courtrooms, and case number two is a vehicle for policy change only if it raises the same policy issues as case number one but manages to adduce better data for decision. Even if the precedent can simply be distinguished, disregarded, or overruled, a court that realizes it has erred may have to wait for a properly framed new case to come along before changing course.

Perhaps most inimical to a sound policy-making framework are the deep structures of tort law — its vestigial moralism, its adversarial, party-centered control of litigation, its radical decentralization and nonaccountability, its glacial accumulation of precedents, its factual diversity and particularity, and its view of problems only in hindsight, transfixed by palpable human suffering. For the new functionalism to reject most of these features is for it to deform tort law into something very different.

Even if courts could readily determine the correct social policy for distributing risk, they would be hard put to implement that policy. The relatively few policy instruments they possess tend to be weak, inflexible, or both. In tort cases, their principal tools are general prohibitions enforced by money damages. With the exception of nuisance cases, all they can do is order A to pay B a prescribed sum of money for breaking a rule. Leaving aside certain cases in which government is the defendant, they cannot impose fines or taxes, subsidize, educate, reorganize, inform, hire, fire, insure, establish bureaucracies, build political coalitions, or coerce third parties. The damage remedy they can deploy is undeniably important in shaping some kinds of behavior, but it affects quite a narrow band on the broad spectrum of human motivation.

The need to decide cases on principled grounds also limits courts' ability to implement even sound policy intuitions. When modern courts abandon the traditional regime of contributory negligence, for example, they nearly always feel constrained to adopt the alternative approach of "pure" comparative fault, which can be derived from general tort principles, rather than any of a number of "modified" approaches that might make better policy but would require the court to select arbitrary cut-off points. Legislatures that enact reforms in this area, by contrast, virtually always choose "modified" systems.[9]

Courts have one significant advantage: they can ordinarily count on strong political support from the public. As institutions, they enjoy greater respect than markets, legislatures, or most bureaucracies inside or outside government. But adherents of the new tort ideology should not take too much comfort from this public support. It is probably more a vestige of what courts traditionally did than a tribute to what they are now attempting to do. In fact, the tasks of legislatures and agencies are generally more intellectually demanding, more politically sensitive, and harder to implement than the traditional functions of courts in resolving tort claims. It should come as no surprise, then, that the other governing institutions have seemed to fail while courts remain popular, for they are playing very different games by altogether different rules. As courts increasingly assume the more comprehensive and problematic tasks that their new ideology thrusts upon them, and as the public learns more about how effectively they perform them, one may expect their failure rate — and the general level of public disappointment in them — to rise as well.

Notes

1. Kenneth Abraham, *Distributing Risk: Insurance, Legal Theory, and Public Policy* (New Haven: Yale University Press, 1986).
2. Asbestos Insurance Coverage Cases, Judicial Council Coordinating Proceeding No. 1072, Superior Court, San Francisco County (29 May 1987).
3. Grant Gilmore, *The Death of Contract* (Columbus: Ohio State University Press, 1974).
4. Peter H. Schuck, *Agent Orange on Trial: Mass Toxic Disasters in the Courts*, enl. ed. (Cambridge: Belknap/Harvard University Press, 1987).
5. See David Rosenberg, "The Causal Connection in Mass Exposure Cases: A 'Public Law' Vision of the Tort System," *Harvard Law Review* 97 (1984): 849–929.
6. Oliver W. Holmes, Jr., *The Common Law* (Boston: Little, Brown & Co., 1881), 111.

7. Schuck, *Suing Government: Citizen Remedies for Official Wrongs* (New Haven: Yale University Press, 1983), 90–91.

8. George Priest, "The Invention of Enterprise Liability: A Critical History of the Intellectual Foundations of Modern Tort Law," *Journal of Legal Studies* 14 (1985): 461–527; idem., "The Current Insurance Crisis and Modern Tort Law," *Yale Law Journal* 96 (1987): 1521–90.

9. See Marc Franklin and Robert Rabin, *Tort Law and Alternatives: Cases and Materials*, 4th ed. (Mineola, N.Y.: Foundation Press, 1987), 381–82.

Beyond the Litigation Panic

MARC GALANTER

For the past decade there have been growing complaints that American society has suffered a hypertrophy of its legal institutions. It has become a commonplace that the United States is the most litigious country on earth, indeed in human history. An obsessively contentious population, egged on by an intrusive activist judiciary, is said to be enthralled with adversary combat. As the volume of law, lawyers, and lawsuits has risen, there is said to have been a concomitant erosion of self-reliance, of the sense of community, and of the informal mechanisms by which society once regulated itself. The excessive resort to law, in short, is said to threaten not just needless expense but also moral decline and far-reaching political and economic ills.

The Meaning of Higher Caseloads

The core observation that supports the "litigation explosion," or "hyperlexis," reading of contemporary American life is that Americans are bringing lawsuits at an unprecedented rate. Per-capita rates of filing civil cases have risen in most localities in recent decades. But these rates are only a surrogate measure for the propensity to litigate. Presumably, such a propensity depends on the proportion of occasions — troubles, injuries, problems, claims, or however one characterizes instances of possible litigation — that do lead to filings. Population is only a crude measure of the volume of such troubles and disputes.

Cases that wind up in court can be seen as the apex of a vast and uneven pyramid, whose base is formed by all human experience that might be identified as injurious. Many injuries (by any account) go unperceived. Of those that are perceived, some are attributed to deserved punishment, assumed risk, or fickle fate. Some, however, will be viewed as violations of some right or entitlement, caused by a human agent (individual or collective) and susceptible of remedy. Some victims "lump it" rather than complain. Other victims voice claims to the offending party. Some of these claims are granted; those that are not become disputes. Such disputes may be pursued in the social setting where the dispute arose (e.g., workplace, school) or in some other forum. Some disputes are taken to lawyers, and some of these are filed in courts. At every stage along the way, disputes may be abandoned or settled.

Since there are no data on how the lower layers of the dispute pyramid have changed over time, one cannot compute changes in the rate at which troubles become disputes or disputes become lawsuits. Before the recent increases are taken as proof of runaway litigiousness, it should be noted that these rates are not historically unprecedented. Several studies document higher per-capita rates of civil litigation in nineteenth- and early twentieth-century America. It appears that rates of recourse to courts were even higher in colonial America.

More than 98 percent of all civil cases are filed in the state courts. Hence any major rise in the propensity to litigate should be detectable in the caseload trends in those courts. But until recently comprehensive and reliable data on state court caseload trends have been unavailable. The National Center for State Courts (NCSC) has recently produced the best profile so far available of state caseload trends, covering a number of states for the years 1978 to 1984, as summarized in table 1. The litigation-explosion view would lead one to expect this to be a period of steeply rising caseloads. But the NCSC figures, based on all courts that reported comparable data for the years 1978, 1981, and 1984, portray nothing that resembles the supposed explosion. Filings of civil cases surged faster than population from 1978 to 1981, but from 1981 to 1984, when litigation-explosion lore would have litigiousness intensifying, per-capita rates of filing actually declined. During this period, filings in small-claims courts — the courts most readily accessible to ordinary Americans — also fell. Tort filings rose steadily, but over the

TABLE 1

Percentage Changes, Population and State Court Filings, 1978–84

Type of Cases	3-Year Period 1978 to 1981 Population/Filings		3-Year Period 1981 to 1984 Population Filings		6-Year Period 1978 to 1984 Population Filings		Base (Number of courts reporting comparable data for all 3 years)
Total of torts, contracts, real property	+3%	+14%	+3%	− 4%	+5%	+ 9%	29 courts in 20 states
Torts	+4%	+ 2%	+4%	+ 7%	+8%	+ 9%	17 courts in 13 states
Contracts	+5%	+14%	+4%	−15%	+9%	− 4%	11 courts in 10 states
Small claims	+2%	+18%	+2%	− 6%	+4%	+11%	29 courts in 25 states

Source: National Center for State Courts, Court Statistics and Information Management Project, *State Court Caseload Statistics:* Annual Report 1984, part II (1986), pp. 177, 181, 184, 186.

six-year period they grew by 9 percent, while population grew by 8 percent. In the 1981–84 period, tort data were available for nineteen courts. In five of these courts filings increased significantly faster than population, while in eight of them filings actually decreased.

This evidence does not suggest that current American rates of civil litigation are dramatically higher than in the recent past. Nor is it the case that American rates are unmatched in other industrial countries. Many advanced countries have much lower rates of litigation, but per-capita use of the courts appears to be in the same range in Canada, Australia, New Zealand, England, Denmark, and Israel as in the United States.

Filings are not an entirely satisfying measure of litigiousness. Since it is plaintiffs who file, one tends to think of filing as measuring plaintiffs' propensity to sue. But it is well known that most disputes are resolved without filings. A filing represents not only a claim but a refusal by the defendant to satisfy it. Thus, changes in the rate of filing may represent changes not only in plaintiff propensity to claim but also in defendant propensity to resist. Or changes in filing may mark changes in the local legal culture — for example, a growing tendency not to begin serious negotiations until a case has been filed. In other words, there is no assurance that a filing represents the same stage of a dispute from one place or time to another.

Filings in the Federal Courts

Although only a small fraction of all American litigation takes place in the federal courts, there are several reasons for focusing on those courts in assessing current trends. First, information on federal courts is more comprehensive and continuous than on state courts. Second, figures on federal courts are frequently cited as proof of runaway litigiousness. Third, the recent rise in filings has been more dramatic in federal than in state courts. During the six-year period 1978–84, in which civil filings increased 9 percent in state courts, they increased 88 percent in federal courts. Thus, if there are portents of doom in the filing statistics, they ought to be discernible there. Finally, federal court litigation involves higher-status actors and is more visible to and through the media, so the portion of the symbolic public space it occupies is far larger than its share of the total caseload.

Taking 1975 as a convenient baseline, table 2 shows a striking 122 percent increase in filings over that nine-year span. Does this increase manifest a generalized heightening of the litigiousness of the American population, a lowering of public thresholds of legal irritability? Does it evidence the "increasing tendency of Americans to define all distresses, anxieties and wounds as legal problems [and to] turn to the courts for relief whenever things work out badly?"[1]

The overall increase in filings over the nine years is heavily concentrated in a few areas. Almost three-quarters of the entire increase is accounted for by just five categories: prisoner petitions, torts, civil-rights cases, Social Security appeals, and recovery cases (suits by the federal government to recover overpayments of veterans' benefits and defaulted student loans).

TABLE 2

Federal District Court Filings, Selected Categories, 1975 and 1984

Category	1975	1984	% Change	Increase [Decrease]	Share of Total Filings Increase 1975–84
Total filings	117,320	261,485	122.9%	144,165	100%
1. Prisoner petitions	19,307	31,107	61.1%	11,800	
A. State	14,260	26,581	86.4%	12,321	8.5%
B. Federal	5,047	4,526	−10.3%	[−521]	
2. Recovery of overpayment, etc.	681	46,190	6,682.7%	45,509	31.6%
3. Civil rights	10,392	21,219	104.2%	10,827	7.5%
A. Public accommodation	601	291	−51.6%	[−310]	
B. Employment discrimination	3,931	9,748	148.0%	5,817	4.0%
4. Social Security	5,846	29,985	412.9%	24,139	16.7%
A. Black lung	2,793	59	−97.9%	[−2,734]	
5. Torts	25,691	37,522	46.1%	12,831	8.2%
A. Products liability	2,886[a]	10,745[b]	272.3%	7,859	5.5%
Total of five "Gainers" (1A, 2,3,4,5)				105,627	72.5%
Some "losers"					
6. Antitrust	1,431	1,201	−16.1%	[−230]	
7. Fraud, including truth-in-lending	2,237	1,842	−17.7%	[−395]	
8. Class Actions	3,061	988	−67.7%	[−2,073]	

[a]Includes 278 contracts cases.
[b]Includes 619 contracts cases.

Indeed, half of the total increase is accounted for by giant increases in two categories: Social Security and recovery cases. Each is the result of deliberate and calculated official policy. On the Social Security side, officials decided to curtail disability benefits by summarily removing beneficiaries from the rolls. Terminated recipients then had to sue for restoration. The impact on the caseload was compounded by the Reagan administration's policy of "nonacquiescence," whereby it insisted on fighting each subsequent claim in spite of fresh opposing precedents. (This policy was modified in June 1985.) Is the 412 percent increase in Social Security cases to be understood as an outbreak of litigiousness among Social Security claimants? According to a *New York Times* account, "the disability reviews were halted in April 1984 in response to harsh criticism from many members of Congress, Federal judges and governors, who said the Reagan Administration was improperly throwing thousands of disabled people off the rolls."[2] In 1985 there was a precipitous 34 percent drop in Social Security cases — from 29,983 to 19,771.

The recovery cases arose from federal efforts to recover overpaid benefits through litigation. Does it make sense to take the 6,682 percent increase in these cases as evidence of an outbreak of litigiousness among federal officials? Indirectly, it reflects an increase in the number of student borrowers and veterans receiving benefits. More directly, it reflects a shift in federal policy: in 1980, the Veterans Administration (VA) was empowered to sue directly to collect debts without referring the matter to the Department of Justice. A VA official estimated that about half the collection cases filed by the VA would not have been brought had the agency not been given authority to institute such actions on its own.

Cases that reflect individual initiative rather than the changing contours of executive policy may provide a better reading of the national propensity to litigate. Prisoners are understandably prone to bring lawsuits: the stakes are high, the alternatives few, and the costs (to them) negligible. From 1975 to 1984, prisoner petitions increased 61 percent. During this period the prison population of the United States grew by 74 percent, so the number of petitions per 1,000 prisoners dropped from 73.4 to 67.1. The rate of case filings rose slightly among state prisoners but dropped sharply among federal prisoners. Whatever the explanation for these trends, it seems more likely to reflect responses to specific circumstances than the rise or fall of an inclination for litigious contest or a proclivity to define issues as legal wrongs.

If it is assumed that discrimination declined in many areas of American life between 1975 and 1984, the increase in civil-rights cases might be seen as evidence of increasing general litigiousness. But disputes over discrimination have a very distinctive profile, compared with disputes about other matters. Lowering some barriers multiplies the potential occasions for experiencing discrimination. Once members of a minority are hired, for example, there are for the first time possibilities for on-the-job discrimination. In discrimination grievances, there is a pronounced demand for vindication of principle. One suggestive study reported that in contrast to other kinds of problems, where most respondents sought "satisfactory adjustment," a strikingly high proportion of those experiencing discrimination problems sought "justice."[3] Yet those with a discrimination grievance are inclined to "lump it." The Civil Litigation Research Project found that discrimination grievances were far less likely to be translated into claims than other kinds of grievances. In all types of middle-range disputes combined, 1,000 grievances led to 718 claims; but 1,000 discrimination grievances led to only 294 claims. When discrimination claims were made, a high proportion ended up as disputes. Only 62.5 percent of claims overall became disputes, but 73.4 percent of discrimination claims did so. But a relatively low proportion of discrimination disputes were taken to a lawyer, and a low proportion of them resulted in court filings. Overall, 1,000 grievances of other types led to 50 court filings, but 1,000 discrimination grievances led to only 8 court filings. Pursuing a discrimination complaint is an extremely painful process, exposing the claimant to social discreditation and self-doubt. Thus, in the area of discrimination, a high demand for vindication is balked by formidable obstacles to making and pursuing such claims, leaving a great pool of grievances that could become cases if those obstacles were overcome. The increase in civil-rights cases suggests that the pursuit of these claims is being successfully institutionalized.

This does not mean that a continuous exponential growth of discrimination cases is to be expected, for practices are changing, too, in the direction of the anti-discrimination norms embodied in the law. Eventually, disputing about discrimination may become more "normal," and the number of cases may stabilize at a level similar to those in other areas. One kind of civil-rights case has already shown a marked decline in filings: public-accommodations cases fell by 51 percent during this nine-year period. There were also declines in other categories of cases, including several that represent major expenditures of resources for the courts. Antitrust cases declined by 16 percent. Fraud and truth-in-lending cases fell by 17 percent. Class actions, often viewed as an engine of legal aggression against business, fell by 67 percent — from 3,061 in 1975 to 988 in 1984, that is, from 2.6 percent of filings to 0.4 percent. Within the burgeoning Social Security area, black-lung cases fell by 97 percent from their 1975 level, as that particular group of victims worked their way through the system — much as the victims of asbestos are doing now.

The area that has excited the most concern in recent debate about litigation is that of torts. Unlike other categories, which have loomed large in federal courts only in recent years, torts have always made up a substantial portion of the cases entering federal courts. The influx of other business in the past generation has sharply reduced the percentage of tort cases. In 1960, 36.2 percent of all civil filings were torts. But because of increases in other categories, only 14.3 percent of federal court filings in 1984 were tort cases.

In this nine-year period, the number of tort filings increased from 25,691 in 1975 to 37,522 in 1984. Almost two-thirds of this increase was due to a rise in products-liability cases. To many observers, this is the fiery heart of the litigation explosion. In identifying "Burgeoning Tort Liability as a Major Cause of the Insurance Availability/Affordability Crisis," the attorney general's Tort Policy Working Group cited as its first item of evidence that "the growth in the number of product liability suits has been astounding. For example, the number of product liability cases filed in federal district courts has increased from 1,579 in 1974 to 13,554 in 1985, a 758 percent increase. . . . There is no reason to believe that the state courts have not witnessed a similar dramatic increase in the number of product liability claims."[4] But the table 1 figures from the state courts, showing a modest overall rise in tort filings during most of this period, give some reason to suspect that the increase in product claims there has been less dramatic. Unfortunately, none of the data on state courts break out products-liability filings separately. If product cases are becoming more common in state courts, their growth is not reflected in figures on actual trials. In two large urban counties for which there are data on the number of jury trials over a twenty-five-year period, the number of products-liability trials fell from the 1970s to the first half of the 1980s (as did the number of jury trials generally).

Products-liability cases have been counted separately in the federal courts since

1974. From 1974 to 1985, other tort claims of all kinds rose from 22,662 to 28,039 — an increase of 23.7 percent. Products-liability cases, on the other hand, rose 758 percent over this period — thirty-two times as fast. The pattern of products-liability claims in federal courts is far from typical of the pattern of other tort claims there — much less the pattern of products-liability or other tort claims in state courts.

What are these products-liability cases? Asbestos cases make up a significant share, as they have during the whole period since products-liability cases began being counted in 1974. In 1985, the first full year in which asbestos cases were counted separately, they made up 31.3 percent of all products-liability filings. In 1986, asbestos filings rose 28 percent while other products-liability filings declined by 7 percent, so that asbestos cases accounted for 43 percent of all products cases. It was estimated in 1985 that more than 16,000 asbestos cases had been filed in the federal courts, which would amount to more than a quarter of the cumulative total of 60,508 products-liability filings counted from 1974 to 1985.

These asbestos cases are a kind of litigation whose growth is not plausibly explained by an increase in the proclivity to sue. By the early 1980s, broad dissemination of information about the injurious nature of asbestos, the presence of an experienced asbestos bar, and concern about possible cutoffs of liability to future claimants were mobilizing large numbers from the pool of asbestos victims. This pool is destined to diminish over the coming decades — in no small measure because asbestos litigation has helped to reduce exposure!

If a single set of related products cases makes up a quarter of the total, other major clusterings may possibly be found in the category. At least one other product — the Dalkon Shield — was the subject of thousands of cases during this period. In October 1984, the A. H. Robins Co. moved to form a class of more than 3,500 pending cases with punitive damage claims. The total number of Dalkon Shield suits filed by early 1985 exceeded 8,700. The major movements of the products-liability category may be expected to reflect the flow and ebb of waves of litigation about specific products and the ways in which these populations of related cases are aggregated.

The products-liability category is often visualized as one in which suits over "thousands of products" have "jeopardized the health of many industries."[5] Its growth is then presented as an index and portent of the general growth of litigation. But if it is a category populated largely by several epidemics of suits about specific products, its growth may be less easily generalized. The available data do not indicate whether the cases in the products-liability category are widely dispersed across the whole range of manufactured products or instead contain large clusters of suits over a relatively small set of products. A 1986 Conference Board survey of risk managers of 232 major United States corporations found that products liability impinges in a major way only on a small number of specialized firms and concludes that products liability and the related crisis of insurance availability "have left a relatively minor dent on the economics and organization of individual large firms."[6]

The Users and Uses of Litigation

Does the course of these cases, once they get to court, suggest an increase in the proclivity for litigious combat? By far the majority of civil cases in both federal and state courts are settled before they come to trial. There has been a great increase in the proportion of cases that terminate early in the process. In the federal courts a declining percentage of cases proceed to trial or even survive until the holding of a pretrial conference. In 1960, 11 percent of civil cases reached the trial stage and another 13.9 percent reached the pretrial conference. In 1986 only 4.4 percent reached trial and 11.3 percent reached pretrial. In state courts, too, a smaller proportion of cases were decided by full contest than in the past. Both trends reflect a long historical decline in the proportion of cases that run the whole course of possible contest.

What do these patterns reveal? If a generalized litigation fever were loosening the restraints that inhibit people from making claims, one would expect to find a general increase in the proportion of cases that are pursued through the full possibilities of contest. But although more disputes are arriving at court, proportionately fewer of these — though more cases in absolute numbers — proceed to later stages of the judicial process. The vast majority are resolved by negotiation rather than full-blown adjudication. Indeed, some critics contend that although lawsuits abound, there are too few opportunities to vindicate claims and elucidate principles through full adjudication.

The world of litigation is composed of subpopulations of cases, some increasing in number and others decreasing, that seem to respond to specific conditions rather than to global changes in climate. The distinctive traits of each subpopulation of cases reflect such factors as the number, concentration, or diffusion of the injuries or troubles in question, the presence or absence of other ways of dealing with these troubles, the availability of information about legal remedies, the development of lawyer expertise, and so forth. Such a subpopulation is not just a statistical collection of discrete cases observed against a fixed (or slowly changing) backdrop of law. It has a career. It is a changing stream whose course shifts and turns as lawyers gain expertise and develop specialization, new knowledge is generated and disseminated, and parties change their expectations. The underlying behavior also changes, as do insurance practices, record keeping, and so forth. New types of cases come on the scene; some expand into sizable populations; some stabilize and remain relatively constant for long periods (like automobile-injury cases and divorces); others fade away (like black-lung and truth-in-lending cases). The careers of these changing populations in turn cumulate into major changes in the makeup of court caseloads.

These changes reflect and reinforce changes in public beliefs and expectations about the legal system. The shifting patterns of filings are compatible with the notion of a general but uneven spread of higher expectations of justice and the growth of a sense of entitlement to protection from, or recompense for, many kinds of injury. But this sense is not self-activating, and its growth does not sufficiently account for the patterns of court use. Its translation into litigation depends on the values and resources of claimants, and on the remedial options available to them. These in turn reflect changes in the wider institutional context in which disputes arise.

The aggregate data reviewed above suggest a moderate and modulated rather than a feverish and unrestrained use of litigation. This picture is confirmed by what is known of the experience of individual litigants. Wary of risks, delays, and costs, litigants do not act as if propelled by an unappeasable urge for contest or public vindication. There is little evidence to suggest that more than a tiny minority of claimants correspond to that figure of folklore, the schemer who wants to turn a trivial injury into a bonanza. For plaintiffs as well as defendants, litigation is usually a miserable, disruptive, painful experience. Few litigants enjoy it or bask in the esteem of their fellows — indeed, they may be stigmatized. Even those who prevail may find the process costly. As a firefighter who quit her job after winning a discrimination complaint (she had been forbidden to breastfeed her infant during free time on duty) explained: "Ever since my suit I was fair game . . . I was the brunt of all their hostilities."[7]

The mythic nature of the notion that Americans are suffering from a litigation mania is revealed by a humble example. The greatest single source of the bulge in filings is the increase in divorce (and postdivorce) proceedings. According to the Council on the Role of the Courts, "domestic relations cases dominate state court dockets."[8] This conclusion is based on a survey of courts of general jurisdiction in eight states in 1976. In all but one state, domestic-relations cases made up more than 50 percent of the total caseload. In California the proportion was 38.5 percent. Of all the common types of disputes studied in the Civil Litigation Research Project, postdivorce disputes were most likely to end up in court. Everyone knows many people who are parties in these cases, but few know many who sought divorce or postdivorce remedies because they were enamored of litigation or beguiled by lawyers. What attracts users is not the desire to use the legal system but the hope for a solution to what they consider an otherwise intractable problem.

For other groups of law users, too, the courts appear the best of unpleasant alternatives. In a study of disputing in three neighborhoods of a New England city, Sally Merry and Susan Silbey concluded that their respondents

> seek to avoid court for a variety of reasons from fear of antagonizing the people they live with every day to the loss of control that court entails. When people do bring interpersonal disputes to court, they tend to be complex, intense and involuted problems in which the moral values at stake appear sufficiently important to outweigh the condemnation of this behavior.
>
> . . . For all respondents turning to court and police with problems is a last resort to be used only if "the problems are very serious," "can't be avoided," "it is absolutely necessary," and "you have tried everything else."[9]

Why, then, do people sue? In his famous June 1978 commencement address at Harvard University, Alexander Solzhenitsyn expressed his misgivings about various features of Western society, including its tendency to assert legal rights to solve every conflict: "A society based on the letter of the law and never reaching any higher fails to take advantage of the full range of human possibilities. The letter of the law is too cold and formal to have a beneficial influence on society. Whenever the tissue of life is woven of legalistic relationships, this creates an atmosphere of spiritual mediocrity that paralyzes man's noblest impulses."[10]

A group of admirers who sought to assemble a volume of commentary "to place Solzhenitsyn's ideas in historical, political, and philosophical perspective" found the author unwilling to allow the speech to be reprinted:

> Thinking that we were forbidden to use only the published version of the address, we then had a new translation made. . . . This process of seeking permission and producing a new translation consumed the better part of a year.

> Finally, in January 1980, the book was ready to go to press. We sent page proofs to Solzhenitsyn and invited him and his wife to come to Washington at our expense to attend a press lunch launching the book. The reply was a phone call and a follow up telegram from Harper & Row asserting that our publication of the address in any translation would be considered a violation of the author's copyright and theirs. We then tried, both directly . . . and through intermediaries, to get Solzhenitsyn to relent. He would not.

> On April 30 of this year a legal complaint was filed on our behalf in the U.S. District Court for the District of Columbia, asking that Solzhenitsyn and Harper & Row be prohibited from charging us with copyright infringement if we published the address in our book. The complaint alleged that the threats of copyright infringement against us violated our First Amendment rights and the "fair use" provisions of the copyright law. A week later Harper & Row notified our lawyers that we had been granted permission to reprint the Harper & Row version of the speech. Our complaint was withdrawn. . . . [11]

It need not be imagined that Solzhenitsyn abandoned his scorn of Western legalism to understand the attraction of the threat to sue as a way of controlling the unwelcome attentions of this band of strangers. The admirers, too, were presumably sympathetic with his views. But, having made a major investment and ending up stymied, finding no other avenue of relief that supplied any leverage over the recalcitrant author, they found filing suit an available and viable way to solve the problem. The result conformed to the classic pattern of American litigation: the filing created a setting for serious negotiations between the parties; positions were assessed "in the shadow of the law" — that is, by anticipating what courts might do, including the shadow of the costs and risks of the proceeding; concessions were made, and, as in most American litigation, the process culminated in a settlement without any direct official input.

Those who are distressed at the United States's excessive litigiousness often gaze longingly at Japan, which is thought to have remained uncorrupted by excessive legalism. Japan, they think, has few lawyers, avoids conflict, disdains legalism, and resolves disputes by conciliation. The country plays a central role in litigation-explosion mythology as a benign black hole of antilitigiousness. In reality, Japan's antilegalism is more complex and ambivalent. The capacity of Japanese courts to provide adjudicatory remedies has indeed been deliberately constricted for generations. But the alleged paucity of lawyers in Japan will not withstand examination. Twelve thousand — the number often cited — is the number of *bengoshi* certified to act as advocates in court. But there are a number of other law occupations in Japan: in-house legal advisers, judicial scriveners, administrative scriveners, patent attorneys, tax attorneys, and so forth. An American lawyer working in Japan estimated the total number of persons doing legal work there in 1982 as 95,342, which would put the ratio of legal workers in Japan in the higher rather than the lower part of the comparative range. The supposed Japanese lack of interest in the law is belied by the observation of a Japanese law professor that "there is in Japan a massive diversion of younger talent into the world of law. Every year more than 38,000 youngsters graduate from law faculties in Japan as compared to 36,000 who graduate from U.S. law schools. Since the population of Japan is approximately half that of the United States, there are proportionately two times more law graduates produced in Japan."[12]

In late 1985, *Reader's Digest* terminated its Japanese edition. The *New York Times* reported:

> On Dec. 17, the union appealed to the Tokyo District Court to seize movable assets such as furniture as security for retirement payments owed to union members; the court executed the order the next day. The union has also filed complaints with Japan's Ministries of Labor, Finance, Foreign Affairs, and International Trade and Industry. It is preparing a lawsuit charging the company with violations of its employees' civil rights, and plans to extend its suit to the parent company in the United States. It has also appealed to the Tokyo labor relations committee to intervene, charging Reader's Digest with attempting to destroy the union. . . . [13]

What would make the unlitigious Japanese so eager to resort to all-out legal warfare? Dispute-resolution theory suggests a number of possible explanations. First, the stakes for the workers are extremely high — their very livelihood — and it is well established that even those disinclined to use the courts will do so when faced with a threat to vital and irreplaceable resources, such as land, power, and reputation. Second, there is nothing to lose. Since *Reader's Digest* is leaving, there is no continuing relationship to be threatened. Just as important, there is no continuing relationship to serve as a locus for alternative remedial actions. Finally, the employer's perceived violation of responsibility — its overtly self-regarding stance and refusal to consult over its decision — provided the spur of indignation that can overcome reluctance to litigate. Once the Japanese overcome this reluctance they can pursue litigation with great moral intensity for long periods, as in the collective litigation campaigns conducted by groups of victims against corporations that are perceived to have conducted themselves badly by denying responsibility to those they have injured.

The Solzhenitsyn and *Reader's Digest* stories are a reminder that even those ideologically disinclined to use the courts sometimes do so. They find themselves in situations where they are affected by others but have no leverage to control those others or hold them accountable — typically in dealings with strangers but sometimes with intimates as well. In such a predicament, they may turn to courts for recourse, usually with reluctance. And modern society presents more of these predicaments. Modern technology increases the likelihood that remote actions will impinge on persons. An increasing proportion of dealings and of disputes is with remote actors, especially with corporate organizations as opposed to other persons. Thus, a growing share of serious disputes are between entities of very different size — typically between individuals and large organizations. The advance of knowledge enables people to trace out more of the connections between actions and their ramifying consequences. Education and wealth make people more competent at visualizing remedies and enlisting the help of the law to control and hold accountable remote and overwhelming actors. The law is used *ex ante* in the "wholesale" form of legislation and administative regulation and also *ex post* in the "retail" form of litigation.

Current discussions of the litigation system display a sensitivity to the various kinds of costs, direct and indirect, that attend the system. One hears much of bizarre claims, immense jury verdicts, undeserved windfalls, the engorgement of contingency-fee lawyers, the financial devastation of defendants, and other horrors that befall the participants in specific cases. One also hears much about the deleterious effects of litigation in the large — that it dampens enterprise, distracts managers, makes doctors practice defensive medicine, increases the cost of products, keeps useful products off the market, and so on. One hears much less of the benefits of litigation: that in addition to its direct provision of compensation, it supports a vast system of bargaining in which almost all disputes are resolved by negotiation and that it stimulates a host of preventive activities by threatening and educating those engaged in the various activities that underlie injuries and disputes.

It is not claimed that the system is optimal, that its benefits outweigh all its costs, or that the current patterns of litigation represent the best way to achieve those benefits. But it should be recognized that the benefits are real and that any assessment of the social value of litigation must take them into account in comparing the net effects of present litigation patterns with those of proposed or likely alternatives.

Conclusion

Respect for the available evidence suggests a more benign reading of the current situation than inhabits discussions of the lawsuit crisis or litigation explosion. The United States is not faced with an inexorable exponential explosion of cases but with a series of local changes, some sudden but most incremental, as particular kinds of troubles move in and out of the ambit of the courts. Higher caseloads do not reflect a heightened desire for adversarial combat; they occur as people try to cope with problems within a given array of remedial alternatives. Litigation, like the alternative ways of handling such troubles, includes among its effects a mix of both benefits and costs. The net effects of each method cannot be ascertained by deduction or supposition.

Why the consternation about litigation? Why is the bad face of law evident and its good face hidden to many? The answer is surely complex, but two points deserve mention. First, litigation implies accountability to public standards. This heightening of public accountability in the courts can be seen as a counter to deregulation in the executive branch of government, and as such is unwelcome in many quarters. The sense of being held to account has multiplied far more than the number of cases or trials, for it depends not on the direct imposition of court orders but on the communication of messages about what courts might do. Law as a system of symbols has expanded; information about law and its working is more widely and vividly circulated to more educated and receptive audiences. As a source of symbols and bargaining counters, litigation patterns have changed too. The kind of litigation that once dominated the system — lawsuits to enforce market relations — has given way to tort, civil-rights, and public-law cases that "correct" the market. It is litigation aimed "upwards" — by outsiders, clients, and dependents against authorities and managers of established institutions — that excites most of the reproach of this litigious society.

The sense that the United States is uniquely cursed by rampant legalism that destroys community, unravels the fabric of trust, distorts markets, and confounds authority is yet another manifestation of the cliché of the United States as a land of alienation and oppression. Instead of unfavorably comparing the reality, in all its puzzling complexity, with some imagined harmonious and organic society, one should take the United States's variform and changing patterns of litigation as a challenge to explore the central and distinctive features of this society.

NOTES

1. Mark Cannon, "Contentious and Burdensome Litigation: A Need for Alternatives," *National Forum* 63 (1983): 10–11.
2. Robert Pear, "U.S. Starts Culling Ineligibles From Disability Benefit Rolls," *New York Times,* 14 May 1986.
3. Leon Mayhew, "Institutions of Representation," *Law & Society Review* 9 (1975): 401, 413.
4. Report of the Tort Policy Working Group on the Causes, Extent, and Policy Implications of the Current Crisis in Insurance Availability and Affordability, Feb. 1986, p. 45.
5. Pear, "Draft Bill Is Set on Liability Suits," *New York Times,* 21 Apr. 1986.
6. Nathan Weber, *Product Liability: The Corporate Response* (New York: Conference Board, 1987), 2.
7. "Battle Won, War?," *New York Times,* 18 May 1980.
8. Council on the Role of Courts, *The Role of Courts in American Society* (1984), 38, 166.
9. Sally Merry and Susan Silbey, "What Do Plaintiffs Want? Reexamining the Concept of Dispute," *Justice System Journal* 9 (1985): 151, 172–73.
10. Ronald Berman, ed., *Solzhenitsyn at Harvard: The Address, Twelve Early Responses and Six Later Reflections* (Washington, D.C.: Ethics and Public Policy Center, 1982), 7–8.
11. Ernest LeFever, "Foreword," in ibid., viii–ix.
12. Junjiro Tsubota, "Myth and Truth on Non-Litigiousness in Japan," [University of Chicago] *Law School Record* 30 (Spring 1984): 8.
13. Susan Chira, "Reader's Digest Leaves Japan," *New York Times,* 26 Dec. 1985.

The Crisis Is Injuries, Not Liability

RICHARD L. ABEL

Most commentators who invoke the shibboleth "tort crisis" maintain that the problem is too much liability and that this is a recent and temporary phenomenon. They blame trigger-happy litigants, greedy lawyers, irresponsible juries, and bleeding-heart judges. They deplore the increased cost of insurance, its unavailability to some, the willingness of others to "go bare," and the impact of all this on the production of vital goods and services. Like all effective propaganda, this account contains a kernel of truth. Victims obtain more favorable outcomes in the tort system today than they did in the past — although recovery is still based on fault. Juries occasionally award large verdicts, but many are reduced by judges, and most verdicts are small (for example, half were less than $8,000 in Cook County, Illinois, between 1960 and 1979). Indeed, if the largest verdicts are excluded, the median has actually been declining.[1]

Propaganda does not mislead through lies, however, but through partial truths. The jeremiads about the "tort crisis" ignore the fact that fluctuations in insurance premiums, which affect everyone, are at least as much a function of interest-rate cycles as of changes in liability rules or jury awards. And they greatly exaggerate the extent to which inflation in the price of goods and services is attributable to higher insurance premiums, which normally constitute an insignificant fraction of total costs.[2]

I see the problem very differently — as an epidemic of injuries with deep historical roots and structural causes. Successful tort claims do not create accident costs; they merely shift them from victims to tortfeasors. It is tortfeasors who inflict costs on society by injuring victims. Liability costs are high because injuries are frequent and serious. Several independent surveys reveal that a majority of people suffer at least one serious injury during their lives.[3] Far too few of them recover damages from a tortfeasor. The present tort system is largely responsible for this failure, which leaves victims uncompensated, allows entrepreneurs to continue creating unreasonable risks and causing injuries, and permits moral dereliction to go unpunished.

Many Injury Victims Fail to Claim

The few studies that attempt to determine what proportion of those legally entitled to tort damages actually recover amply support the conclusion that many eligible victims fail to claim. A joint study by the American Bar Association and the American Bar Foundation ascertained that only 16 percent of those who reported tort problems consulted lawyers about them.[4] Another investigation, comparing expert judgments about injuries caused by medical malpractice with subsequent claims, found that only 10 percent of victims claimed, and only 4 percent recovered damages. Even among those who suffered a significant permanent partial disability, less than 15 percent claimed damages, and only 6.5 percent recovered.[5] A third study of hospital records found that only 6.7 percent of significant injuries caused by medical malpractice led to claims and noted that even this figure was inflated, since the cause of many injuries could not be identified from the records.[6] And a fourth inquiry found that 40 percent of the incidents that physicians reported to their own insurers as malpractice never resulted in claims.[7]

Medical patients may fail to claim because they do not recognize they have suffered a compensable injury or are (perhaps justifiably) pessimistic about the speed and likelihood of recovery. Injured workers fail to claim for a different reason: fear of employer retaliation for the liability costs, increased insurance premiums, or intensified scrutiny by agencies charged with protecting worker safety. Although the National Safety Council estimated that there were 11,600 workplace deaths in 1985, employers reported only 3,750 to the U.S. Bureau of Labor Statistics. Chrysler recently paid over $300,000 in fines to settle charges that it willfully failed to report worker injuries, and the U.S. Department of Labor has filed similar charges against other major corporations, including Union Carbide, Monsanto, Shell Oil, Fina, and USX Corporation.[8] The California Supreme Court has allowed employees to sue the Johns-Manville Corporation in tort (rather than claiming workers' compensation, usually the exclusive remedy), because for decades the company concealed health records showing that those workers were suffering from asbestos exposure.[9] And a study whose methodology resembled that of the medical malpractice research cited above found that only about 37 percent of work-accident victims claim workers' compensation, which is available by law regardless of employer or employee fault.[10]

Even road-accident victims often fail to claim, although police generally record the event, most tortfeasors and victims are strangers to each other, and liability insurance is widespread. In New York City in the late 1950s, 64 percent of those suffering slight shock or contusion recovered some compensation within two years; but it seems likely that recovery was less frequent among that half of the victims who could not be located by the researchers.[11] In Michigan in the 1960s, only 14 percent of automobile-accident victims even retained a lawyer, although half of those suffering more serious injury did so.[12]

The most comprehensive study of claims by the injured was conducted in England in the late 1970s.[13] Among those who suffered at least two weeks of incapacity, 47 percent of road-accident victims considered claiming, as did 46 percent of work-accident victims and 9 percent of victims in other accidents. A third of road-accident victims consulted lawyers, along with a quarter of work-accident victims and 3 percent of other accident victims. Victims obtained some recovery from tortfeasors in 29 percent of road accidents, 19 percent of work accidents, and 2 percent of other accidents. Because 86 percent of all accidents fell within this last category, only 12 percent of those who suffered two weeks of incapacity from injuries recovered any damages.[14] Although this study did not attempt to ascertain which accident victims were legally entitled to damages, the proportion must have been far greater than 12 percent.

There are several reasons to expect claiming to be less frequent in England than in the United States: the imposition of costs on unsuccessful plaintiffs, lower damage awards, the prohibition of contingent fees, and the prevalence of social insurance. Yet there are also reasons to expect English victims to claim more often, such as the availability of legal aid in tort cases and the award of costs to a successful plaintiff (which allows the victim to keep all damages, undiminished by lawyers' fees). In fact, claims seem to be about as frequent in the two countries: less than half of road-accident victims, significantly fewer work-accident victims, and hardly any victims in the residual category, which accounts for the vast preponderance of injuries.

Qualitative studies in widely varied social environments confirm victim reluctance to claim. Residents of a rural community in southern Illinois reported strong pressures against suing for torts, even when the defendant was a foreign corporation.[15] Small-town Missouri lawyers were reluctant to sue local notables — often the only defendants capable of compensating tort victims.[16] The predominantly Baptist population of an Atlanta suburb was restrained from suing by strong cultural norms.[17] Upper-middle-class inhabitants of a bedroom community outside New York City rarely complained about outrageous behavior by neighbors.[18] These inhibitions remained pervasive in a large city like Boston,[19] although working-class victims were more assertive in each of the last two environments.[20] Even New Yorkers failed to live up to their reputation for contentiousness, passively tolerating progressively more offensive affronts in a series of psychological experiments.[21] Inaction is also found when other legal rights are violated: among dissatisfied consumers and the victims and witnesses of crimes.[22]

Methodological objections could undoubtedly be raised to each of these studies. But the wide variety of populations observed and the broad range of investigative techniques used overwhelmingly suggest that a large proportion of injured victims fail to claim — certainly more than half, probably more than three-fourths, and possibly as many as nine-tenths.

The Value of Participation in Social Life

In order to argue that tort victims *should* claim, I want to consider several other realms of behavior where we strongly value and encourage participation: politics, the market, cultural life, and social services.

All theories of democratic politics demand citizen participation. Direct democracy—in the New England town meeting or the voluntary association—constitutes the core of our political mythology. Because the growth of political units makes representative institutions unavoidable, the level of participation in electoral politics has become a central index of the quality of political life. It is a source of shame that America long disenfranchised women and racial minorities and that turnout among eligible voters remains low. Some countries make voting compulsory, just as the United States requires other forms of political participation, such as service on juries and in the military. We do encourage participation in elections by publishing ballots and voter information pamphlets in several languages, facilitating registration, extending polling hours, and striking down gerrymandering that would dilute the influence of votes. And we have become increasingly concerned about the extent to which access to and influence within the political arena now depends on acquiring the economic resources to purchase exposure in the mass media.

It is almost tautological that the health of a market economy is measured by the degree of participation. Economists daily scrutinize indices of production, employment, investment, borrowing, and consumption. They deplore anything that interferes with market activity, whether state regulation, private monopoly, or restrictive practices. Socialist and Third World economies increasingly tolerate some free enterprise in order to enlarge participation. And at least some producers and sellers actively encourage consumers to complain in order to improve quality and enhance consumer confidence.

We demonstrate the importance of participation in our common culture by making public education free and compulsory. We are proud that the proportion of our population obtaining some higher education is larger than that in any other country. Literacy and numeracy not only confer intrinsic rewards but are also essential for participation in political and economic life. Although we often disagree about means—as in the debates over bilingual education or the back-to-basics movement—no one would disparage the goal of promoting the highest level of involvement in public affairs. Even those who deplore the banality and commercial degradation of mass culture must concede that audiences do not passively consume radio, television, movies, and popular music but engage them actively, often critically.

Attitudes toward the consumption of social services are more ambivalent. Politicians and the media often invoke the image of the welfare scrounger to argue for cuts in such services. Yet we make education compulsory, viewing high-school dropouts as systemic failures and offering them substantial incentives to return and obtain their diplomas. We require inoculation against infectious diseases and strongly encourage the use of public prenatal care and other preventive health services. We measure the value of publicly and privately subsidized cultural and recreational activities by consumption levels: museum attendance figures, public library circulation, the viewing audience for public television programs, crowds at public celebrations, and the number who visit state and national parks. Western

European nations ideologically more committed to social welfare view high "take-up" rates for all social services as indices of governmental achievement, not failure.

Law is simultaneously an inherently political activity, an essential framework for economic life, an expression of basic cultural norms, and an important social service. Litigation allows parties to mobilize political authority; it conveys information to consumers and producers by altering prices and correcting market imperfections; it declares and changes social values; and it is a social service whose consumption we encourage by subsidizing the institutions that create and apply it—legislatures, courts, administrative agencies, executive bodies, and lawyers. In a society with relatively weak historical traditions, roiled by continuous and rapid change, composed of a very heterogeneous population characterized by great inequalities of class, race, gender, ethnicity, and region, dominated by highly concentrated economic power, and directed by national, state, and local governments that inevitably threaten individual freedom, litigation is an essential constituent of social order. For all these reasons, I believe we should value public participation in the legal system.

Tort Victims Should Claim Damages

Even if civil litigation should generally be valued as a form of participation in social life, it is necessary to focus more narrowly on what particular legal claims accomplish. Most scholars agree that tort law has three principal objectives: redressing the violation of important norms, compensating victims, and discouraging unsafe behavior.

All torts are normative violations. The tortfeasor has behaved unreasonably and caused injury to another. To preserve and strengthen the violated norm it is imperative to publicize the violation and punish the wrongdoer. Émile Durkheim argued that transgressions offer society an opportunity to punish, thereby reasserting its commitment to the broken norm.[23] Repeated failure to punish violations invites nullification. There is also evidence that expectations about the availability of compensation strongly influence the victim's attribution of moral blame.[24] Increasing victim confidence in the possibility of recovery, therefore, would have the salutary effect of reinforcing moral censure.

Normative violations must also be redressed for the sake of the victim's psychological well-being. Some societies require tortfeasors to apologize to victims as part of the remedial process.[25] In others, honor compels victims or their kin to seek revenge.[26] American social structure and culture may preclude these responses, but the victim's hurt and anger still demand legal redress in *every* case. Unredressed wrongs allow resentment to fester, breeding feelings of pervasive injustice and persecution and sometimes leading to acts of violence. This is one reason why the American criminal justice system has recently sought to reinvolve victims in the prosecution of criminals.

Nineteenth-century American law made the defendant's (and sometimes the plaintiff's) *moral* fault a central element of all tort claims.[27] Contemporary tort law tends to emphasize compensation instead. Some advocates of compensation are motivated by compassion for the victim; others are more concerned with restoring victims to productive life so that they do not become dependent on public or private welfare. But both perspectives deem it essential that every needy victim have the greatest possible opportunity to claim tort damages. Disagreements about the quantum of damages — pain and suffering, punitive damages, collateral sources, and ceilings — do not diminish the importance of increasing the frequency of claims.

Tort law fails to fulfill its stated goal of restoring victims to the status quo ante. In English households whose principal wage earner suffered two weeks of incapacity as a result of an injury and remained unemployed or seriously disabled, income was only half the national average.[28] Tort remedies provide less adequate compensation to those who are already socially disadvantaged. Because English women suffered fewer of their injuries on the road or in the workplace (where claims are more frequent), they obtained damages only half as often as men. The young and the elderly recovered less often than those in between, and the unemployed less often that the employed.[29]

In the United States, a higher proportion of blacks than whites are disabled and a higher proportion of women than men.[30] Yet the leading study of "legal need" found that men reported experiencing tort problems more often than women, whites more often than blacks and Latinos, and the wealthier and better educated more often than the poor and less educated. Furthermore, the likelihood of retaining counsel and obtaining damages varied directly with income and education.[31] The existing tort system, therefore, not only fails to compensate victims but also reproduces inequalities of race, gender, and class.

Although there is disagreement about whether tort liability should be fault-based (negligence) or strict (predicated on mere causation), no one would deny the importance of discouraging dangerous behavior. Indeed, scholars who differ in most other respects agree that this is its most important function.[32] Even if we were willing to allow victims to choose whether to seek an apology or compensation, we could not be equally indifferent about whether they mobilized the deterrent sanction of tort liability. Dangerous behavior is a continuing threat to people other than its immediate victim. The importance of tort liability as an incentive for safety is magnified by the conservative attack on government regulation (most devastating during the Reagan administration), complemented by the perennial suspicions of liberals about the capacity of industry to capture its regulators. We have no choice, therefore, but to make tort law the most effective regulatory instrument possible.

Research has repeatedly confirmed that the likelihood of suffering punishment is at least as important in influencing behavior as the severity of the penalty, and probably more important. In any case, there are limits on our ability to increase severity: the compensatory objective of tort law places a ceiling on damages, and the higher the damages the less likely they are to be imposed. Critics of the tort system who want to curtail or eliminate punitive damages or compensation for pain and suffering and deduct payments by collateral sources should welcome any proposal to recoup the loss of deterrence by increasing the frequency of claims.

Tort liability is not equally powerful in shaping all behavior. It has the greatest effect on profit-seeking enterprises engaged in repetitive activities and operating in competitive markets. Therefore, it probably has little impact on automobile drivers, whose behavior is rarely deliberative and who, in any case, tend to endanger themselves as much as others (so that self-preservation is the strongest incentive for safety). And tort liability can almost never be imposed on American employers, because workers' compensation is the exclusive remedy.

It is in the residual category of accidents — those suffered by consumers and bystanders as a result of the production and sale of goods and services for profit — that tort liability is most likely to reduce risk. Here, damage awards not only encourage potential tortfeasors to be safer but also inform consumers about dangerous goods and services. Lawsuits responding to toxic shock syndrome, injuries caused by IUDs, and airplane crashes undoubtedly shape consumer choice. Free-market advocates who deplore government regulation should welcome the role of tort claims in reducing market imperfections by increasing consumer information. The data strongly suggest, however, that the very claims that could do the most to reduce injury are rarely made. The definitive English study found that 86 percent of the injuries that incapacitated their victims for at least two weeks occurred in environments other than the road or the workplace. Yet only 3 percent of those victims claimed, and only 2 percent recovered damages.[33] Although some of this difference reflects the fact that no one was legally liable rather than the failure of victims to claim damages to which they are legally entitled, any profit-seeking entrepreneur operating within a competitive market would have to discount the threat of tort liability very heavily in deciding how much to spend on safety. This indifference to safety is not a matter of personal callousness, because it does not reflect individual choice; an entrepreneur who fails to cut safety costs whenever the tort system permits it will be put out of business by a competitor who does.

Increasing the frequency of claims is imperative, therefore, if tort law is to perform its undisputed functions. The failure of victims to claim erodes the norm against injuring others, allows anger and resentment to fester, leaves the most disadvantaged victims uncompensated and often impoverished, and tolerates — indeed encourages — dangerous behavior. A higher claims rate could improve the functioning of the tort system more dramatically than *any* other politically feasible change. If all injury victims claimed, the English study suggests, the impact of tort law could triple in road accidents, quadruple in work accidents, and increase thirtyfold in the residual category, which represents 86 percent of all accidental injuries (the actual effect, of course, would depend on how many of these claims prevailed).

Helping Victims to Claim

There are many ways to increase the proportion of injured victims who claim. We could make legal services more readily available through either the market (by lowering the entry barriers erected by the legal profession) or government action (by extending legal aid to personal injury cases and increasing its availability). Courts could resolve tort claims more expeditiously. And we could increase the likelihood of victim recovery by making liability strict and eliminating defenses.

Although I favor all these reforms, there is another way to increase the level of claiming that is both more effective and politically more feasible: lawyers should actively reach out to assist victims. The English study showed that the greatest attrition among accident victims occurred at the earliest stages of the claims process: considering whether to claim and deciding to consult a lawyer. Two-thirds of road-accident victims, three-fourths of work-accident victims, and a staggering 97 percent of other accident victims failed to take these steps. Furthermore, it is here that bias is introduced: fewer women than men consulted lawyers and fewer young and elderly than those in between.[34] Once victims consulted lawyers, however, most recovered: 88 percent in road accidents, 76 percent in work accidents, and 67 percent in other accidents.[35] These patterns of claiming are not natural phenomena: lawyers construct the public's sense of legal entitlement by institutionalizing their services in some situations and not others. Lawyers have the power, and therefore the obligation, to alter existing patterns of legal mobilization by intervening at the early stages of the claiming process.

Most producers of goods and services seek to stimulate consumption through promotional activities. Professional associations prohibited lawyers from doing so until 1977, when the Supreme Court granted some First Amendment protection to lawyer advertising.[36] Unfortunately, the Court has refused to extend such protection to individual lawyer solicitation, and no state allows it.[37] Nothing prevents professional associations from engaging in collective solicitation, however; indeed, statements by the Court strongly suggest that such activity would also enjoy First Amendment protection.[38] Collective action would avoid intensifying intraprofessional competition, which the lower strata of lawyers fear. It could also enhance the public image of lawyers, a preoccupation of elite practitioners. Indeed, collective solicitation simply extends the concept of lawyer referral services, which the profession has enthusiastically supported for years.

A highly successful experiment in collective solicitation of accident victims was initiated in England in 1979 by the Greater Manchester Legal Services Committee. It distributed 30,000 leaflets in six languages through hospitals, public libraries, and Citizens' Advice Bureaus. The leaflets explained the legal rights of accident victims and offered to arrange a free initial interview with a solicitor. Comparison of those who responded to the leaflets with those who had contacted lawyers in the earlier English survey revealed that the program not only increased the rate of claiming but also significantly altered who claimed. The survey had found that male victims of serious accidents were nearly twice as likely to recover damages as female, but 55 percent of those who responded to the program were women. The survey had found that victims between the ages of thirty-one and fifty were three to six times as likely to claim as those younger or older, but the program reached higher proportions in these latter categories. The survey had found that those in full-time employment were three-fourths of successful claimants even though they were only half of all victims, but those employed full time constituted only 40 percent of respondents to the program.[39]

The program reduced bias by reaching victims of "other" accidents, whom the existing tort system serves inadequately. The survey had found that of those who sought legal advice previously, road-accident victims had constituted 43 percent, work-accident victims 46 percent, and other accident victims 11 percent; but of respondents to the program, road-accident victims constituted 27 percent, work-accident victims 34 percent, and other accident victims 38 percent—more than a threefold increase in the "other accident" category. And while the survey had found that the likelihood of recovery varied inversely with injury severity (among those who claimed), program respondents tended to be seriously incapacitated, including a significant number who had been disabled for more than two months. This statistical evidence that the program succeeded in reaching victims previously unserved by the tort system was confirmed by their own evaluations: two-fifths said they had not considered claiming before they saw a leaflet, and nearly two-thirds had never before consulted a solicitor.

Collective solicitation must anticipate the objection that it will encourage frivolous, unfounded, or trivial claims. The solicitors who interviewed injury victims in Manchester advised 80 percent of their clients to claim. At the time of the survey, those solicitors reported that 42 percent of the claims had been settled, 41 percent were the subject of continuing negotiations, and only 16 percent had been abandoned. Among the claims that had been settled, the average recovery was £1,120 (about $2,000 at the prevailing exchange rate).

Both clients and solicitors felt that the program had enhanced the public image of the legal profession. Some thirty other local law societies adopted similar schemes over the next eight years, and in May 1987 the national Law Society decided to extend it throughout the country.[40] Such programs can do far more than persuade the particular victims who receive leaflets to seek compensation for their injuries. First, numerous studies have revealed that claiming is learned behavior; those who succeed are more likely to claim in the future.[41] Second, their success can inspire other victims. And, third, increasing the number of claims will compel the institutions that process them — courts, police, lawyers, and physicians — to become more responsive to the needs of the victims.

Conclusion

For at least a decade, insurance companies, the medical profession, and corporate defendants have been deploring the "litigiousness" of Americans, who allegedly file unjustified claims for trivial or imaginary injuries. The media have disseminated this view, and many members of the public have uncritically accepted it. But the myth is false.[42] The real problem with the tort system is the *failure* of accident victims to claim.

The most significant reform of the system — far more consequential than incremental changes in substantive or procedural law — would be an increase in the rate of claiming. This would strengthen the norm against endangering and injuring others, relieve the anger of victims, ameliorate their financial plight, and encourage safety. Collective solicitation of victims would be an important step in this direction. All lawyers, but especially those who represent the injured, have a strong interest in launching such a program. It is inexpensive and requires no governmental action. Opponents of such a reform will have great difficulty explaining why lawyers should not advise injured victims of their legal rights. Lawyers, who long have been on the defensive, will be visibly engaged in helping victims. They will be increasing access to the legal system and reducing the bias against those disadvantaged by race, gender, age, and class. And they will be curtailing the risks to which all of us are exposed. Asserting tort claims and helping others to do so is a vital civic duty.

NOTES

1. Mark Peterson and George Priest, *The Civil Jury: Trends in Trials and Verdicts* (Santa Monica, Calif.: Rand Corporation, 1981).

2. George Eads and Peter Reuter, *Designing Safer Products: Corporate Responses to Product Liability and Regulation* (Santa Monica, Calif.: Rand Corporation, 1983), 30–31.

3. Barbara Curran, *The Legal Needs of the Public* (Chicago: American Bar Foundation, 1977), 117; Donald Harris et al., *Compensation and Support for Illness and Injury* (Oxford: Clarendon Press, 1984), 31; "Census Study Reports 1 in 5 Suffering from a Disability," *New York Times*, 23 Dec. 1986.

4. Curran, 145.

5. Patricia Danzon, *Medical Malpractice: Theory, Evidence, and Public Policy* (Cambridge, Mass.: Harvard University Press, 1985), 19–20, 23.

6. L. Pocincki, S. Dagger, and B. Schwartz, "The Incidence of Iatrogenic Injuries," *Appendix to Report of the Secretary's Commission on Medical Malpractice* (Washington, D.C.: U.S. Department of Health, Education and Welfare, 1973), 50–70.

7. Office of the Secretary, U.S. Department of Health, Education and Welfare, *Study of Medical Malpractice Claims Closed in 1970* (Washington, D.C.: U.S. Department of Health, Education and Welfare, 1973).

8. Holcomb Noble, "Certain Numbers Can Kill," *New York Times*, 28 November 1986; idem, "Chrysler Will Pay $295,000 Fine for Violations in Injury Records," *New York Times*, 31 Jan. 1987.

9. *Johns-Manville Products Corp.* v. *Superior Court*, 27 Cal.3d 465, 612 P.2d 948, 165 Cal.Rptr. 858 (1980).

10. Lois Sincere, "Processing Workers' Compensation Claims in Illinois," *American Bar Foundation Research Journal* (1982), 1073, 1105.

11. Robert Hunting and Gloria Neuwirth, *Who Sues in New York City: A Study of Automobile Accident Claims* (New York: Columbia University Press, 1962), 4–8, 36–39.

12. Alfred Conard, "The Economic Treatment of Automobile Injuries," *Michigan Law Review* 63 (1964): 279, 285.

13. Harris et al.

14. Richard Abel, "£s of Cure, Ounces of Prevention," *California Law Review* 73 (1985): 1003, 1012–13.

15. David Engel, "The Oven Bird's Song: Insiders, Outsiders, and Personal Injuries in an American Community," *Law & Society Review* 18 (1984): 551.

16. Donald Landon, "Clients, Colleagues, and Community: The Shaping of Zealous Advocacy in Country Law Practice," *American Bar Foundation Research Journal* (1985), 81.

17. Carol Greenhouse, "Nature Is to Culture as Praying Is to Suing: Legal Pluralism in an American Suburb," *Journal of Legal Pluralism* 20 (1982): 17.

18. M.P. Baumgartner, "Social Control in Suburbia," in *Toward a General Theory of Social Control*, ed. Donald Black, vol. 2 (New York: Academic Press, 1984), 79.

19. Leonard Buckle and Suzann Thomas-Buckle, "Self-Help Justice: Dispute Processing in American Neighborhoods" (unpublished manuscript, 1981).

20. Baumgartner; Sally Merry, "Going to Court: Strategies of Dispute Management in an American Neighborhood," *Law & Society Review* 13 (1979): 891.

21. Thomas Moriarty, "A Nation of Willing Victims: Urban Danger and Urban Insult," *Psychology Today*, April 1975, 44.

22. Arthur Best and Alan Andreasen, "Consumer Response to Unsatisfactory Purchases: A Survey of Perceiving Defects, Voicing Complaints, and Obtaining Redress," *Law & Society Review* 11 (1977): 701, 716; Curran, 146; Erhard Blankenburg, "The Selectivity of Legal Sanctions: An Empirical Investigation of Shoplifting," *Law & Society Review* 11 (1976): 109; U.S. Department of Justice, Bureau of Justice Statistics, *Criminal Victimization in the United States, 1983* (Washington, D.C.: GPO, 1985), 85.

23. Émile Durkheim, *The Division of Labor in Society* (Glencoe, Ill.: Free Press, 1933), chap. 2; Kai Erikson, *Wayward Puritans* (New Haven: Yale University Press, 1968).

24. Abel, 1022.

25. Frank Upham, "Litigation and Moral Consciousness in Japan: An Interpretive Analysis of Four Pollution Suits," *Law & Society Review* 10 (1976): 579; Hiroshi Wagatsuma and Arthur Rosett, "The Implications of Apology: Law and Culture in Japan and the United States," *Law & Society Review* 20 (1986): 461.

26. J.G. Peristiany, ed., *Honour and Shame* (London: Weidenfeld & Nicholson, 1965); F.G. Bailey, ed., *Gifts and Poison* (Oxford: Basil Blackwell, 1971), Maarti Gronfors, "Finnish Gypsy Blood Feuding," *Journal of Legal Pluralism* 24 (1986): 101.

27. Oliver Wendell Holmes, *The Common Law* (Boston: Little, Brown, 1881), 94–96.

28. Abel, 1021.

29. Abel, 1008–10.

30. Curran, 148, 151 n., 123, 156, 159.

31. U.S. Department of Transportation, *Economic Consequences of Automobile Accidents* (Washington, D.C., 1970), 54; Curran, 122–28, 197–99.

32. Guido Calabresi, *The Costs of Accidents* (New Haven: Yale University Press, 1970), 24–29; Richard Posner, *Economic Analysis of Law*, 2d ed. (Boston: Little, Brown, 1977), 135–42.

33. Abel, 1012–13.

34. Abel, 1008–9.

35. Abel, 1013; William Felstiner, Richard Abel, and Austin Sarat, "The Emergence and Transformation of Disputes: Naming, Blaming, Claiming . . . ," *Law & Society Review* 15 (1981): 631.

36. *Bates v. State Bar of Arizona*, 433 U.S. 350 (1977).

37. *Ohralik v. Ohio State Bar Association*, 436 U.S. 447 (1978).

38. *In re Primus*, 436 U.S. 412 (1978); *United Mine Workers v. Illinois State Bar Association*, 389 U.S. 217 (1967); *Brotherhood of Railroad Trainmen v. Virginia ex rel. Virginia State Bar*, 377 U.S. 1 (1964); *NAACP v. Button*, 371 U.S. 415 (1963); *United Transportation Union v. State Bar of Michigan*, 401 U.S. 576 (1971).

39. Hazel Genn, *Meeting Legal Needs? An Evaluation of a Scheme for Personal Injury Victims* (Oxford: SSRC Centre for Socio-Legal Studies, 1982); Abel, 1008–10.

40. *Law Society's Gazette* 83 (3 Dec. 1986): 3648–49.

41. Hunting and Neuwirth, 11; F. Raymond Marks, Robert Paul Hallauer, and Richard R. Clifton, *The Shreveport Plan* (Chicago: American Bar Foundation, 1974); Curran, 190; Royal Commission on Legal Services, *Final Report*, vol. 1 (London: HMSO, 1979), 185, 210; Royal Commission on Legal Services in Scotland, *Report*, vol. 2 (Edinburgh: HMSO, 1980), 55, 58.

42. Marc Galanter, "Reading the Landscape of Disputes: What We Know and Don't Know (And Think We Know) About Our Allegedly Contentious and Litigious Society," *UCLA Law Review* 31 (1983): 4.

Overdeterrence and the Problem of Comparative Risk

WALTER OLSON

Of all the goals of the liability revolution, the most promising is that of reducing the rate of accidents. The modern tort system may, as its critics charge, fall short in every other respect. It may be an inefficient means of providing money to injury victims. It may depart drastically from legal precedent and from widely shared ideas of moral fault; it may dampen the spirit of enterprise and innovation; and it may be cumbersome and capricious in its workings. But if it deters needless accidents and injuries, many will find its expenses and burdens to be worth tolerating. Most people would like society to pay a high price to avoid injuries, more, perhaps, than the prospective victims of accidents themselves would be willing to spend if it were up to them.

The case for liability as a means of risk deterrence is clear, intuitive, and up to a point unassailable. Unless the victims of oil spills can go to court to win compensation, tanker owners will be less careful than they ought to be, and too often oil that should have been sent through pipelines or conserved will be shipped by sea. (To put it more formally, both the level of care and the level of activity will be suboptimal.) Some other form of regulatory control will have to be exerted over tanker owners if they are to be given proper incentives. But even a well-thought-out effort along these lines—perhaps embodied in a thousand-page rule manual for tanker captains— is apt to be clumsy, intrusive, and incomplete compared with the sublimely simple rule: "Pay when you spill."

The costs of underdeterrence, then, are plain enough. The symmetrical risks in the other direction are less obvious. Why not make tanker owners pay fifty times the cost of the harm done by the oil they spill? The answer must be that the public would then face too small a risk of oil spills or, put more commonsensically, would spend too much on prevention and pay too much at the gasoline pump. Injuries are not a positive good, but reducing them beyond a certain point would require society to give up too much of other values.

What are these other values that are being given up when the law is too stringent, when it deters too much? A general answer to that question requires an enormous and frustrating empirical inquiry. The inquiry is enormous because virtually every corner of society has been reached by the liability revolution, and frustrating because each story is unique, with much of the evidence anecdotal in nature and hard to document or quantify. How would one go about ascertaining the number of investigative reports that are never published because of the chilling effect of libel law? Or set a price tag on their value to the public? An added frustration to the researcher is that many potential defendants are understandably reluctant to discuss the sensitive subject of how often they get sued or what tactics they use to avoid coming to the attention of the plaintiffs' bar.

Even so, some of the costs of overdeterrence can be measured fairly directly, if partially, and given monetary price tags of a sort. The amounts spent on lawyers' time can be calculated with some accuracy, though this expense is far from the dominant economic impact of litigation. Specific areas of litigation can be linked to observable expenditures. Diverse sources agree that hundreds of millions of dollars, if not more, are spent on medical tests that have been ordered less to prevent misdiagnosis than to stave off liability. Personnel managers report that large chunks of staff time are now spent setting up proper defensive paper trails to guard against wrongful-discharge lawsuits, and one may speculate that further infusions of staff time go into the equally pressing task of erasing, deleting, and shredding alternative paper trails that could prove embarrassing.

Many of the economic values society sacrifices in pursuit of fuller liability are less easily translated into cash terms: the enjoyment of rock faces and hiking paths now put off limits to outdoor enthusiasts, the full usefulness in expert hands of a machine hobbled by "idiot-proofing," the advice value of a retired business leader who quits a hospital board for lack of insurance. These costs do not show up as direct expenditures on anyone's books but are just as real and in principle might be assigned a price tag.

Nothing should discourage researchers from doing their best to quantify the costs of liability. But concentrating on the monetary costs perpetuates the misimpression that the fundamental choice is between life and limb on the one hand and dollars on the other. The most salient choices are those between lives and lives, injuries and injuries, illnesses and illnesses. The most typical outcome of going too far in pursuit of one form of safety is to give up some other form of safety.

Several of these trade-offs between risk and risk have become familiar. The costs of defensive medicine, for example, go beyond needless testing. According to Dr. Vincent T. DeVita, Jr., director of the National Cancer Institute, many physicians refuse to prescribe potentially curative doses of chemotherapy for fear of litigation over side effects, and thousands of cancer patients may die needlessly each year as a result.[1] Many vaccine makers have withdrawn from the market because of litigation over side effects, increasing the risk that children will go unvaccinated, at peril to their health. Many consulting engineers, terrified of being sued, are reported to be holding back from cleaning up toxic-waste sites.

Cases like these may appear to be exceptional instances of liability gone haywire, but they are not. The problems are systemic, the predictable results of the fact that virtually every risk serves as a substitute for other risks. No liability rule, however harsh, can ever deter risk in itself; it can only deter behavior that gets people sued, which is not at all the same thing. Potential defendants go to extreme lengths to avoid getting sued, and if cornered they will save themselves by inflicting far bigger risks on society than were originally at issue. And the customers and patients they deal with do not sit still, either. When the threat of liability deters a transaction, they migrate to other alternatives, which are sometimes safer and sometimes not. Whatever they were trying to get from the transaction — entertainment or outdoor exercise, child care or cheap liquor — they will try to get somewhere else. The result is that when courts try to suppress one hazard, the sum total of societal risk does not usually fall as much as expected and often rises.

The liability system in its newly expanded form is ill suited to tackle the problem of comparative risk. And its failures are more than casually related to its refusal to distinguish between chosen and unchosen risks.

Reformulating a Risk

Perhaps the simplest way a producer can respond to liability is to redesign or redeploy its product or service, adding a new safety feature or subtracting an old risk that has led to litigation. Put in such general terms, it might sound as if the system is working as intended to make life safer. Sometimes it is. But when it comes down to the details, the risk barometer could actually be headed in either direction.

A drugmaker sued by patients who suffer a side effect reformulates the product at a lower and less effective dosage. An automaker sued because its seat belts let users add slack, thus reducing the belt's efficacy, does away with the slacking device — and some comfort-minded drivers start going beltless. Developers sued for negligent security after a mugging respond by avoiding multiple convenient exits in building designs — good for crime safety but bad for fire safety.

Adding a safety feature costs money; subtracting a risky feature that many consumers had valued costs market position. Either way, a producer will generally try to compensate through some combination of cuts in other quality dimensions and increases in price. Both affect safety. The case of quality cuts is straightforward enough. In hospitals, nurse time devoted to defensive medical paperwork competes directly with nurse time devoted to more direct ways of helping patients. The extra paperwork doubtless has genuine value in preventing mistakes and tracing blame when mistakes occur. But it is also costing something in safety. Malpractice plaintiffs have already started to charge that nurse understaffing contributed to their negative medical results.

Discussions of liability frequently assume that prices will rise rather than that quality will fall and that this is a preferable outcome from a safety standpoint. Yet the two are not easy to distinguish in practice. When prices rise, consumers move downscale in their quality preferences. Average quality may decline even if no single producer reformulates its product for the worse. When automobile prices rise steeply, buyers economize by trading down to smaller and lighter models, most of which are distinctly less safe in crashes. Others keep their old cars longer, raising the average age of the vehicles on the road, with equally negative implications for safety. If landmark court decisions expanding design liability drive up automobile prices, some boomerang effect is automatic.

Consumers find one automobile a close substitute for another, but when some products are under litigation pressure they can readily switch to dissimilar products that serve the same purpose. The virtual disappearance of the intrauterine device (IUD) has driven many women who are poor risks for birth-control pills to use that form of contraception, according to Planned Parenthood experts.

At some point, the liability dynamic that wipes out one risky product will tend to turn against its far-from-safe substitutes. The birth-control pill, like the IUD before it, faces persistent attack in court. But the new target will not always go the way of the old one, even if it is no more safe, because the liability system is far from consistent in its treatment of different products. The reasons for these discrepancies are varied, even whimsical. The plaintiffs' bar has launched a major attack on disposable cigarette lighters but seems not to care much about their major substitute, matches, although it is far from clear that the lighters are involved in more fire injuries per use. The reason may be that matches are less likely to survive as evidence. Or it may be, as Peter Huber has written, that juries are known to treat old and familiar risks more indulgently at trial than new and complicated risks.[2] If plaintiffs come back for try after try, however, the overall survival rate of products may be quite low, as customers switch to one substitute and then another and attorneys follow.

The Immobile and the Immune

At the end of the downward spiral, the producers left in an inherently risky field will tend to be the immobile and the immune — those who cannot escape liability and those who need not fear it. Consider first the immobile. The chief provider of last resort is the government. Because physicians, wary of liability, are reported reluctant to accept charity patients, indigent sufferers are showing up at municipal clinics that cannot turn them away.[3] Because private landowners are barring the use of their land for fear of suit, backpackers and hunters use public land instead. In both cases, the users' previously expressed preference for the private operator gives reason to think that quality (of which safety is one part) has probably not improved and may have declined.

Among the products that cannot be pulled off the market by their makers are those that have already been sold and are now in users' custody or on the second-hand market. Elevator manufacturers report frequent liability claims on machines installed more than seventy years earlier, and litigation has substantially driven up the price of newly sold long-lived goods like machine tools and light aircraft. Because of these price increases, many users hold onto old drills and pre-World War I crop dusters that might in a less judicially adverse world be sent to the scrap heap. Unfortunately, the obsolete models get into far more accidents than the new ones. If some sudden stroke of judicial leniency exempted manufacturers of these items from liability, the accident rate might paradoxically fall.

A subtler form of immobility is that of the sunk costs of product development, such as research. These investments cannot be retrieved when liability renders them retrospectively unprofitable. Products based on old research, whose current variable cost of production is low, may thus be kept on the market despite a wave of adverse liability judgments that deters new research.

The still-in-progress courtroom saga of insulation offers an interesting look at the courts' treatment of old and new technology. The greatest safety triumph of the modern liability system, it is widely believed, is the litigation that has bankrupted major processors of asbestos. Asbestos in conjunction with smoking is extremely dangerous to those who install it. Ironically, the mineral itself is the archetypal safety material, known since ancient times for its fire-resistant properties. Without its widespread use, countless people would have lost their lives at an early age from fire, smoke, and cold, as well as from enemy action: much of the careless use of asbestos that later came back to haunt American producers took place in the World War II crash shipbuilding program.

Now asbestos has given way in many applications to a far safer substitute, fiberglass. But fiberglass is alleged to cause inhalation problems similar to those of asbestos, though far less severe. Some scientists see the fault as the physical structure, common to both substances, of inert fibers with extreme resistance to biological and chemical decay. It is alleged that lung tissue cannot easily break them down as it does most other inhaled matter, and the fibers remain for long periods, wicking up cigarette smoke and other carcinogens. The very virtue that makes these substances effective over time in their safety missions, in short, may present a health risk that science cannot reduce to zero.

By all accounts, fiberglass is vastly safer than asbestos, and its invention has saved a great many lives. But if it poses even one-tenth as much risk as asbestos, the legal system will probably make its inventors come to regret ever having brought it into the world. Juries will return their common mix of positive and negative verdicts, and someone, somewhere, will win the first award of punitive damages. The scientists working on the next-generation innovation in the field — with risks even lower than fiberglass, though still higher than zero — will then get an unmistakable signal that their efforts will be judged not against the industry standard but against the unattainable goal of perfect safety.

Consider next the immune. Among the likeliest providers of last resort are those who are effectively unreachable by liability law. Canadian physicians who dispense IUDs to American women presumably do so on the assumption that they will not be sued under American law. As Douglas Besharov has pointed out, smaller foreign producers may be doing very well in markets where products liability is a major threat to United States producers.[4] To be sure, huge multinationals like Toyota and Nestlé, with ongoing United States operations and brand-name presence, are fully exposed to liability in American courts, at least for their sales in this country. The same does not hold true for independent Taiwanese or Brazilian producers that sell off-brand merchandise and maintain few or no assets in the United States reachable by the orders of American courts.

Other providers gain an advantage, whether deliberately or not, by being so thinly capitalized that they are not worth suing. When insurance rates rise and established child-care operations are priced beyond the reach of more families, part of the slack is taken up by less formal unlicensed providers — neighborhood mothers, grandmothers, and teenagers — whose virtues do not include the ability to furnish deep pockets in case of catastrophe.

When liability becomes a major factor in market survival, providers who are illegal or anonymous enjoy a distinct competitive edge. Major retail chains are inevitably exposed to full liability; street vendors usually get away without offering even a money-back guarantee, let alone a health-back guarantee, if their merchandise turns out to be faulty. Irregular channels of liquor production and distribution, such as "blind pigs" and home brewing — still common in some parts of the United States — get a new lease on life when the expansion of "dramshop liability" tightens the screws on legitimate taverns and when attorneys target commercial breweries for suit.

Black-market distribution of therapeutic drugs is widespread in the Third World but still rare in the United States (except for psychoactive compounds). But there are signs that such underground markets are getting under way in the case of more and more compounds suppressed by litigation pressure or regulation. They are likely to flourish if lawsuits or regulations drastically restrict access to promising acquired immune deficiency syndrome (AIDS) drugs or to Accutane, a drug desperately sought by acne sufferers that appears safe for patients so long as they do not become pregnant while using it. Just as tax cuts can bring people up from the underground economy, litigation pressure can drive them back down.

There is every reason to think that the departure of mobile, exposed producers from a market and their replacement with the immobile and the immune have perverse consequences for both safety and insurance objectives. Favorable things can be said about the here-today-gone-tomorrow producers that bob in and out of many markets, competing on price alone with no intent to build reputation. That they are known for intensive safety engineering and careful quality control and that they stand ready to compensate injury victims generously when injuries occur are not among them.

The most important risks whose creators are immune from litigation, however, do not arise from organized enterprise at all. One major culprit, and a big source of risk in general, is do-it-yourself activity. When organized playgrounds close down or put their jungle bars and other attractions into storage, more children play on the street, as they did a century ago. When liability drives up the price of stepladders, more people climb on boxes and chairs. Electricians have not yet become major targets of litigation, if only because the makers of electrical equipment offer a more inviting deep-pocket target. If they do, however, the prognosis for safety is not good. One study has shown that where the supply of electricians is restricted, more people electrocute themselves at home, a result that is believed to be due to the greater prevalence in those places of do-it-yourself electrical work.

Most hazardous products around the home represent improvements in safety over the generic or homemade remedies of previous generations. Commercial cleaning fluids and pesticides remain dangerous, but less so than old-time lye and arsenic. Store-bought hair-setting products have definite hazards, but amateur approaches are worse. At present the commercial products are so well established, and the original home methods so nearly forgotten, that the danger of mass regression seems minuscule. On the other hand, who would have guessed before the 1970s that the most pollutive and hazardous of all home-heating sources — the burning of wood — would make a comeback?

The Risks of Nothing

The ultimate substitute, the end of the line, is the option of nothing at all. When nothing else serves the intended purpose or nothing else is affordable, people will buy, use, or do nothing and divert their time and money to some entirely different objective. Sometimes the effects on safety are clearly positive. If a ski resort closes or a diving board is taken away, some enthusiasts of these sports will choose safer forms of recreation or stay home with a good book. Not many, it may be assumed, have such a positive taste for danger that they will search out an equally hazardous pastime. From the standpoint of safety, as opposed to freedom or satisfaction, all is well.

The trouble arises when a product or service improves its users' health or safety overall but is linked to particular hazards, mistakes, or side effects for which the legal system can punish it. When such goods are driven off the market or never get introduced, nature takes its course. In these cases — the stuff of headlines — insurance as well as safety objectives again suffer. A patient may sue if he takes a drug and suffers a side effect not perfectly spelled out in the warning, but there is no one to sue if the drug is unavailable and he dies of his underlying disease. An expectant mother may sue if a small-town obstetrician delivers her baby with birth defects but not if he quits practice and she miscarries on the long drive to the big-city hospital. A young athlete may sue if his football helmet might have been designed differently to give him added protection, but not if helmets have become so expensive that he was playing without one. An accident victim may sue if, while she lay unconscious in the street, a physician gives her an emergency tracheotomy that might have been done more nimbly. But she may not sue if the only physician on the scene sidles away into the crowd.

There is no reason to expect that a system that regularly embraces the risks of inaction in preference to the risks of action, that chooses the risks of nothing over the risks of something, is erring on the side of safety. The general trend in human affairs certainly suggests the opposite. As technology intervenes in one new area after another, death and injury rates continue to drop.

The safety differences between something and nothing, or between a product and its substitute, sometimes hinge on spillover effects. When the substitute is adopted, the safety of third parties may not fare as well. A classic example is the litigation over rival polio vaccines. One reason the health authorities promote the Sabin over the Salk polio vaccine is that the Sabin confers some immunity on unvaccinated persons, who pick up resistance through close contact with those who have been vaccinated. Juries nonetheless award damages against makers of Sabin on the grounds that Salk might have been better for the plaintiff at hand.

Instances of safety spillover are reasonably numerous. In automobile design, what is best for the driver who shows up in court with an injury is not always best for pedestrians, other drivers, and miscellaneous road users. Providing more power or better handling would prevent some accidents; on the other hand, the more a car approximates a high-performance vehicle the more it will tend to be driven as such, menacing everyone else on the road. Sam Peltzman's hypothesis — that when safety improvements are added to a car, a certain number of drivers will reduce their own level of care — is no less likely to apply whether the features are mandated by regulation or liability.

The design of power plants involves safety trade-offs between different pollution victims; the design of toll-booth stations, between workers and drivers; the design of buildings, between residents and outsiders. A fortress-style building that is largely shut off from contact with the street will face fewer negligent-security suits from tenants who get mugged, but a building that is reasonably open to the sidewalk may make the street itself safer for passersby. Instructing juries to consider possible safety spillovers helps make trials immensely complicated but in no way ensures that the interests of those not present in the courtroom are adequately represented.

Such spillover effects are often found in the operation of governmental and charitable services, which may go some distance to explain why courts were so long reluctant to treat these defendants as severely as they treated profit-making defendants. Strictly private endeavors also produce positive spillovers, of course, but the operators by charging full price for their services tend to capture much more of the benefit of what they produce, and at the margin, perhaps, all of it. In a public-health venture — vaccination, pest abatement, or screening for contagious disease — the benefits of the challenged risk accrue in large part to neither the plaintiff nor the charitable or governmental defendant but to citizens not in the courtroom.

In a recent New York City case, the issue was public safety. A terrorist device went off in a Manhattan public plaza while a bomb-squad detective and his partner were working on it. The detective was badly injured and sued the city for failing to train him well enough for the job. A jury awarded him $1.5 million and his wife $300,000.[5] The sympathetic case was overwhelming: who could resist lending a hand to a public servant who had risked his life to save innocent bystanders? And, looked at solely with respect to the safety of future bomb-squad officers, the effects of the decision are likely to be positive.

But the effects on the sum total of risk are not clear. If jury-proofing the training of such squads takes a huge infusion of money and time, cities will train fewer officers, and fewer cities will establish bomb squads in the first place. And if the training issue is perceived as just an excuse for a jury to compensate a brave officer, police departments will come under budgetary pressure to skip the training charade and simply use bomb squads less aggressively. Not much litigation pressure comes from the other side. In general, courts have not held municipalities to an especially high liability standard in preventing crime, and not many terrorist victims will win awards on the grounds that a city has disbanded a bomb squad or failed to deploy officers aggressively in finding or defusing devices. In days past, the officer would have been compensated through a special public collection or legislative appropriation kept separate from the department's budget. That older custom showed a subtle knowledge of incentives; it encouraged heroism in the individual without discouraging it in the department.

The Balance of Terror

One might think the balancing of risk versus risk would come out rationally enough when the same producer has control of all the different risks and can get sued either way. Hospitals should in theory be unaffected by defensive considerations if they can be targeted alike for letting their nurses neglect paperwork or neglect patients; physicians, for treating patients too aggressively or too passively. A soft-drink bottler, faced with a choice between glass bottles that might blow up and plastic bottles that might cause cancer, and certain to be sued whichever happens, might have a good incentive to find the safer option.

Unfortunately, liability often shows signs of backfiring even when all the safety reins are in the same hands. The Public Citizen Health Research Group, a Ralph Nader organization, and other groups have charged that physicians order Cesarean-section deliveries far more often than they should, in part because they overdiagnose "fetal distress" and related conditions that portend possible bad results. Presumably no legal doctrine bars a suit by a mother who has been put through a needless Cesarean or a chemotherapy patient who has been prescribed too timid a dosage. The only plausible explanation is that deterrence is applied unevenly in practice. Perhaps a dramatic side effect in chemotherapy or a birth defect after a Cesarean section was indicated but not used is more likely to enthrall a jury than a failure to cure a disease known to be deadly or trauma in childbirth. Or perhaps courts brush aside informed consent more readily for the surprising injuries than for the more routine ones.

Many supporters of broad liability agree that uneven deterrence leads to perverse safety results but hope to solve matters by making the system even broader and more comprehensive. If thinly capitalized firms are outcompeting deep-pocket participants, they suggest, the answer is to pass "financial responsibility" laws that level the playing field by compelling all producers to post bonds or buy insurance. If biases in litigation patterns lead physicians to prescribe too many Cesarean sections and not enough chemotherapy, the answer is for lawyers to step up the litigation pressure where it lags, thus equalizing the balance of incentives against mistakes in either direction.

Such a symmetry of terrors may be in the future of more and more potential defendants. An employer who awards hiring preferences in order to head off a discrimination lawsuit from one group walks into a costly lawsuit from another. A landlady must anticipate a lawsuit from a tenant if she evicts him because of his alleged criminal tendencies, and a different kind of lawsuit from other tenants if she does not. A physician can be hit with a failure-to-warn lawsuit for not telling the wife of an AIDS patient about his condition or a violation-of-confidentiality lawsuit from the patient himself.

The modern law seems to be increasingly comfortable with the proliferation of legal obligations between which there is much tension if not outright contradiction. The older law was concerned to provide "safe harbors," "bright-line tests," and similar devices by which persons in useful lines of work could arrange their affairs so as to stay out of court. The newer trend is to spike the former safe harbors with floating mines and to replace the bright lines with a vast no-man's-land of uncertain legality in which the liability status of an action can be decided only after the fact in court. An appropriate motto might be a paraphrase of the old Marine Corps saying: sue them all and let God sort them out.

As a means of salvaging safety, however, the attempt to equalize the balance of terror is doomed to fail. Stepping up the pressure on existing producers may help even out imbalances between them, but at the cost of shifting more and more business to the more serious risks that the legal system cannot control, including do-it-yourself activity and nature itself. The landlord and employer, sued from every direction at once, behave judiciously while they lay their plans to go condo or move to Taiwan. The physician, forced to pay for every kind of adverse result, faces reasonably balanced incentives in treating the patient at hand but also far too much incentive to turn away the next gravely ill patient in favor of golf. The judicial carpenters can never be sure of leveling the table when they can reach only some of its legs.

One final, desperate way to try to right the risk imbalance would be to make people liable for their very acts of omission and forbearance, for their failure to stay in markets with risky products or enter them in the first place. The idea would require a sort of safety conscription, the establishment of positive obligations where there is currently no "duty of care." Under such positive obligations, the physician could be sued for leaving the scene of the emergency without doing anything to help; the drugmaker, for withdrawing an oft-litigated compound; the landowner, for refusing to allow local children to use his swimming hole, though he knows it is safer than the abandoned quarry.

Such proposals are sometimes dubbed "Good Samaritan statutes," a label that is a bit confusing, since those who emulate the kindly biblical figure are already subject to liability when they do inadvertent harm, and the point of the proposals is to extend liability to everyone else. A number of academic commentators have endorsed the general principle. But the legal system has been fairly resolute in resisting urgings to move in this direction. It has peered into the implications of Good Samaritan statutes and seen an abyss.

Taking the logic of such liability even a few steps would require government's domain over human affairs to be all-encompassing. It would mean not only compelling producers to go on marketing beneficial goods but also maintaining price controls on those goods, since overly high prices — in effect, partial withdrawals of a good — can discourage buyers who might benefit. It would be noteworthy for the wealth and variety of its violations of personal liberty and constitutional values, involving such things as curbs on the ability of physicians to retire, requirements that they move to the litigious communities where they are most needed, and legally enforceable obligations that newspapers chilled by libel law conduct investigative journalism on topics of public concern. Hardly anyone wants to follow the principle wherever it leads, and even the warmest supporters of Good Samaritan statutes seem to agree that no more of the camel should be admitted to the tent than the nose.

The Persistence of Choice

What the legal system keeps running into, on both the producer and the consumer sides, is the intractable phenomenon of individual choice. The underlying legal revolution in this field — the declaration that risks of personal injury could not be made the subject of binding contracts and would be transferred to the domain of tort law instead — arose from an assumption that all the real choice was on the producers' side, that most product and medical risks were inflicted on consumers in much the way that oil spills are inflicted on beachfront owners. Yet the courts do not have the eyes or ears, let alone the nerve or stomach, to police all choices by producers.

And it is becoming increasingly apparent that the dismissal from consideration of the choices of consumers and third parties is no way to optimize the accident rate either. If courts hold producers liable in clear cases of product misuse — as when a user has removed the safety guard from a piece of machinery — they are misallocating the incentives of all three parties: the company that made the machine, the user who removed the safety guard, and the one who came in contact with it afterward. Inviting one of the parties to adopt a level of care that is too high, and the others to adopt one too low, does not average out to an optimal policy of accident prevention.

This point has special force in the fast-growing area of business liability for crimes committed by third parties. More and more courts, following the lead of the 1970 case *Klein* v. *1500 Massachusetts Ave. Apartment Corp.*, are willing to hold a business defendant liable for someone else's criminal act that it might have prevented, such as an airline hijacking, a headache-pill tampering on store shelves, and muggings at a supermarket's parking lot or a bank's automatic teller machine. The Dupont Plaza Hotel arson of New Year's Day 1987 was followed by a spate of negligent-security suits against the owners.

Such lawsuits need not interfere with vigorous prosecution of the actual criminals. But in practice, nearly all the money, time, and legal-investigative talent on the scene is spent going after the business rather than the criminals, simply because the business is the one with the money. The litigation directs the indignation of the victims and their survivors toward those who did not commit the crime and away from those who did. When, as in the Dupont Plaza arson, the criminal attack was meant to intimidate the business itself, the irony is complete. By menacing the owners with ruinous liability verdicts, negligent-security doctrine makes such intimidation more credible and thus more likely to be used.

The purely unchosen, gratuitously inflicted hazard — bowling balls rolling off a roof, to borrow an image from Tom Wolfe — is responsible for only a small portion of all injuries. Yet this is the mold into which many courts now insist on forcing all manner of accidents that arise from consensual interactions, from surgery to the purchase of cigarettes. Once courts insisted on ignoring the component of choice in the assumption of risk, they were bound to run into the problem of comparative hazard. If bowling balls are secured and their precipitation ceases to be a matter of urban menace, neither pedestrians nor, in all likelihood, building owners will fly to some new hazard. But when courts suppress a risk that is voluntarily entered into, they encourage the parties to conspire to defeat the law's paternalist efforts — a conspiracy whose success often spells defeat not just for paternalism but for safety itself.

Notes

1. Ronald Kotulak, "Cancer May Feed on Malpractice Fear," *Chicago Tribune*, 25 March 1986.

2. Peter Huber, "Safety and the Second Best: The Hazards of Public Risk Management in the Courts," *Columbia Law Review* 85 (March 1985): 277–337.

3. Sara C. Charles and Eugene Kennedy, *Defendent: A Psychiatrist on Trial for Medical Malpractice* (New York: Free Press, 1985), 226.

4. Douglas Besharov, "Forum-Shopping, Forum-Skipping, and the Problem of International Competitiveness," in this volume, pp. 139–48.

5. "Injured cop awarded 1.5 M," *New York Daily News*, 18 June 1987.

The Causes of the Insurance Crisis

KENNETH S. ABRAHAM

Every crisis combines danger and opportunity. If it is not resolved, the problems it poses may worsen. But the public attention it evokes may also help to solve problems that would otherwise go ignored. This essay examines the danger and opportunity created by the liability insurance crisis of 1985 and 1986. During that time the price of commercial liability insurance escalated dramatically, and some businesses and professionals found they could not obtain coverage at any price. Some blamed the tort system for the crisis, others what they saw as collusion by the insurance industry. Dozens of states responded by enacting the first tort-reform statutes of general application they had ever adopted and by revising their insurance laws and regulations.

The crisis is by no means completely resolved. Premiums remain high compared with previous levels, many enterprises still find it hard to obtain adequate coverage, and most participants in the debate — though they may disagree on other issues — recognize that none of the actions taken thus far ensures that similar crises will not recur.

To make sense of the insurance crisis, one must unravel the various short- and long-term developments that brought it about and assess their relative contributions. Four explanations have been widely given for the crisis, and each has different implications for reform. In fact, no single explanation fully accounts for the problems that have arisen, and no single reform is likely to prevent their recurrence. Most important, the principal long-term cause of the crisis — a legal climate that makes insuring businesses and professionals a risky enterprise — cannot be rectified through the kind of "quick-fix" tort and insurance-law reforms that have been adopted thus far.

The Underwriting Cycle

Fluctuation in price and supply is a fact of life in commercial liability-insurance markets. This fluctuation results from changes in such factors as interest rates, the supply of reinsurance capital, the value of the dollar against foreign currencies, and the attractiveness of alternative investments. Although insurance consumers tend to complain during the "hard" portion of this cycle, they benefit during the "soft" portion. Between 1979 and 1984, for example, premiums for commercial liability insurance generally remained unchanged, although double-digit inflation prevailed for much of that time. Intense price competition during these years was brought on at least partly by high interest rates that led insurers to engage in "cash-flow" underwriting — writing business at a sizable underwriting loss that they would recoup by earning investment income on premium money before claims came due. Cash-flow underwriting held premium levels in check for several years, with insurance consumers reaping the benefits.

In late 1984, however, several developments broke this pattern and sent premium rates upward. First, interest rates had been declining for more than a year, and investment returns were certain to fall as a result, which meant that less income would be coming in to offset underwriting losses. Second, the value of the dollar against European currencies reached a peak. That made the American market less attractive to European reinsurers, whose willingness to reinsure American risks helps determine the total underwriting capacity of the American market. Finally, as both of these factors began to break the competitive hold on premium levels, the players began to realize that the predominant component of liability insurance payouts — the costs of the tort system — was rising fast.

Although it is difficult to disentangle the separate effect of these developments on premiums, the least influential was probably the decline in interest rates. Changes in interest rates alone should not have a major effect on premium levels, because they tend to parallel changes in the cost of the components of tort liability. During periods of high interest rates, for example, there is usually high inflation, including inflation in medical costs and wages — two of the principal components of tort recoveries. Similarly, when interest rates fall and investment income declines, the rate of inflation of medical costs and wages is also likely to decline. When all these rates of change move in the same direction, as they generally do, a decline in expected investment earnings need not produce a fully offsetting increase in premiums. In some circumstances it might not require any increase at all.

A second cyclical reason for the crisis, one that would seem more important in practice, was the strength of the United States dollar at the end of 1984, which partially explains the withdrawal of European reinsurers from the American market. But that withdrawal was also motivated in part by the surge in tort costs, which lies outside the insurance-cycle explanation.

It should not have been surprising that when the cycle finally turned upward, premium levels rose substantially. Indeed, if premiums had only, say, doubled between 1984 and 1986 and all businesses had found adequate coverage reasonably available at those prices, the course of the underwriting cycle might fully explain the problems in the market. Unfortunately, however, some enterprises could not obtain insurance at any price, and many that could were faced with premium increases of several hundred percent. The underwriting cycle alone is an implausible explanation for market conditions this severe.

Primarily in response to the real and perceived ills that are generated by the insurance cycle, some states adopted a regulatory device known as "flex-rating."

The rationale for flex-rating is that wide fluctuations in insurance prices are intolerably disruptive in settings where insurance coverage is a practical or legal prerequisite to doing business and can be moderated by setting both a floor and a ceiling on rate changes in each line or subline of coverage. Rates may fluctuate, or flex, within the range, but they may not rise or fall outside the range without special justification and prior approval by the state's regulatory authority (usually an "insurance commissioner"). The idea is to curb the excesses of open competition in insurance pricing (which had itself replaced the "prior approval" approach to rates) and thus moderate both the up and down portions of the cycle.

There are reasons both in practice and in principle to question the value of flex-rating. First, a flex-rating scheme probably cannot be sufficiently detailed to control actual pricing decisions in commercial liability insurance lines, and many different criteria are used to set prices for business customers. Different coverage levels, deductibles, and classifications of risk are common in these markets, and much coverage is customized. The rules of a flex-rating scheme are not likely to govern a particular pricing decision specifically enough to have any bite, and many pricing decisions are unique.

Second, even if a flex-rating scheme were formulated in sufficient detail to govern each pricing decision, few state insurance regulators would have the eyes and ears needed to make it work. Even New York, whose insurance commissioner's office is well staffed and financed, is likely to run into trouble enforcing its flex-rating system. Most other states, which have smaller, already overworked staffs and much lower budgets, would find the task overwhelming.

Third, even if flex-rating did work, it could exacerbate the problems created by the underwriting cycle. During the past decade, premium rates in commercial insurance have been largely unregulated. Flex-rating would reintroduce many of the undesirable side effects of price control that open competition has eliminated. During the soft portion of the underwriting cycle, when flex-rating limits price cutting, insurers competing for premium dollars are likely to lower their underwriting standards to accept applicants for coverage whom they might otherwise reject. Ultimately, this behavior will increase underwriting losses in much the same way as does price competition. The increased underwriting losses incurred later will justify added price increases during the up-cycle, and the system will have recaptured the torque that flex-rating is designed to eliminate.

Similarly, during the hard portion of the cycle, when flex-rating limits premium increases, insurers can camouflage price increases by lowering the quality of coverage provided or by raising underwriting standards and thereby making coverage unavailable to the marginal risks who would have obtained it if increases above the flex-ceiling were permitted. In both cases, flex-rating will be formally enforced, but insurers will have found methods of circumventing it.

Finally, in addition to the practical limitations on flex-rating's feasibility, there is a strong argument in principle against the device. At its most general level this argument is against the cross-subsidies entailed in a flex-rating scheme, but it is best understood at a more specific level. Suppose that all the customers who pay more during the soft portion of the cycle, when flex-rating keeps rates from falling as low as they would, are the same customers who benefit later from below-market prices. Then flex-rating operates like an enforced savings scheme for insurance buyers.

The paternalism of such a scheme may itself be objectionable. But the original supposition is also invalid. There is no reason to imagine that the customers whose coverage is flex-priced at different times are identical. Businesses come and go, and their need for liability insurance varies throughout their existence. Consequently, a business that pays an above-market price for liability insurance at one time is not necessarily the same business that takes advantage of a below-market price a few years later. In effect, sometimes the first business is not only participating in an enforced savings scheme but buying an advantage for a second business without receiving any particular benefit for doing so. It has simply been taxed for the benefit of the second business.

In short, flex-rating is a flawed method of dealing with price fluctuations. In fact, most industries that rely on inputs with fluctuating prices do not depend on price control for protection; they recognize its dangers and employ other, nonmandatory devices to mitigate the effects of price swings. For example, they may hedge by investing in a futures market for the commodity, or they may accumulate an inventory of the commodity. Interestingly, a futures market in insurance would be infeasible for the same reason that flex-rating is likely to be ineffective — the product in question is heterogeneous, not uniform from one buyer to the next.

On the other hand, the insurance analogue to accumulating inventory — the purchase of long-term policies at fixed premiums — might cushion the disruption resulting from swings in the underwriting cycle. The fact that this device is not widely used is a strong signal that premium increases are caused not only by swings in the underwriting cycle but also by other forces that would endanger any insurer that sold a long-term policy. These other disruptive forces are analyzed in the following sections.

Collusion

A second prominent explanation for the crisis of 1985–86 is that it was caused by collusion within the insurance industry. In this view the cause of the problem is the industry's exemption from federal antitrust regulation by the McCarran-Ferguson Act of 1945. The industry's return to profitability in 1986 and its support of tort reform are often cited in support of the collusion theory.

As a general explanation for the crisis, the theory is implausible. First, as recently as 1983 a price war raged in commercial liability insurance. Second, by the most prominent measure used by antitrust analysts, the degree of concentration in the insurance industry is comparatively low. Maintaining a cartel in commercial lines would be especially difficult, because cartel members could so easily cheat on the agreement in nonobvious ways — by offering higher-quality coverage instead of lowering prices, for example. In reality, the experience of the market has been opposite during the recent crisis. The quality of coverage, measured by the limits of coverage, the type and number of exclusions included in policies, and the coverage of claims that arise after the policy period ends, has not improved but markedly deteriorated. Third – and in some ways most revealing – an important feature of the early stages of the current crisis was that liability insurance was not merely very expensive but completely unavailable to certain businesses. It would be an unusual cartel that refused to sell its product at the high prices that its monopoly power enabled it to charge.

Despite these indicia of competition, critics of the industry often cite two other pieces of evidence in support of the collusion hypothesis. The first is that the insurance industry returned to profitability in 1986, after, as critics see it, pleading poverty to justify raising rates. If the crisis were real, the insurers would still be losing money. One reply to this charge is that unless the industry is profitable it will not attract new capital, its capacity to provide new coverage will dry up, and customers will be worse off in the long run. The insurance industry is not remarkably different from others in its concern for profitability, and its long-term return on capital is probably slightly lower than comparable industries.

An even more persuasive reply, however, is that we do not really know whether the property/casualty insurance industry was profitable in 1986, because its profit and loss figures are based on uncertain assumptions about the future. Insurance profits are a function of both investment and underwriting experience – that is, earnings on invested premiums and payments and expenses on insured events – and few of the claims arising out of liability policies sold in one year are paid by the end of that year. In medical malpractice and products liability, for example, the "loss development" period averages five to seven years; not all claims are filed immediately, and once a claim is filed it may take years to resolve. On such "long-tail" policies, as they are called, calculating underwriting profit on policies sold in the past year or two is only an exercise in guesswork.

Such advance profit-and-loss estimates often turn out to be substantially inaccurate. Early calculations are heavily dependent on an accounting category known as IBNRs, or claims "incurred but not reported." These are the claims that will eventually be paid or adjusted by a given year's policies but have not yet been lodged. When claim frequency and severity are holding steady, or changing at a predictable rate, estimates of IBNRs are reliable and the profitability statements made by insurers tell a reasonably accurate story. In periods of unsteady change, however, IBNR estimates can be misleading.

Because IBNRs are such a sizable component of estimated underwriting profit or loss in "long-tail" lines like medical malpractice and commercial liability, the reports that the property/casualty industry as a whole turned a profit in 1986 are a bit misleading. Given accepted accounting conventions, which include estimating IBNRs, the industry was far more profitable than the previous year. Since premiums had just risen dramatically and most claims against policies sold that year in long-tail lines had not yet been lodged, it would have been surprising to see any other result. Whether this profitability forecast is accurate, however, will depend on the frequency and severity of future claims against 1986 policies.

The second piece of evidence frequently offered for the collusion hypothesis is the insurance industry's strong support for tort reform during the crisis. Having raised premiums on the pretext that its liabilities were expanding, critics say, the industry used the crisis to secure liability reforms that could be expected to lower its costs, thus profiting twice at the expense of the consumer.

There should be no doubt that the industry's campaign for tort reform was consciously collective; the issue is whether the crisis itself had been contrived to make the lobbying possible or whether less conspiratorial forces were at work. Here one may note a paradox. In principle, the insurance industry should favor a broad rather than narrow application of tort liability, so as to increase demand for its product. Why would the industry support reforms that would dry up much of the demand for liability insurance? One possible reason is that the industry simply prefers the short-term profit to be had in tort reform — paying fewer claims on policies already written — to the long-term profit to be made from a bigger market with more money at stake. But how all the major insurers could have considered such a strategy, and then reached consensus on it without any leaks about their internal debates, is a mystery.

A second possible reason for the industry's stance is that it knows there are practical limits on how much businesses and professionals will spend on insurance. Once these limits are exceeded, the industry may be blamed for rate increases for which the legal system is actually responsible. By 1986, in fact, the industry was under attack in exactly this way; its support for tort reform both focused blame in a different direction and held out hope to customers that future premium increases would be slowed by tort reform.

A third view, by contrast, rejects the proposition that expanding tort liability is always in the insurance industry's long-term interest. An industry that thrives on the certainty afforded by the law of large numbers may favor expansion of tort liability when it is slow, steady, and predictable, but not when the expansion creates unpredictable new liabilities that cannot be insured with any confidence. In the latter case, placing limits on liability that make prediction easier may be the only way to continue insuring customers. On this view the motive behind the insurance industry's tort-reform campaign was exactly what it claimed — the desire to restrain the surge in tort costs that had contributed to the crisis and to add greater predictability to the liability-insurance system.

In sum, the collusion hypothesis is not persuasive. The structure and recent history of the commercial liability-insurance market reveal no evidence of a cartel; the fact that the industry was "profitable" in 1986 says little about whether premiums for that year will ultimately prove to have been excessive; and although the industry acted as one in supporting tort reform, this collective behavior is equally open to noncollusive explanations based on the individual interests of each company. In short, collusion as an explanation for the insurance crisis is implausible in theory and unlikely in practice. The hypothesis falls not only because the arguments for it are weak, but also because the alternative explanation for the crisis — the combination of the surge in tort costs and the predictability problem — is persuasive.

Tort Costs and Predictability

A third explanation for the insurance crisis is that it arose from two developments in the tort system: a surge in tort payouts and changes in the rules of tort and insurance law that make it harder to predict future liabilities. Over the long run, both developments are likely to cause the cost of liability insurance to increase, since both the scope and the predictability of tort liability inevitably influence premium levels.

The first development — the surge in tort costs — translates directly into higher premiums. Almost all available data indicate that the cost surge has been substantial: figures on tort payouts by insurers, figures on payouts by self-insured businesses, and indices of the cost of components of tort liability like medical costs and wage rates. Between 1981 and 1985, for example, amounts paid in nonautomobile liability claims rose by 15 percent a year; between 1979 and 1985 New York City, which is self-insured for tort liability, experienced a 400 percent increase in settlements and judgments; and between 1979 and 1984, tort payouts by commercial liability insurers increased 130 percent. Similarly, between 1975 and 1984, the real or inflation-adjusted level of per capita income and of health-care costs, two major components of tort awards, grew by 17 percent and 23 percent respectively.

It should come as no surprise that liability premiums, although they might remain generally level for some years under the influence of the underwriting cycle, would eventually have to rise substantially to reflect cost increases of this magnitude. When the five-year downswing in the underwriting cycle ended in 1985, the cost pressures finally burst out in dramatic premium increases. In a sense the short-term effects of the underwriting cycle and the long-term effects of the tort-cost surge together magnified the increases that each alone would have produced. In addition, as premiums increased, comparatively low-risk insureds were probably more willing to give up coverage than comparatively high-risk insureds, and some low-risk insureds found alternatives to the commercial market through self-insurance or risk-retention groups. This "adverse selection" effect may well have further magnified premium increases.

The forces within the legal system that have caused the cost surge have been widely analyzed and debated. Increases in the frequency of suits, in the size of settlements and jury verdicts, and in the cost of litigation all seem to have contributed to the surge. But another feature of the system, the predictability of liability, deserves attention, because it has a special effect on liability insurance. To set accurate premiums, insurers must predict the scope of liability that a policy will cover, anticipating not only ordinary cost increases but also changes in liability rules. When insurers have confidence in their predictions, the market is likely to be stable. But when the future state of the law is uncertain, insurers must charge what amounts to an additional premium to cover the risk that their predictions about the scope of future liability are inaccurate.

In fact, legal changes during the last decade have severely undermined insurers' ability to predict the nature and scope of future liability with confidence. This has added a third upward pressure on premiums accompanying the underwriting cycle and the tort-cost surge. As a result, in the lines of insurance with the greatest uncertainty, the price at which supply would meet demand was probably so high that for practical purposes coverage was simply unavailable for a time.

The legal changes responsible for these developments reveal much about the kinds of reforms that are and are not likely to succeed in preventing the insurance crisis from recurring. Five such developments are worth detailing. First, scientific and medical advances have made it possible for the first time to draw inferences about the causes of certain kinds of diseases. In particular, the relation between exposure to hazardous substances and the occurrence of certain types of cancer and other diseases is now better understood than it was only a decade ago. A proliferation of tort suits alleging liability has followed these medical advances.

Ironically, instead of making the scope of liability more predictable, the growth of medical knowledge has had the opposite effect. In the past there would have been no serious threat of liability for many hazardous exposures, because a claimant had no way to prove the requisite causal connection between a particular exposure and his disease. Today that connection can sometimes be proved, at least to the satisfaction of a tort jury. But the retrospective task of linking today's diseases to yesterday's exposures is far easier than the prospective task of predicting how today's exposures will influence the frequency and severity of tomorrow's diseases. Insurers are consequently finding themselves liable for losses that often could not have been predicted when the policies were originally sold; at the same time, they are being threatened with future liability for diseases whose contours are difficult to predict today. Naturally, insurers build into their calculations of the cost of today's coverage a premium to guard against this threat.

Second, some courts have begun to impose retroactive strict (no-fault) liability for flaws in the design or marketing of consumer products or drugs. This amounts to liability for failing to discover or warn of imperfections in products at a time when doing so was not technically possible. The leading decision is the New Jersey asbestos case of Beshada v. Johns-Manville Products Corp. Although the Beshada decision has been limited in New Jersey to asbestos claims, other jurisdictions have applied its principle to other products. The rationale behind these decisions is that the threat of retroactive strict liability provides an incentive for companies to conduct research on product hazards and that in any event manufacturers and sellers are better placed than consumers to obtain insurance against losses caused by product imperfections. The weakness of this rationale, however, is that an insurer cannot calculate a premium for open-ended coverage against unknowable risks. All insured parties must therefore pay what amounts to an uncertainty tax as part of their premiums, to cover the risk of currently unpredictable retroactive strict liabilities.

Third, the doctrine of joint and several liability is being employed more frequently and liberally in tort suits and is a central feature of the liabilities created by the federal Superfund Act of 1980 and its 1986 amendments, which insurers fear will serve as a model for further expansion of tort liability. The doctrine holds that under certain circumstances when the actions of several parties combine to cause a plaintiff's loss, each can be held liable for the entire amount of the loss. For example, when pollution from several sources combines to harm a plaintiff, each source might be held jointly and severally liable for the entire damage. The doctrine is often invoked to make a single defendant pay for losses caused by other injurers who cannot be identified or are insolvent, exempt from liability, or otherwise unable to pay.

Predicting the scope of any given policyholder's potential joint and several liability is very difficult for insurers. Whether a policyholder is held jointly and severally liable at all depends partly on what other parties do, and how much of a judgment one party must pay depends on whether those other parties are solvent and on the scene. Thus, setting a price for insurance against joint and several liability is largely guesswork. Consequently, insurers must assess an additional premium much like the uncertainty tax created by retroactive strict liability.

Fourth, a number of courts have begun allowing plaintiffs exposed to danger to recover damages before they have suffered any tangible physical harm. The leading decision is *Ayers* v. *Jackson Township*, a New Jersey case in which residents whose water supply was contaminated by toxic pollutants from a township landfill recovered more than $13 million for medical monitoring expenses and damage to their quality of life, even though no residents proved that they had suffered physical injury or disease from the contamination.

No court has yet awarded recovery for the imposition of risk alone—*Ayers* avoided the issue by focusing on medical monitoring and quality-of-life damages. But plaintiffs in dangerous-exposure cases continue to claim compensation for fear that they will suffer disease and for their mere exposure to risk with no showing of injury in any of these respects. Of course, many times more persons may be exposed to risk by an act of misconduct than eventually suffer actual injury because of that act. Even if liability for risk alone is not imposed, medical-monitoring costs and losses resulting from fear and anxiety are likely to be larger and less determinate than losses from actual physical harm. Consequently, predicting the scope of future payouts based on these new kinds of claims will also involve considerable—and perhaps intolerable—indeterminacy.

Finally, a very different kind of legal change has also undermined the predictability essential to a properly functioning system of liability insurance. This change involves insurance law itself rather than tort law. In a series of different contexts, the courts have interpreted insurance contracts so as to expand coverage beyond what the language of the policies and the insurers who drafted them originally contemplated. The tendency of the courts to resolve coverage disputes in favor of policyholders is not new. But typically the courts indulged this tendency mainly to favor individual policyholders, generally taking the view that insured businesses stand on a more equal footing with insurance companies and should have to live with the language in their policies.

Recently, however, there has been a proliferation of "judge-made insurance" in coverage disputes involving business customers as well. This use of anti-insurer interpretive strategies is much more threatening for insurers, since the liabilities in question — often involving alleged mass torts — tend to be enormous. Moreover, the courts sometimes adopt these fluid and malleable readings of contract language in the very cases that first expand the frontiers of tort liability, making the liabilities created by tort law doubly difficult for insurers to predict and further hampering their ability to revise coverage language to clarify or limit their obligations.

Each of these developments in tort and insurance law has added unpredictability to the calculations insurers must make in setting liability-insurance premiums. Since the aggregation of predictable risks is the essence of the insurance function, it is extremely probable that the market's instability during the crisis of 1985 and 1986 — and a portion of the premium increases of that time — can be traced to these developments.

Yet, notwithstanding the widespread legislative response to the crisis, little has been done to return predictability to the market. A few states have limited the use of joint and several liability, but most of the tort-law reforms enacted by the states during 1986 (such as changes in the collateral-source rule, periodic payment of judgments, and sanctions for frivolous suits) are directed at controlling the tort-cost surge rather than relieving the predictability problem. Even the most far-reaching reform adopted — ceilings on recovery of noneconomic damages — will have much more effect on the cost surge than on the prediction of claim frequency.

It is therefore understandable that the limited data available on the effect of tort reforms on premium levels suggest that the sort of reforms enacted thus far are likely at best to slow the rate of premium increases over the long run. As long as tort law continues to expand into new areas of liability and judges continue to expand the coverage of policy language, it is unlikely that tinkering with tort-law doctrine will put an end to the upward trend in liability-insurance costs. Small-scale reforms may slow the trend, but they cannot stop or reverse it, because the underlying problem is the accelerated pace of legal change.

The important question, then, is whether any *formal* reform can affect the willingness of a generation of judges and juries to change the law — and to change it quickly — if that willingness is at the heart of the predictability problem. Formal rules may caution judges and juries against rapid legal change, but they cannot, in our system of law, prevent it. The most that can be expected from typical state tort reforms, therefore, is that they will serve as a warning, a symbolic shot across the bow of the expanding tort system. Of course, symbols can sometimes be powerful. Although the tort reforms of the past two years cannot by themselves solve the insurance crisis, they are a sign of legislative concern that could convince courts to slow the pace of legal change in order to reintroduce predictability to the system.

Incentives to Litigate

A fourth explanation for the insurance crisis takes a comparative approach that complements the preceding explanations as much as it contradicts them. It does not purport to explain why the most recent crisis struck when it did. Rather, it takes a long-term view and compares the American civil-liability experience with that of other industrial countries, most of which are not experiencing a similar crisis. This view suggests that the incentives to litigate tort claims in the United States are so strong that tort liability will continue to expand and insurance costs to increase over the long term.

Three distinctive features of the American civil-liability system create incentives to litigate tort cases: the availability of contingent percentage fees for plaintiffs' attorneys; the rule that a losing party does not pay the winner's costs or attorney's fees; and the absence of the widespread, comparatively generous forms of social insurance found in other Western democracies.

Each incentive has its influence. The contingent-fee system gives plaintiffs' attorneys an intense interest in filing and winning cases. That system, along with the "American rule" that parties bear their own costs, also makes instituting a lawsuit much less risky for an American plaintiff. If he loses, he need not pay the counsel fees of either set of lawyers. An unsuccessful European or Commonwealth plaintiff, by contrast, may have to pay both sides' counsel fees. Similarly, the absence of generous and nearly automatic social insurance for medical costs, rehabilitation, and lost wages in the United States gives the American accident victim more reasons to bring suit and makes his case more sympathetic than it would be in other systems, where these out-of-pocket losses usually have been paid long before a suit comes to trial.

This combination of incentives to litigate gives the American system its distinctive character. Plaintiffs' attorneys have very strong incentives to file suits that seek to expand the bounds of tort liability. Even if success in doing so is infrequent, the occasional victory sets a precedent, garners publicity, and opens a field of new litigation, some of which will afford opportunities to test the limits of the new rules. A new theory of liability is therefore more likely to be developed in the United States; a series of cases floating the new theory are more likely to be brought in American courts; and these courts are more likely to accept a new theory than are the courts elsewhere. Inevitably there are more tort claims and higher awards than in other systems, and the cost of tort liability and insurance increases accordingly.

Some state reformers have begun to consider the role of litigation incentives in fueling these costs, but there are severe constraints on what an individual state can realistically do. Limiting contingent fees would cause plaintiffs' attorneys to take on fewer cases, and forcing losing plaintiffs to pay defendants' costs would deter plaintiffs from filing suits, including some that would have proved successful. But both devices would discourage not only creative lawsuits that seek to expand the frontiers of tort liability but also meritorious lawsuits that arise under mainstream liability rules.

In addition, many of the fastest-growing types of tort litigation, such as products-liability and toxic-tort suits, tend to be filed against nationwide businesses. By enacting reforms that decrease litigation incentives and limit recovery, a state disadvantages its own citizens and benefits out-of-state defendants. Individual states are likely to be reluctant to carry on this form of altruism unless other states do the same. Social scientists will recognize this problem as the "prisoners' dilemma"; only some form of reciprocal state legislation or a uniform federal rule is likely to solve it.

Contingent-fee limits and cost-shifting, however, are only two of the three possible ways to discourage tort litigation. The third would be to provide some other means of compensating plaintiffs for their losses. As noted, the United States has no comprehensive scheme of social insurance. Most accident victims with serious injuries are likely to have a portion of their medical expenses and lost wages paid through a combination of private health and disability insurance, Medicare, Medicaid, Social Security, and a few other benefit sources. But this patchwork mixture of private and public, group and individual coverage hardly assures an accident victim full compensation for his out-of-pocket losses. No judge or jury would reasonably assume that a plaintiff had already been fully compensated for such losses and no alternative system that would provide such compensation is on the legislative horizon.

If most accident victims were covered by generous private or social insurance, the tendency of the courts to expand liability rules and the inclination of juries to award damages in sympathetic but nonmeritorious cases might be held in check. Yet boosting the level of activity in the private, voluntary market for health and disability insurance is not a promising way to achieve this goal. The problems of risk underestimation, adverse selection, and moral hazard are probably too severe to be completely overcome. And of course the institution of mandatory national health and disability insurance to circumvent the problems of the private market would be equally if not more problematic. As a solution to the tort-law problem, such a system would be massive overkill; and it is not at all clear that such a system should or would have a high priority when set alongside other social welfare goals.

The implication is that the forces behind the expansion of tort liability in the United States will not be easily quelled. The American tort system is a device that a society without full social-welfare protection uses, though often inconsistently, to fill gaps in the social-welfare safety net. As long as those gaps exist, the establishment of severe disincentives to civil litigation will probably be unpalatable, and the tendency of victims and their attorneys to call upon tort law as a surrogate source of social-welfare protection is likely to persist.

Conclusion

No single explanation fully accounts for the insurance crisis of 1985 and 1986, and no single reform can effectively remove the threat of further crises. The American liability insurance market reflects economic forces, legal developments, and the social-welfare policy of the United States, and only a combination of major substantive reforms in each area is likely to provide a long-term solution to the problems uncovered during the recent crisis. Whether preventing insurance crises would be worth the cost of such a combination of reforms is another question. Until a consensus on that issue develops, it is likely that the most recent insurance crisis will not be the last.

Directors' and Officers' Liability Insurance: What Went Wrong?

ROBERTA ROMANO

In late 1984 and 1985, after four years of expanding coverage and falling prices, the market for directors' and officers' (D&O) liability insurance tightened dramatically. Premiums skyrocketed, deductibles increased, and coverage was reduced. There were reports that growing numbers of directors were resigning from boards, or declining invitations to serve on them, because firms had lost insurance coverage. In addition, the proportion of outside directors on boards—persons not employed by the corporation—had decreased, reversing a trend of two decades. A survey of corporate customers for D&O insurance shows the shift toward a perceived crisis. In 1984, the most commonly given reason for not carrying such insurance was that it was not needed; in 1987 the most common reason was that it was unaffordable.

By mid-1986, the crisis conditions in D&O insurance were subsiding, and the trend toward higher rates and lower capacity was slowing. While many corporations reported difficulty in securing D&O insurance coverage in 1986, only a few found the problem intractable. One source of new capacity was the emergence of the insurers owned by the policyholders themselves. In 1986, these insurers accounted for more than a quarter of the premiums in the primary D&O insurance market and about half of all premiums in the excess market.

This essay attempts to explain what went wrong in the D&O insurance market. After a thumbnail sketch of the dimensions of the problem, it discusses how general economic conditions affect directors' liability, how the structure of the market for D&O insurance is related to the crisis, and how the legal system generates uncertainty in this area. The essay's policy recommendation is prosaic, though important: courts ought to refrain from rewriting D&O insurance contracts, for their efforts to aid insureds have unintended, perverse effects of reducing coverage. The conclusions on the causes of the crisis are at times tentative, however, and there are several significant loose ends, because the data are quite limited, D&O liability insurance not being reported as a separate line. In addition, although there is a superb literature on the tort-liability crisis, little attention has been directed specifically to D&O insurance, and the analyses of the tort literature are not always applicable in the D&O context. Finally, compounding the difficulties for analysis, the economics of some crucial aspects of the insurance crisis, such as the disappearance of reinsurance and the nature of the insurance cycle, are only dimly understood.

Trends in Claims against Directors

Directors and officers of for-profit corporations face two types of claimants: shareholders and third parties. Shareholders can sue either on behalf of the corporation — in a "derivative suit"— or in their own right. Directors and officers are liable to shareholders for breaches of their fiduciary duty. This duty has two components: the duty of care, which enjoins negligence in decision making, and the duty of loyalty, which enjoins certain self-interested transactions. Third-party claimants include employees, creditors, suppliers, customers, and government agencies. In this litigation, the corporation is frequently also a defendant, and there is no necessary conflict between the interest of the corporation — the shareholders — and individual defendants.

Because of this difference in defense posture, state law typically distinguishes between the two kinds of lawsuits in permitting corporations to indemnify directors. In third-party actions, companies may reimburse directors for all they pay out in settlements, judgments, and legal expenses. In stockholder derivative suits, by contrast, they may indemnify only expenses. There are two standard reasons for permitting indemnification from the shareholders' perspective: ensuring that the ablest individuals agree to serve as directors, since a director's compensation is small compared with the risks of liability; and ensuring that directors take appropriate risks, since they might otherwise be too cautious in their decision making for fear of liability from a decision that proves harmful in hindsight.

The same state corporation codes permit corporations to buy liability insurance to reimburse their directors and officers for the losses they cannot directly indemnify. The knowledge that they will not be able to ask for direct reimbursement in shareholder suits gives directors and officers a powerful incentive to have their companies purchase D&O insurance. They also have reason to seek insurance to cover two other situations: where the firm is insolvent and unable to indemnify them and where it is unwilling to do so, as when new management takes over that is unsympathetic with the old. Insurance need not lead to increased misconduct: even if insurers cannot monitor insureds perfectly, they can adjust contract terms and offer partial insurance to mitigate the moral-hazard problems by which insurance can induce a suboptimal level of care.

D&O policies were introduced after the stock-market crash of 1929 and the enactment of the federal securities laws in the 1930s to protect directors from shareholder suits. Shareholder claims still constitute the largest category of claims against directors, but their share is slightly less than 40 percent. The second largest category of claims — those filed by employees — has been growing, making up 26 percent of all claims in 1986, compared with an average of 16 percent historically. In recent times the proportion of claims filed by customers has almost doubled, although there has been an offsetting decline in the percentage of claims by prior owners of acquired companies.

Probably the most important cause of the recent upturn in D&O insurance premiums is the increase in the number of claims filed against directors. By one account, four times as many such suits were filed in 1985 as in the previous year. From 1974 to 1984, the number of companies reporting in the Wyatt Co. surveys that they had experienced a liability claim against a director rose from 7 percent to 18 percent. Moreover, for *Fortune*-listed corporations, claim susceptibility, which is defined as the probability that a corporation will have one or more claims against it over a nine-year period ending in the stated year, increased from 21 percent in 1978 to 26 percent in 1980, 27 percent in 1982, 33 percent in 1984, and 41 percent in 1986. Claim frequency, "the total number of claims per [company] during the nine-year interval in question," increased even more dramatically—from .31 in 1978 to .44 in 1980, .48 in 1982, .63 in 1984, and .91 in 1986.[1] Thus, over the nine years to 1986, for every ten *Fortune*-listed corporations, slightly more than nine claims were filed. Because of inherent problems in the survey data, it is hard to estimate how fast claim frequency is really going up. The best guess is that as of 1986 claims were increasing annually at a rate of 10 to 25 percent a year.

Claims against directors include an extraordinarily broad range of allegations: civil-rights violations, antitrust violations, interference with contractual rights, misleading representations, imprudent investment, inadequate supervision of underlings, and illegal payments to officials. Although the Wyatt Co.'s 1987 survey breaks D&O claims into seventeen categories, 17 percent of the allegations could still not be classified: that is, they constitute unique types of allegations. Under a different system of classification based on the circumstances surrounding an allegation, 17 percent again could not be fit into any of twenty-seven specified classes. Under both types of classification, the number and proportion of miscellaneous claims not susceptible to categorization rose from 1984 to 1987. Although this phenomenon is most likely a testament to creative lawyering, the growth in hard-to-classify claims, which given their uniqueness are presumably unexpected claims, undoubtedly makes it difficult for directors and their insurers to assess future D&O liability risks.

Just as crucial to insurers in pricing future policies is the growth in the cost of an average claim. The average cost for paid claims in the Wyatt surveys, excluding legal fees, was $1,988,200 in 1986, up from $1,306,000 in 1984 and $877,361 in 1980. Adjusted for inflation, the increase is still more than 50 percent. While less than half the claims against directors resulted in a payment to the claimant, a proportion that has remained fairly constant, the number closing with a payment in excess of $1 million has been rising, leading the Wyatt Co. to conclude that settlement amounts are continuing to increase.

Even when there is no payout to a claimant, D&O insurance pays for directors' and officers' legal-defense costs. The cost of defending an average claim was an estimated $592,000 in 1986, up from $461,000 in 1984, $318,255 in 1980, and

$181,508 in 1974. Adjusted for inflation, the increase is a sizable 35 percent. While data on these costs are sketchy (so that all figures are really best guesstimates), the trend is clearly upward. The annual rate of increase, based on the 1986 survey data, is 10 percent.

Shareholder suits, the largest category of claims, are less frequently successful than other claims, but they are larger. Although 74 percent of shareholder claims are settled without payment to the claimant, in every large category of award amount — those greater than $500,000, $1 million, or $5 million — the percentage of shareholder claims is greater than the percentage of virtually all other classes of claims. In addition, shareholder suits have consistently cost more to defend than the average claim against directors. While employee suits have become more numerous, the damages sought and received in such cases, as well as the costs of defending them, are considerably below average. Hence, so far as personal liability is involved, directors' single greatest fear is still the shareholder suit. In this regard, recent state legislation limiting directors' monetary liability to shareholders for negligence might ease the insurance crisis by reducing the number of claims in one of the more costly claim categories.

Trends in D&O Policy Coverage

The rise in premiums for D&O insurance reversed a downward trend of several years. More than half the firms renewing policies from mid-1985 through 1986 reported premium increases of more than 200 percent. The effective rate of premium increase was actually much higher, because the new policies provided less coverage than the old. Taking 1974 as a base year, the Wyatt Co. has computed an index that incorporates deductible levels and other factors in determining premium levels. The 1987 index stood at 682.4 percent of the 1974 level, compared with only 54.3 percent in 1984.

Coverage has been restricted by means of raising deductibles, adding exclusions, and revising provisions on coverage extension. D&O policies consist of two parts, a "company reimbursement" portion that reimburses the company for indemnification it pays to directors and officers for losses covered by the policy and a "directors' and officers' liability" part that provides direct personal reimbursement to individual directors and officers for unindemnified payments. Most claims fall under the corporate-reimbursement portion. Corporate-reimbursement deductibles in the average policy surged more than thirteenfold from 1984 to 1987. Personal deductibles, after declining steadily for a decade, also began to drift upward after 1984, increasing an average of 44 percent in the next three years, although these levels are still lower than those of the 1970s.

There have always been exclusions in D&O policies, covering such matters as losses caused by dishonesty and improper personal enrichment, in order to mitigate obvious moral-hazard concerns. But the proportion of policies with exclusions has sharply increased, and so has the number of exclusions in an average policy. In particular, traditional exclusions — such as exclusions for losses due to pollution, pending and prior litigation, and failure to maintain insurance —

appeared in about twice as many D&O policies in 1987 as in 1984. Newer exclusions for losses linked to mergers and acquisitions, tender-offer resistance, actions by regulatory agencies, securities transactions, and litigation between insured parties appeared in more than 10 percent of D&O policies in 1986. Some of the more common provisions, such as the pollution exclusion, are evidently meant to prevent D&O policies from being used as umbrella, or substitute, general-liability policies. But others, such as the exclusions for acquisitions and takeover resistance, undercut the very rationale of the product, because they eliminate from coverage shareholder claims that have been a traditional impetus for purchasing insurance.

The standard D&O policy has two key provisions dealing with the duration of coverage: the insurer-cancellation clause and the "extended discovery," or "extended reporting," clause. Cancellation provisions, which give the insurer the right to cancel the policy after a specified advance notice period, have not been used very much to limit coverage. The number of new policies with cancellation periods of less than forty-five days is barely higher than in the past. Extended-discovery provisions, however, have been redrafted so as to reduce coverage significantly.

Extended-discovery provisions come into play when an insurer has exercised its right to cancel a policy or has decided not to renew it. They permit the customer, by paying an additional premium, to obtain continued coverage of claims filed during the extension period that are based on wrongful acts committed during the original policy period. The occasion for such a clause arises because D&O policies are written on a "claims-made" basis, in contrast to the "occurrence" basis traditional for general-liability policies. An occurrence policy covers all the losses arising out of the customer's actions during the policy period, even if the policy expires before the claim is filed. A claims-made policy covers only those losses that arise from claims filed against the insured during the policy period. The claims-made policy exposes customers to a potentially serious gap in protection: if they lose coverage they are exposed not just to suits for their ongoing activities, which they might alter, but for past activities that it is too late to take back. Extended-discovery-period provisions make a claims-made policy more like an occurrence policy and thus offer valuable protection to many customers.

Since the crisis began, the extension period in the average policy has been getting shorter. For instance, only 41 percent of new policies had an extended discovery period of a full year, compared with 57 percent of old policies, and 41 percent of new policies had only a ninety-day period, compared with 30 percent of old policies. This particular revision imposes a significant cost on customers, because insurers often cancel policies when a claim appears imminent. No fewer than one-third of the directors who submitted D&O insurance claims reported that the insurer tried to cancel the policy or narrow its coverage. Cancellation under these circumstances can create serious problems for an insured, since new policy applications ask whether the insured knows of any past acts that could produce a claim and typically exclude losses from any acts so disclosed.

Finally, there have been sharp cuts in policy limits, that is, the maximum loss covered by a policy. From early 1985 to mid-1986, an increasing number of companies found they could renew their D&O policies only at a fraction of the former coverage level, despite increases in premiums and deductibles. The average decrease in policy limits on renewal was 50 percent in the first quarter of 1986. Nearly all insurers remaining in the market reduced their capacity from 1984 to 1986. By the end of 1986, the situation had improved somewhat, as newly organized policyholder insurance groups offered increased policy limits for their members. As a result, there was a net reduction in policy limits of only 10 percent in the last quarter of 1986, and average limits, counting ongoing policies as well as renewals, were higher than before 1984.

Business Conditions and D&O Liability Risks

Both the demand for D&O insurance and the cost of supplying it depend on the volume of the sorts of business transactions that give rise to litigation. The 1980s have seen a high incidence of three major categories of events that breed shareholder suits: acquisitions, initial public offerings, and bankruptcies.

Corporate acquisitions, attempted or successful, frequently spawn lawsuits against directors by shareholders who object to the terms of the deal, the disclosure surrounding it, or the defensive tactics used to thwart it. Although there is some disagreement, it is generally thought that corporate mergers and acquisitions have come in waves, which appear to crest when stock prices are high. One of the largest waves of acquisitions has occurred in the 1980s, with the advent of new financing techniques that have left no corporation too big to be taken over and of revisions in the Justice Department's merger guidelines that have expanded the number of permissible mergers. Observers in both the bar and business press appear to agree that this merger boom is one primary cause of the D&O insurance crisis. The behavior of insurers lends some support to this contention. In policy applications, insurers inquire into the past and future acquisition activity; in renewing policies, they increasingly demand exclusions for losses due to acquisitions and resistance to takeovers; and they sometimes cancel policies of customers that become takeover targets. In addition, the leading judicial decisions in corporate law in the 1980s have involved acquisition battles.

The pace of initial public stock offerings, like the pace of merger and acquisition activity, can affect D&O insurance rates. The strong stock market of the early and mid-1980s prompted a flurry of public offerings, particularly in high-technology industries. Lawsuits can follow if the price of a new issue drops, as investors try to recoup their losses by alleging violations of the federal securities laws. One commentator has attributed the 1985 increase in shareholder litigation to public offerings that went sour.

Finally, directors and officers of bankrupt companies are often sued by bankruptcy trustees and shareholders. Because insolvent entities are so prone to litigation, the most desirable risk is said to be a company "in sound financial condition with a good earnings record."[2] Insurance applications require customers to submit financial statements, and rates are correlated with profitability, with companies paying substantially higher premiums if they have reported losses. The early and mid-1980s have seen a rash of business failures, primarily among oil companies and banks, especially banks with a high proportion of energy loans in their portfolio. Moreover, the Federal Deposit Insurance Corporation has increasingly sued bank directors in order to tap the failed institutions' D&O insurance. As might be expected, banks had particular difficulty obtaining D&O insurance during the recent crisis, but the entire market for D&O insurance seems to have been affected as well.

By increasing the underlying risks that breed liability, the business conditions of the 1980s account for some aspects of the D&O insurance crisis, especially the large premium increases. But they do not explain the shrinkage of capacity and the exit of insurers from the market. Withdrawal of the product, as distinct from a rise in its price, suggests that insurers perceive some risks to be uninsurable. The number of bankruptcies, acquisitions, and public offerings may be rising, but such losses fall within the realm of the predictable and could be controlled by rate adjustments. Moreover, since some of the environmental factors increasing the number of lawsuits are specific to a few industries and kinds of companies, it is puzzling that the crisis was felt so widely across the market. To the extent that all corporations are affected by these factors, however, the increased liability risks will not be independent. Interdependency of losses disrupts insurance markets, because it means losses are no longer subject to the law of large numbers. The level of premiums will correspondingly rise and capacity may shrink as well.

Market Structure Considerations

One explanation for rising premiums is collusion among insurers. Conspiracy theories of the general insurance crisis have been popular, in part because the industry is largely exempt from the antitrust laws. As recently as the 1960s Lloyd's of London provided the only market for D&O insurance. Although the line is far more competitive now, it is still a highly specialized product offered by fewer carriers than other lines of business insurance. The 1987 Wyatt survey identified fewer than fifty providers, and their capacity and activity in the market vary greatly. Tallies of the major active D&O insurers range from six to eighteen.

Some sense of the concentration in the D&O insurance industry and thus the potential for collusion can be derived from the Wyatt survey data. The data compute market shares on two separate bases, number of policies written and premium dollar volume, for two separate markets, primary and excess insurance. By the Herfindahl-Hirschman index, the leading technical measure, the industry's degree of concentration is quite low, ranging from a low of 900 for excess insurance (measured by number of accounts), through 1100 for excess insurance (measured by premium volume), and 1600 for primary insurance (measured by number of accounts), to a high of 2500 for primary insurance (measured by premium volume). These figures suggest that collusion is unlikely, since under the Justice Department's guidelines a market within the range of 1000 to 1800 is classified as only "moderately concentrated." However, the four-firm concentration ratios are high, ranging from a 52 percent market share for the top four firms in excess insurance (by number of accounts), through a 59 percent share in excess insurance (by premium volume), and a 70 percent share in primary insurance (by number of accounts), to an 85 percent share in primary insurance (by premium volume). The two measures' estimates are not inconsistent: the market contains several firms with infinitesimal market shares and a few firms with large though relatively equal market shares.

But at least as important as market shares in assessing competitiveness is the stability of market shares. Concentration ratios are a static measure that may obscure the degree of dynamic competition and turnover among top firms in an industry. There have been dramatic shifts in D&O market shares in recent years. Eight insurers that had been ranked in the top ten by number of accounts from 1975 through 1984 left the market by 1985. Chubb Group, currently the second largest insurer by number of accounts and third largest by premium volume, was not even in the D&O market in 1980. Two of the newly formed policyholder-owned insurers are among the top four companies by premium volume and the top eight firms by number of accounts. In addition, two major commercial insurers began writing D&O insurance in 1987. When one considers the combination of market information, the low Herfindahl-Hirschman index, and the fluidity in entrance, exit, and market shares, despite the high concentration ratios, the picture that emerges is most consistent with competition.

The measures of concentration and mobility do not indicate the level of competitiveness in the reinsurance market, which is an important influence on D&O rates. A high percentage of the D&O insurance written by American companies is reinsured. In the 1970s, American companies entered the D&O field in competition with the London market, with the aid of aggressive European reinsurers. Reinsurance enabled the American companies with no D&O claims experience to offer substantial amounts of coverage while retaining only modest exposure.

Because D&O reinsurance is of the "facultative" variety, in which each policy is separately and specially negotiated with a reinsurer, it is especially susceptible to changes in the reinsurance market. This factor contributed to the D&O crisis. When reinsurers absorbed substantial losses and the worldwide reinsurance market tightened in the mid-1980s, high-risk lines, such as D&O, were the most severely affected. On their 1985 renewals, American insurers could no longer obtain inexpensive reinsurance. They responded by reducing their capacity and retaining a larger share of risk.

This reduction in apparent capacity is among the more puzzling aspects of the D&O insurance crisis. Conventional markets are supposed to adjust to cost increases with price increases and not product withdrawal. Yet in D&O, as well as other professional liability insurance, desired terms of coverage (and for some companies *any* coverage) became unavailable. Perhaps commercial buyers were simply unwilling to pay the higher premiums necessary to induce insurers to supply coverage. Some, however, attribute the capacity problem to the regulatory requirement that insurance companies maintain a specified premium-to-surplus ratio. In a tightening market where prices are rising, to hold capacity constant requires that insurers increase reserves to correspond to the additional premiums. If maintaining these reserves is inconvenient, insurers may instead avoid having to increase reserves by dropping their riskier lines, such as D&O.

Because the input of insurance capacity is wealth, which, unlike the tangible capital of a factory, is not subject to immediate physical limits, a capacity-constraint explanation seems intuitively implausible. For such an explanation to be compelling, some barrier must be preventing the entry of new insurers or of reinsurers, who are the traditional outlet for insurers seeking to spread risk and to reduce reserve requirements attributable to new business. The shifting market shares and turnover of companies in the direct-insurance market, as well as data suggesting that most firms are not pushing up against the premium-to-surplus ratio constraint, indicate that there is no formidable barrier at that level. Although entry into the reinsurance market might be expensive, it is difficult to see which aspect of the business would create such a barrier. Reinsurers encounter even less regulation than direct insurers, and established reputation would seem to be less important in swaying the insurers to whom reinsurers market their services than it is to underlying customers.

An alternative market-structure explanation views the insurance crisis in both D&O and general-liability lines as simply the peak of a recurring competitive insurance cycle of the sort that has been charted for many lines in many countries. The apparent capacity shortage and the pattern of entry and exit in the D&O market could fit into this view. According to this explanation, the D&O cycle started in the late 1970s when prices were high. These prices attracted new entrants into the market in the 1980s. As they competed for business, prices dropped. At the same time, interest rates were rising, which made insurers willing to price policies below underwriting cost to obtain more premium dollars to invest at the higher rates. In 1984, when interest rates turned back down, low-premium D&O policies became unprofitable. As a result, some insurers left the market; those remaining raised their prices. Thus the peak-to-peak cycle ended as it began, with rising premiums and shrinking capacity. Lured by the higher prices, new entrants arrived in late 1986, and the rate of price increases slowed, presaging a cycle phase of lower prices ahead.

Cycle explanations typically treat the period of low premiums, such as 1982 through 1984 for D&O insurance, as reflecting a conscious underpricing of risks and the period of higher prices as a realignment in accord with cost. The cost function parallels changes in interest rates. Since premiums are set to equal the discounted value of expected losses, a rise in interest rates — hence the discount rate — should reliably bring about a fall in premiums and vice versa. The unexamined premise is that losses remain constant when interest rates change. This premise, however, is dubious. If, as seems likely, a significant part of the rise in interest rates is caused by expected inflation, it follows that expected losses will increase as well, and premiums will not necessarily decline. The increase in expected payouts may be less than the increase in investment earnings, perhaps because not all components of payouts are fully exposed to inflation. But although an inverse relationship between interest rates and premiums may still hold, it is unlikely to explain the full magnitude of premium shifts during the recent crisis. In fact, payments on D&O claims increased throughout the cycle period, and they increased faster than inflation. Moreover, real interest rates have been at historic highs throughout the 1980s, including 1984–85, and while the real rate was lower in 1985 than 1984, it was also lower in 1983 than 1982. These factors lessen the persuasiveness of an underpricing argument for the period preceding the crisis, as well as the explanatory power of the cycle theory as a whole, for the D&O line.

In addition, the incentive that high interest rates give insurers to cut premiums and expand their business is weaker for claims-made than for occurrence policies, because claims are paid much sooner after receipt of the premium under a claims-made policy, so there is less time to earn investment income. Undoubtedly, interest-rate savings have had some effect on the D&O market, since there is still some lag between receipts and payouts even under claims-made policies. According to one account, the average time required to settle a D&O claim is 6.6 years, and the average age of claims reported in the Wyatt surveys has been 4 to 5 years. But, given the course of interest-rate changes in the 1980s, the effect of those changes for D&O insurance could not account for the entire reported increase in premiums.

Changes in the Courtroom

The most persuasive explanation of the wider crisis in general-liability insurance emphasizes changes in tort doctrines of liability and damage recovery. In the case of D&O insurance, however, the substantive doctrines that underlie the largest and most expensive category of claims — shareholder claims — have not undergone radical expansion or even major change since the 1970s.

Companies began to purchase D&O insurance on a widespread basis toward the end of the 1960s, at a time when director-liability rules were in flux. The best available data indicate that in 1965 less than 10 percent of corporations carried D&O insurance. By 1971, 70 to 80 percent of major corporations were buying it. In addition, the amount of insurance written went from an insignificant quantity in 1963 to more than $1 billion in 1968. This growth in the D&O market coincided with two major developments in the field: the entry of American companies into the London-dominated market, heightening competition, and two 1968 court decisions that found directors and officers to have violated the federal securities laws, *Escott* v. *BarChris Construction Corp.* and *SEC* v. *Texas Gulf Sulphur Co.*, which were thought to herald a new era of D&O liability.

The projections proved to be accurate: D&O liability expanded in the succeeding years, largely through suits under the federal securities laws extending the reach of rule 10b-5 of the Securities Exchange Act of 1934, the linchpin of the *Texas Gulf Sulphur* decision. In addition, the federal rules of procedure for class actions were liberalized in 1966, and courts interpreted the rules favorably to plaintiffs, further facilitating claims against directors. While D&O premiums rose with the increasing liability risk, companies apparently did not have much difficulty obtaining insurance, and no one perceived a crisis in the market.

The trend toward wider liability was reversed, however, by the mid-1970s, in a series of Supreme Court rulings that restricted the reach of the securities laws. Federal courts also became less accommodating to class action and derivative suits brought under the securities laws. The contraction in D&O liability under the federal securities laws has continued in the 1980s.

State fiduciary doctrine has changed even less during the past two decades than federal securities law, and what changes there have been have tended to shrink the scope of liability. For example, at the turn of the century, shareholders could void managers' self-interested transactions at will. By 1910, self-interested transactions were generally valid unless a court found them unfair, and statutes enacted in nearly all of the states since the 1960s prescribe procedures, such as informed approval of a disinterested board, that can preclude a fairness review. Further, courts have steadfastly applied the business-judgment rule in duty-of-care cases, which gives directors the benefit of the doubt when their decisions are informed and taken in good faith. In a more recent innovation, courts have allowed special litigation committees, which are appointed by boards, to terminate a derivative suit.

The one important case that arguably expanded directors' liability for negligence over the past two decades was *Smith* v. *Van Gorkum*, in which the Delaware Supreme Court found directors grossly negligent in accepting a bid for their company. This case was decided in 1985, after the insurance crisis was well under way. The business-judgment rule did not cover the *Van Gorkum* case, because the court found that the directors had not properly informed themselves concerning the company's value. The court indicated that if the board had followed specific procedures, such as obtaining an investment banker's fairness opinion, there would have been no liability. Providing as it does such a safe harbor for nervous boards, one not wildly in conflict with prevailing business practice, the opinion should not be seen as a scandalous harbinger of increased exposure. Quite to the contrary, the decision arguably lowered the standard of conduct by defining breaches of the duty of care to require "gross" rather than "ordinary" negligence.

Changing the standard of liability is not, however, the only way a legal system can create the uncertainty that disrupts insurance markets by making prediction of losses difficult. The application of a liability standard can also be a source of uncertainty. Even settled law can be a source of uncertainty in a case of "first impression," one with a pattern of facts sufficiently novel that earlier cases do not enable the parties to predict what a court will do. Rapid innovation in the forms of doing business can thereby produce a level of doctrinal uncertainty at least as severe as that generated by a shift in the actual standard of liability.

The *Van Gorkum* decision illustrates how uncertainty in the legal system can take different forms. Although the decision did not alter any substantive liability rule, it provoked a strong critical reaction from boards, commentators, and the Delaware legislature. Debate among commentators focused on how the law had been *applied*: Did the facts evidence gross negligence by the board or the sort of ordinary negligence that in the past was not in practice subjected to liability? The reaction to *Van Gorkum* suggests the decision created uncertainty concerning how the liability standard would be applied in the future, the effect of which on litigants is the same as that of an uncertain standard. Uncertain application of the directors' liability standard generates acute problems for corporate practice, which in recent years has been characterized by rapid-paced innovation in the structuring of deals. Because litigation in a fast-paced innovative environment will inevitably raise numerous difficult issues involving application of the liability standard, the variability of the standard will increase, making D&O losses harder to predict. While an increase in uncertainty of itself should not be of moment to insurers, who unlike insureds are risk neutral and concerned only with an increase in the expected value of a loss, this sort of legal uncertainty affects all insureds and creates a dependence across D&O risks, vitiating the applicability of the law of large numbers to D&O policies' pricing. Rates can therefore rise even though the core of the standard of conduct has remained the same. And as the economist Ralph A. Winter of the University of Toronto has shown, if there are imperfections in the capital market making the issuance of equity temporarily to increase capacity expensive, then the increased dependency in risks will severely reduce capacity as well.[3]

For D&O insurers, the uncertainty problem is exacerbated by court rulings on insurance contracts that are all too often, to be blunt, lawless. In reading D&O policies, courts frequently rewrite the allocation of risk against the insurer. For example, they have ordered insurers to pay customers' defense costs as incurred even though the loss may not be covered by the policy, the insureds refuse to respect the insurers' reservation of rights, and policies explicitly give the insurer the option to make defense advances. They have forbidden insurers to litigate the applicability of a dishonesty exclusion when the underlying action has been settled without an adjudication of guilt. They have also forbidden insurers to exercise their cancellation rights when the insured is bankrupt. They have consistently found related transactions to constitute "separate loss occurrences," increasing the liability of the insurer, and they have held knowing misrepresentations in financial statements not to void policies, because the documents were not explicitly incorporated by reference in the application's cognizance warranty. Furthermore, they have held insurers liable for losses arising from suits involving an outside directorship—where an insured individual serves on the board of an entirely different company—when the policy was silent on the issue.

Courts have also construed the broad language of D&O policies as placing the risk of all new perils on insurers, so that liability arising out of novel D&O litigation is borne by the insurer. This ensures that the growth of innovative claims in D&O litigation translates directly into upward pressure on rates. A prime example is the recent spate of novel cases in which banks have sought to recover on the D&O insurance policy by directly suing their own officers and directors for negligently approving what with hindsight were bad loans. The liability on such claims has been substantial. Chase Manhattan settled a $175 million claim for $32 million covered by insurance; Bank of America settled a $95 million claim for an $8.2 million payment from insurers; and Seafirst Corp. entered into a $110 million settlement with its directors and officers limiting recovery to its $70 million in remaining policy limits. Insurers could not have anticipated such claims in pricing policies, because it was until lately unthinkable for a corporation to sue its own employees for negligence. Yet in *National Union Fire Insurance Co. v. Seafirst Corp.*, the court cavalierly rejected the insurer's contention that the policy was not intended to cover such a claim, citing the policy language in which the insurer pledged to pay losses suffered as a result of "any" claims against directors.

The corporate strategy followed in the bank cases, when successful, converts what is priced as third-party insurance into first-party insurance. In effect, the corporation can trigger a payment to itself from its own policy. Because a corporation suing its own employees has access to far more records and information than the typical plaintiff, the defendants are more likely to lose than they are in a normal case. The inevitable consequence of such litigation is higher premiums. In addition, judicial acceptance of such claims magnifies moral hazard and adverse selection problems, because the insured is often better informed than the insurer about such risks and has a degree of control over some of them.

Insurers have sought to escape the vulnerability presented by the bank cases by attaching an exclusion for lawsuits brought by one insured against another. This reaction exemplifies George Priest's thesis that insurers use exclusions to control adverse selection problems produced by the courts' expansion of liability,[4] although in this case the source of the problem is a change not in substantive liability but in the reading of the insurance contract. The new exclusions are not precisely tailored to the problem: their typical wording is broad and applies equally to losses that have traditionally been insurable, such as shareholder derivative suits and suits brought by a terminated officer who feels wronged by the board. The failure of a policy to cover derivative suits especially limits its value, because companies are generally not permitted to indemnify directors for payments in those suits, and this means future plaintiffs will recover less because they are typically paid only out of insurance proceeds. The "insured versus insured" exclusion thus illustrates how by attempting to expand insurance coverage courts can perversely cause it to shrink.

Decisions like *Seafirst* place insurers in a dilemma. They may not be able to limit their exposure simply by writing policies that specify in more detail what risks are covered, because just as courts construe coverage provisions broadly, so they construe exclusions narrowly. The judicial provision of a safety net for insureds is a well-intentioned but misguided use of the insurance-law maxim that ambiguity in a contract is construed against the drafter. This rule of construction makes sense when the contract is a standard form and the party who drafted it has superior and cheaper access to information. But these features are certainly not present in the D&O context, where buyers employ professional brokers to negotiate particularized policy language and both contracting parties are sophisticated enterprises. Here again the courts' efforts to expand coverage ironically hinder it by leaving negotiators with fewer bargaining points with which to facilitate the crafting of mutually acceptable contracts.

Neither this doctrine of construction nor the courts' sometimes lawless interpretation of insurance contracts are new phenomena. Before the mid-1980s, however, very few decisions involved D&O policies, because insurers rarely litigated D&O contract disputes. While the new litigiousness may reflect the entry of new D&O insurers and reinsurers, it may reflect the scarcity and availability problems of the insurance crisis. And in turn the litigation may itself be helping to cause the insurers' problems, in two ways. First, when courts enforce a contract different from the one insurers intended to write, the price they receive will not be commensurate with the risk they bear. New policies will bear higher premiums than identical older policies to compensate insurers for the court-added risk. Second, to the extent that courts require insurers to cover losses that are in the insured's control, as in the *Seafirst* case, the new risks may be uninsurable and may therefore lead some insurers to withdraw from the market.

Conclusion

No satisfactory understanding of the cause of the D&O insurance crisis is at hand. But one need not dig very deep to conclude that any satisfactory explanation will be multicausal. This essay has sought to identify some of the causal factors. In the 1980s, unexpected and undesired exposures were increasingly forced on insurers by economic conditions that shifted the underlying D&O liability risk by increasing the number of bankruptcies, acquisitions, and public offerings and by judicial decisions that altered the contractual allocation of that risk. These factors made loss prediction harder in the D&O line, which decreased its profitability. At the same time, interest rates were falling and world reinsurance markets were contracting; these developments further restricted D&O insurers' flexibility. One of the few clear policy recommendations in this murky area is for courts to enforce D&O insurance contracts. For judicial reallocation of risk in D&O insurance contracts is the one most controllable factor in the confluence of factors that produced the increases in premiums and deductibles, reductions in policy limits and substantive coverage, and capacity shortages, that staggered the D&O consumer in the mid-1980s.

Notes

1. Wyatt Co., *1987 Wyatt Directors and Officers Liability Insurance Survey* (Chicago, 1987), 11–12.
2. "What Existing D&O Policies Cover," *Business Lawyer* 27 (February 1972): 147, 155.
3. Ralph A. Winter, "The Insurance Cycle: Economics and Policy" (manuscript, January 1988).
4. George L. Priest, "Modern Tort Law and the Insurability Crisis," *Yale Law Journal* 96 (1987): 1574–75.

Not-for-Profit Organizations and the Liability Crisis

FRANK J. MACCHIAROLA

Not-for-profit organizations are remarkably varied, ranging from museums and orchestras to day-care centers and clinics to philanthropic foundations and schools. And while it is difficult to generalize about their problems across the board, virtually all these groups were affected by the insurance crisis of late 1985. Insurance companies refused to provide some not-for-profit organizations with coverage, and rates skyrocketed when insurance was available. The crisis is a continuing one, though its urgency has abated somewhat because of largely stopgap measures.

The variety of not-for-profit organizations makes it difficult to consider them similarly. On one end of the spectrum are the rich and prestigious museums, libraries, and cultural associations staffed by many paid professionals, their boards graced by wealthy and influential patrons, usually boasting thousands of members and annual operating budgets in the millions of dollars. On the other end are the not so generously endowed majority. Their managers have a great variety of duties, many of which they were not trained to perform. Frequently, they exist from hand to mouth, barely managing to scrape together enough to stay in the black, expanding and contracting their staffs on the basis of often elusive foundation and government support. Because they watch their expenses closely, they are distressed to see their fixed costs, such as rent, utilities, and insurance, shoot upward. They must struggle to convince influential people to serve on their boards of directors or trustees and to recruit professional management that can understand both the mission of the organization and the business setting in which it operates.

These not-for-profit organizations are extremely important to a country of joiners, such as the United States. Their services make a major difference in the quality of life for communities and individuals alike. Those who have studied them, worked for them, or had extensive dealings with them agree that without their work necessary public purposes very often would not be served. This is particularly so in the United States, where many public goals are not addressed by either government or the profit-making sector. (In this essay, government is generally excluded from the not-for-profit sector.)

The special role of the not-for-profits inclines their staffs and boards of directors to see their mission as different from that of government and the for-profit sector. While expecting prudent management of resources, they often think that the organization's responsibility is to use its resources rather than to accumulate and husband them. Even when a not-for-profit has considerable assets at its disposal and enjoys immense prestige, its revenues rarely exceed its expenditures.

The experience of premium increases has not been peculiar to not-for-profits, but unlike many other organizations they cannot pass these costs on to their customers as added costs of doing business, nor have they a profit margin that can absorb temporary shocks while they adjust. The increasing cost of insurance since 1985 has therefore been felt as a tremendous burden by most of these groups. One organization typical of the larger not-for-profits, the New York City Partnership, purchased $10 million of directors' and officers' (D&O) protection for $13,000 in 1985. By 1987, just $5 million of protection cost $50,000. Such increases are significant even to a sizable organization like the New York City Partnership and devastating to many groups with more limited resources.

It has become especially difficult for not-for-profit organizations to recruit the best qualified officers and directors. The wealthier a potential board member, the more he or she is likely to worry about being exposed to the risk of liability lawsuits as a result of board membership. In a 1987 study of the liability crisis the Peat Marwick organization surveyed 2,532 executives, more than half of them in the not-for-profit sector.[1] Ninety-two percent of the executives thought that there was an incipient crisis in D&O liability and nearly 90 percent saw a negative effect on the governance of their institutions. Seventy-eight percent of the not-for-profit participants thought liability problems were having a negative effect on governance, and most predicted that rates would increase even higher, further curtailing their ability to conduct their affairs.

Most participants reported large increases in premiums for D&O insurance. About one-third of the entire sample reported that premiums had risen more than 300 percent at the last renewal of their organization's coverage. Another 46 percent indicated that rates had risen by less than 300 percent, while only 6 percent said rates had remained unchanged or fallen. One-fourth of the not-for-profit organizations reported increases in excess of 300 percent, and about half reported increases of less than that percentage. Another widespread feature of the crisis was a decline in the quality of coverage: the amount of liability protection was often reduced, while the required deductible retention was increased. Sixteen percent of the respondents reported increases in deductibles of at least 300 percent.

Access to this type of insurance is often critical in recruiting good board members. In the National Association of Corporate Directors' 1986 survey of 2,800 corporate directors and fifty state insurance and commerce commissioners, only 36 percent said they would be willing to serve on not-for-profit boards without D&O coverage, and only one-fourth said they would serve on corporate boards without it. About one in seven said that he or she would flatly refuse to serve without protection. Nearly half knew colleagues who had refused directorships for lack of D&O insurance. If talented potential directors refuse to serve on the boards of not-for-profit organizations, the sector will lose a significant resource for support and leadership.

Origins of the Crisis

Many not-for-profits were long shielded from liability suits by the doctrine of charitable immunity. The overwhelming trend, however, has been for state courts to do away with this immunity. In *Fitzer* v. *Greater Greenville YMCA*, for example, the South Carolina Supreme Court abolished the defense as one that has "no place in today's society"[2] and held that a charitable institution is subject to tort liability like any other person or corporation. The appellant, Matthew Fitzer, had paid a fee to attend a camp operated by the Greater Greenville YMCA. During his stay at the camp he was injured by a rock thrown by another camper, and he brought a negligence action to recover damages for his injuries. The trial court granted the YMCA summary judgment, holding that the claim was barred by the doctrine of charitable immunity, but the state supreme court reversed it on appeal. Writing for the majority, Justice Julius B. Ness announced an end to the court's once "steadfast adherence" to the "antiquated rule" that grants tort immunity to charitable institutions. The public-policy arguments that tort liability would discourage charitable activities could no longer withstand judicial scrutiny. "There is no tenet more fundamental in our law," Justice Ness said, "than liability following the tortious wrongdoer. Yet, in South Carolina, immunity is the rule and liability the exception. It is time once and for all to lay this anachronism to rest." The judge pointed to the availability of liability insurance for not-for-profits, which would cushion the blow of adverse judgments. In a dissenting opinion, Justice Cameron B. Littlejohn urged that the matter be decided by the legislature rather than the court.

A parallel development has been the decline of traditional immunities for government action, which has put municipalities at greater risk. In the frequently cited case of *Irwin* v. *Town of Ware*,[3] the Supreme Judicial Court of Massachusetts held that a municipality could be sued for the negligent failure of its police officers to arrest someone driving under the influence of alcohol who subsequently injured others.

With the expansion of liability, insurance companies began to pay out huge judgments and grant large out-of-court settlements of damage claims. Equally important, the calculation of those losses in advance became virtually impossible. In this context of uncertainty the carriers have passed the costs — both real and envisioned — on to their customers, including not-for-profit organizations.

Some have charged the insurance industry with deliberately creating the crisis. J. Robert Hunter, former federal insurance administrator, has blamed the "phony insurance crisis" on abusive insurance company practices and on the states' failure to regulate rates properly, which he claims has allowed the crisis to be seen as demanding tort-law reform.[4] Trial lawyers have been particularly vociferous in pressing the idea of collusion. Writing in the *Trial Lawyers Quarterly,* Abraham Fuchsberg said, "In state after state, the insurance industry is indeed using the current panic to eliminate victims' rights." He further charged that "the truth is, none of these measures [tort reforms promoted by the insurance industry] would solve the so-called insurance 'crisis,' because the culprit is not the tort system — it's the insurance industry's desire to maintain its profits at the high inflated level of a decade past."[5]

Along with most commentators, the executives in the Peat Marwick survey assigned some blame for the crisis to both the insurance industry and the general state of tort law. Nearly two-thirds of those responding also blamed lawyers and juries' inclination to give large awards for a great deal of the problem. Other aspects of the judicial system receiving the blame included heavy publicity following big settlements, the concept of joint and several liability, and the behavior of judges themselves. The greatest divergence of opinion between the executives of the for-profit organizations and those of the not-for-profit sector occurred over the question of whether the insurance industry was "mainly responsible" for the crisis. While only 37 percent of the corporate chief executives surveyed named the insurers as a major cause, 53 percent of the not-for-profit officers and 60 percent of independent-sector executives and university presidents did so.

An Atmosphere for Reform

The controversy over the causes of the liability crisis has been largely mirrored in the remedies proposed by various sides. They fall into two principal categories: reform of tort law and regulation of the insurance industry. Tort-law reforms have tended to be more comprehensive and far-reaching and have been more often identified with the political right. Some related measures, like curbs on contingency fees, have been directed against the plaintiffs' bar itself. Steps to bring the insurance industry under greater government control and supervision have generally been milder and have usually been favored by the political left. Many states have pursued remedies in each area. Despite efforts of both sorts, the cost of insurance continues to increase, though at a much reduced rate.

The not-for-profit sector has begun to organize itself and to press for reform of both tort law and insurance regulation. In New York City, organizations like the New York Chamber of Commerce and Industry, the United Way, and the Nonprofit Coordinating Committee of New York have lobbied extensively for reform and have organized the not-for-profit community to present its point of view. Indeed, one of the most important goals of these organizations has been to educate the not-for-profit sector on insurance and liability issues, with the hope of also increasing their officers' and directors' business sophistication. It is generally agreed that many of those working in the not-for-profit sector know little about these issues. Frequently, insurance matters are given over to brokers, with little follow-up from managers themselves. Many not-for-profits do not even have brokers to advise them and go unprotected in many areas of their activities. This is beginning to change as more executives are looking critically at these risks and the costs of insuring them and working to bring both under stricter control.

Insurance Reforms

Agitation by the not-for-profit sector in many states has led to insurance reform and regulation that, it is hoped, will bring about reductions in premiums in the not-for-profit sector. This can be done in several ways. The first is to satisfy insurers — and, where the issue is one of regulation, the state insurance department — that the not-for-profit sector should be treated as a discrete market that can demonstrate a better loss and claims experience than the commercial insureds with which not-for-profits have been generally grouped. If this argument can be proved to the satisfaction of both state regulators and some major insurers, the result might well be a dramatic lowering or at least meaningful stabilization of the liability-insurance premiums of not-for-profits.

A second way of keeping premiums in check is to ascertain how the not-for-profit sector should be divided into subgroups for the purpose of purchasing group insurance. Under the Risk Retention Act of 1986, "like" organizations are permitted to purchase group insurance as long as such a practice is not in violation of state law. As a result, group insurance purchases are now permitted in several states. Group purchasing of any kind is a relatively new development for not-for-profit organizations.

Under recently enacted legislation in New York State, the Department of Insurance must establish, market by market, what maximum increases and decreases in commercial insurance rates may lawfully take place without its prior approval. The regulations implementing this "flex rating" legislation have also established a separate rating band for not-for-profit philanthropic and civic organizations with regard to both D&O and general liability insurance. Furthermore, the "sunshine" provision in the New York statute requires that the Department of Insurance report annually to the legislature and governor on the general state of the liability-insurance market, with a view to deciding whether anything ought to be done to reduce or contain the costs of this insurance. These reports will commence in 1988. The new law specifically requires that they include loss and expense experience that roughly segregate not-for-profit from for-profit activities. These steps offer significant opportunities to affect future rates. It is also hoped that insurance carriers, on their own, will develop a better working relationship with not-for-profits, thus helping to reduce rates.

In addition, numerous reforms have focused on the matter of D&O liability insurance for not-for-profit board members. Here again there is a problem with rating bands. For rating purposes, directors of not-for-profit organizations have been put in the same category as for-profit directors, where they have found D&O liability insurance difficult to obtain and expensive when it is available. The factors largely responsible for the increased premiums for D&O insurance are the growth of lawsuits alleging that directors have not fulfilled their duties with "due diligence" and consequent enormous judgments that have proved costly to insurance carriers. Although director suits of this sort are common in the for-profit sector, they are extremely rare in the not-for-profit sector. The enormous financial stakes involved in many suits against for-profit directors, as in takeover cases, are simply not found in the not-for-profit sector. Furthermore, many of the suits against for-profit board members are derivative suits (that is, suits brought by a shareholder on behalf of the corporation). This kind of suit can rarely be brought against board members of not-for-profit organizations. In addition, as discussed below, recent legislation in New York and other states has established a more lenient standard of duty for not-for-profit directors, further increasing the difficulty of bringing suit against them. Although these legal distinctions are certain to bring about important differences in the frequency and seriousness of director suits, some carriers remain either unaware of or unimpressed with them. Rates for not-for-profit groups remain inordinately high notwithstanding their rather "safe" history and likely future.

Not-for-profits have found some relief because of the new legislation and because of the pressure that has been exerted on insurance companies to offer them coverage. But it is still generally thought that insurance reform alone will be inadequate to protect the not-for-profits without some tort reform as well.

Tort Reform

A principal target for reform is the legal standard that is applied in determining whether directors have breached their duty. The stricter the standard of liability, the harder it is to attract board members. Nearly 90 percent of the directors surveyed by Peat Marwick favored legislation like that first developed in Connecticut, which specifically immunizes a director, officer, or trustee of a not-for-profit who serves without compensation, acts in good faith, and is not found guilty of "willful and wanton misconduct." A related type of reform gives not-for-profit organizations wider latitude in deciding when to indemnify directors who lose liability cases. A typical reform statute provides that they can offer indemnity so long as a director did not act "in bad faith," with "active and deliberate dishonesty," or for "improper personal benefit."

There has been some controversy over these statutes, although — as the casenote concerning the Washington state law in this area indicates — most commentators think that the law is "a reasonable means of balancing the rights of insured persons to recover against tortfeasors and society's need for available and affordable insurance."[6] Clearly, the statutes have helped improve the climate for directors. Along with the new laws easing liability or indemnity standards for not-for-profits, at least thirty states have extended protection to directors of for-profit enterprises. Even a state like New York, which has traditionally been strict with business, permits its corporations to indemnify directors for payments of settlements of derivative actions.

A second common target of tort reformers is the doctrine of joint and several liability, under which a defendant with only the slightest responsibility for an injury can be forced to pay all the damages. At least twenty states have already limited or abolished this doctrine, and more are expected to follow. Joint and several liability gives rise to the "deep pockets" syndrome, in which the defendant with the most assets pays the biggest share of damages, regardless of fault. This syndrome has hurt municipalities, in particular, but poses the same threat to private not-for-profits as well.

A classic case that illustrates the problem is *Sills* v. *City of Los Angeles.*[7] The case arose when a Los Angeles driver under the influence of drugs ran a stop sign and was hit broadside by another motorist. A sixteen-year-old passenger in the first driver's car was left crippled and brain-damaged. In March 1985, a jury awarded a verdict of $2,160,000 jointly against the first driver and the city of Los Angeles, which had been sued for failing to trim bushes that had partially obstructed the view of the drugged driver. Although the city was found liable for only 22 percent of the injury, it had to pay virtually all of the damages. The driver was judgment-proof, and his three codefendants settled for their insurance policy limits — a total of $200,000.

The insurance industry has been outspoken in its criticism of the doctrine, which, it says, makes it difficult to predict any company's ultimate degree of liability risk exposure and makes insurance itself a magnet for liability. William McCormick, chief executive officer of the Firemen's Fund Insurance Companies, has said, "A defendant should be financially responsible only for his own fault in the incident, and not for someone else's fault if that person can't pay." On the other hand, negligence attorneys have argued that it is fairer to place the costs of an accident on an injurer who can afford to pay, even if that injurer is not the only responsible party, than to give the injured person only partial compensation. They add that although the abolition of the doctrine will certainly reduce an individual's ability to collect, it will not necessarily reduce overall insurance costs. They claim it will tend to increase the number of defendants taken to court by placing the burden on an injured person to make sure he has brought all the responsible parties into the action.

Other tort-law reforms that many think would ease the insurance burden include limiting the award of punitive damages; limiting the application of strict liability and replacing this type of liability with traditional negligence standards; permitting damage awards to be reduced to offset the income that plaintiffs receive from "collateral sources," such as workers' compensation and health insurance; paying future damages in installments rather than a lump sum, when the damages are above a certain amount; limiting the dollar amounts of awards in certain cases, such as environmental ones when damages have been significant; and enacting a series of civil-justice procedural reforms, such as allowing two-part trials in personal injury cases (one part to decide the fact of liability and the other to decide damages), capping attorneys' contingent fees, permitting those who successfully defend against lawsuits to recover the cost of their legal defense, and assessing new penalties for frivolous suits.

Some of these reforms could be tailored to the needs of not-for-profits. A state might wish to ban punitive damages in actions against not-for-profits even though it is not prepared to ban them for all defendants. And some reforms, while applying across the board, could hold special significance for not-for-profits. For example, an expanded "assumption-of-risk" defense could go far to reduce the liability exposure of those who operate recreational facilities, among which not-for-profit organizations are prominent. Current case law in several states holds that when consumers knowingly assume reasonable risks—such as being struck by a foul ball at a baseball game or a puck at a hockey game—they cannot generally sue if an injury results. But in recent years, plaintiffs have been increasingly successful in chipping away at this liability defense, particularly as it applies to tourism and related activities, which have been subjected to some of the biggest liability-rate increases of any industry in recent years. Courts have been steadily expanding the theory that there is a "duty owed" by recreational and sports facilities, such as ski areas, to protect customers from injury in inherently risky situations even when the facilities are managed by municipalities or run by not-for-profit organizations. An equitable assumption-of-risk standard would play an important role in reducing the spiraling liability costs of the many not-for-profit organizations that run sports and recreational facilities.

Conclusion

A push for legislative and regulatory reforms has not been the only reaction to the insurance crisis. The crisis has also provided an incentive for not-for-profit organizations to improve some of their management practices and generally to improve their oversight of management performance in order to reduce their potential for liability. Following the "due diligence" cases in for-profit situations, where stricter standards of board action have been imposed, some not-for-profit boards have insisted on more information before making decisions. Further, some of them have instituted procedures to determine whether there is a conflict of interest among the directors. Other not-for-profits have increased the efficiency of their committee structure, adding special committees to oversee sensitive areas within the group's scope of activity. Some have reached beyond the usual candidates for board membership and added experts to the board who might help prevent mistakes that could result in liability. Others have brought in outside experts to counsel the board about specific issues, particularly their own liability. Such improvements mean that there have been some important side benefits to the crisis.

If it has done nothing else, the liability crisis has persuaded the not-for-profit community to review its insurance needs and how they have been met by carriers that provide that protection. In many ways, this review was long needed and welcomed. In the long term, the wider issues of tort reform that remain to be addressed have implications that go far beyond the not-for-profit sector. Whatever its benefits for society as a whole, it is clear that basic reform, if it does occur, will benefit not-for-profit organizations as well.

NOTES

1. Peat Marwick, Mitchell & Main, *D&O Directors and Officers Liability: A Crisis in the Making*, 1987.

2. *Fitzer* v. *Greater Greenville YMCA*. 277 S.C.I., 282 S.E. 2d. 230 (1981).

3. *Irwin* v. *Town of Ware*, 467, N.E. 2d. 1292 (Mass., 1984).

4. J. Robert Hunter, "The Phony Insurance Crisis," *Trial Lawyers Quarterly* 17, no. 2 (1985): 6.

5. Abraham Fuchsberg, "Insurance: The 'Seven' Fat Years," *Trial Lawyers Quarterly* 17, no. 2 (1985): 3–5.

6. Jeri A. Carver, "Immunity for Nonprofit Corporations RCW 4.24.264," *Willamette Law Review* 23 (Winter 1987): 321–26.

7. *Sills* v. *City of Los Angeles*, San Fernando Superior Court, 1985.

A Choice-of-Law Approach to Products-Liability Reform

In recent years, interest in products-liability reform has grown. But interest in federal legislation for that purpose has actually declined. Among the reasons are not only the political strength of reform opponents in Congress but also the difficulties inherent to the project. Congress, unlike the fifty state legislatures, generally and wisely refrains from experimental legislation, since federal mistakes are notoriously difficult to correct. It is hazardous to impose a single national "solution" to a problem without a reasonable confidence that the solution can be tolerated for years to come.

Reformers have therefore turned to the fifty states, which Justice Louis Brandeis dubbed "laborator[ies]" for conducting "novel social and economic experiments without risk to the rest of the country."[1] Tort law has always been predominantly a state matter, and the prospects for rethinking the relation between tort liability, on the one hand, and innovation, competitiveness, and prosperity, on the other, would seem far more promising at that level. Indeed, more than thirty state legislatures passed some kind of tort reform in 1986 and 1987.

But there is a major structural obstacle to effective state reform that goes beyond the issue of political will. In a unified economy where products move in national markets, no state can ensure that its own consumers, manufacturers, and workers will capture the major benefits of reform legislation. This essay draws on the insights of the "public choice" school of economics and political science to show how the current legal structure militates against products-liability reform at the state level and, more tentatively, to argue that meaningful reform may require new federal rules governing the choice of law in products-liability cases.

Thanks are due to the Russell Baker Scholars Fund for financial support during the preparation of this essay, to Christopher R. DeMuth and Michael J. Horowitz, who worked with the author on these ideas some years ago at the Office of Management and Budget, and to Lea Brilmayer, David Currie, Richard Epstein, Larry Kramer, Fred McChesney, Bernard Meltzer, Richard Posner, and Alan Sykes for their probing comments on an earlier draft.

The Importance of Choice of Law

In theory, each state is free to set its own products-liability laws. Some states impose strict liability for certain hazards, while others use a negligence standard; some place monetary caps on noneconomic losses, while others allow recovery limited only by the sensibilities of the jurors; and some have relatively liberal standards for awarding punitive damages, while others virtually preclude damage awards of that type. But it is a fiction that any state can actually enforce the products-liability laws on its books. Since most products are made in one state and used in another, at least two states are usually involved, and often more. Obviously, they will not all be able to get their way when their laws differ. Accordingly, an elaborate branch of legal doctrine has arisen, called "conflict of laws" or "choice of law," whose goal is to devise relatively predictable and fair rules for determining which state's law should govern in a multistate transaction.

There is no consensus, to say the least, on the best way to resolve the choice-of-law problem in products liability. As one leading scholar in the field has put it: "There is no conflicts magic that can make sense of the underlying bedlam of rules that passes for products liability laws."[2] Whatever their prescriptions, choice-of-law theorists almost invariably use what could be called static analysis. They take the substantive law of each state as a given and see as their task to select which of the various fixed state laws would be best to apply in a particular case. Absent from the debate have been the dynamic effects of choice-of-law rules: how they influence the substantive legal doctrines the various states will adopt.

A number of normative assumptions should be made explicit. This essay does not assume that any particular substantive standard of products liability is desirable or undesirable in itself. Instead, it assumes that the "right" substantive rules are those a state would choose to adopt if it were an autarky, that is, a self-sufficient economy, all of whose production and consumption took place within its own borders. In such a case, since all manufacturers and all consumers would be citizens of the state, all the costs and benefits of a change in the laws would be in principle taken into account by the state's democratic processes. The legislative outcome reached under those circumstances is akin to what economists would call a market-clearing price in a market without externalities, that is, where participants could not throw off costs onto unwilling outsiders.

The optimal products-liability law might well vary from state to state, just as market-clearing prices vary from place to place, depending on supply-and-demand conditions. But factors that skew this process of political market-clearing — leading states to enact beggar-thy-neighbor laws in hopes of exporting costs to citizens of other states — are here assumed to lower the net satisfaction of the national citizenry with the legislative outcome and thus to be inefficient and undesirable. Products-liability reform, therefore, is legislation that moves in the direction of the laws that a state would adopt if left to its own devices.

Under the current system of choice of law, changes in a state's products-liability laws that reduce the size or probability of plaintiff recoveries injure the interests of consumer-plaintiffs (and plaintiffs' attorneys) within the state, who either have to sue under less-favorable rules or must undergo the cost and inconvenience of suing elsewhere. Yet such reform, at best, is of limited use in protecting the state's own manufacturers. By the standard outlined above this structure of choice of law is inefficient; it artificially inhibits prodefendant reforms in a way that does not reflect the settled views of the citizenry as a whole. This essay therefore focuses on inhibitions to prodefendant reform.

The Structural Bias against Reform

Two economic factors combine to prevent states from protecting their manufacturers through changes in products-liability laws. First, products tend to move in national markets, while people tend to live in one place. Some goods and many services are made for local use, but most products with major liability exposure are distributed nationally or even internationally. A state's decision makers will therefore observe that nearly all the consumers injured in the state are local residents and constituents, while most of those who can be sued for making the products are residents of other states. By contrast, in related fields of tort law, such as medical malpractice and municipal liability, producers as well as consumers are likely to be local residents.

Second, product manufacturers cannot generally price their products differently to reflect the costs imposed by differing state standards of liability. Calculating the dollar cost of different liability rules, where hard data come only years after sale, is a daunting if not impossible task. To compound the difficulty, differential pricing would give consumers and middlemen an incentive to buy products in states with less onerous liability laws (and hence lower prices) and transport them to states with more stringent laws (and hence higher prices). This arbitrage would leave the manufacturer doubly defeated: it would be exposed to just as much liability as before but would collect less revenue for its product.

In addition, the Robinson-Patman Act of 1936 broadly outlaws differential pricing. Although a seller can defend such pricing on the basis of actual cost differences, the burden of proof is stringent and the outcome uncertain. While the Robinson-Patman Act goes virtually unenforced today, its vestigial presence may discourage state-by-state price differentials. Note that the providers of local service (e.g., hospitals, taverns, municipalities) and of the minority of products that are more or less immobile can generally set prices to reflect estimated tort liability with little fear of either transhipment or Robinson-Patman challenge.

It follows from these factors that the cost of a given state's liability laws, as they apply to mass-market products, is borne by consumers nationwide. In effect, consumers in states with less generous products-liability laws pay a portion of the more generous recoveries won by plaintiffs in other states. This imbalance introduces an incentive for strategic behavior that would not be present if states made rules for themselves alone. Each state can profit at the expense of the others by expanding its scope of liability, at least until the others catch up. A rich literature has arisen documenting the states' propensity to succumb to just such temptations. In fields ranging from taxation to antitrust to utility rate regulation, they have avidly embraced policies whose costs are borne by other states.

Resolving suits under the law of the plaintiff's own state would, in itself, create a structural bias toward proplaintiff state laws. But developments in recent years have added a different sort of bias, by making it easier for plaintiffs to shop around for the most favorable law — whether that of their own state, the defendant's, or a third state.

It was once the general rule that tort cases were governed by the law of the state where the injury occurred. Thus, if a consumer living in Ohio purchased a product in Michigan from a New York manufacturer and was injured by it while traveling in North Dakota, North Dakota law would apply. Most often, this meant in practice that the law of the plaintiff's home state would apply, since consumers ordinarily use products, and thus are injured by them, at or near home. The distinctive feature of this choice-of-law rule was its so-called mechanical operation. The applicable substantive law was fixed at the time of the injury without regard to its relative attractiveness to plaintiff or defendant or to subsequent litigation tactics.

This rule came under intense attack by progressive legal commentators and courts. Essentially, their argument was that the rule was arbitrary and failed to take into account the degree of "interest" of the states involved in the conflict. For example, in the hypothetical situation above, it was argued that both Ohio and New York have a stronger interest in the outcome of the case than does North Dakota. Ohio has an interest in ensuring that its residents are adequately compensated for injuries and do not become public charges. New York has an interest in protecting the profitability of its manufacturers and also in seeing to it that safe and wholesome products are produced within its borders. North Dakota's interest in the outcome was said to be relatively slight. In this instance, the reformers concluded, to apply North Dakota law was to sacrifice real sovereign interests to imaginary ones.

The traditional rule of applying the law of the place of injury has therefore given way to "interest analysis," under which the law of the state with the most substantial interest in the conflict will apply. Most often, courts take this to mean either the plaintiff's or the manufacturer's home state. At this level of abstraction, interest analysis seems a major improvement over the prior rule. The prior rule was arbitrary and led to senseless results in some cases. The difficulty, however, is that interest analysis is not neutral; it systematically loads the dice in favor of plaintiffs and against defendants. It tends to select whichever state's law — the plaintiff's or the defendant's — seems likely to allow a higher recovery. (If their laws are equivalent, there is no choice-of-law problem.)

Interest analysis begins with the assumption that states are interested only in obtaining benefits for their own residents. The interests reflected in a proplaintiff law are said to be greater compensation for injured consumers within the state or, alternatively, greater deterrence of unsafe manufacturing within the state. The interest reflected in a promanufacturer law is said to be the promotion of manufacturing within the state.

In roughly half the cases, where the defendant's state law is more favorable to the plaintiff, interest analysis almost automatically favors the plaintiff. The defendant's state is said to be expressing its interest in deterring unsafe manufacturing. The plaintiff's state has no countervailing interest in applying its own promanufacturer law, since the purpose of such a law is not served by extending its protection to an out-of-state manufacturer. And so the proplaintiff law applies. David Cavers has approvingly summarized the situation: "A forum where the victim resided would have an obvious interest in his compensation if its law were pro-claimant. If its law were pro-producer, the court might well conclude that, having a resident victim but no local producer to protect, it should apply the law of the state of acquisition or of production if either were pro-claimant."[3] The exceptions seem to be relatively rare.

In the other half of the cases, where the plaintiff's own state law would allow higher recovery, the analysis gets more complicated. The plaintiff's state has an interest in gaining greater compensation for its injured consumers, but the defendant's state also has an interest in promoting manufacturing within its borders. This situation is called a "true conflict," because both states appear to have an interest in applying their own law. There is no uniformly agreed-upon solution to a "true conflict"; but two leading solutions turn out to be proplaintiff. One is to apply the law of the forum — that is, the state in which the lawsuit is brought. Since the plaintiff chooses where to file suit, he will get to select the most favorable forum, in this case his own home state.

The other solution is more straightforward — to choose the law more favorable to the plaintiff. Legal commentators generally agree that this is the usual result of modern conflicts analysis and that it is a satisfactory resolution. "Among the factors that should be borne in mind in framing choice-of-law rules," as Willis Reese has put it, "are the policies underlying the relevant substantive field." In the field of torts this points to "a policy favoring compensation for injury and spreading the risk."[4] This is not the place for a full discussion of the merits of importing substantive "policy" into choice of law. But if one sees the aim of liability policy as striking a balance between values, rather than simply maximizing compensation, one will wish to guard against errors in either direction, toward either too much or too little compensation for injury. And one will not so easily dismiss state laws that are less favorable to plaintiffs than others as obviously mistaken or illegitimate. At any rate, introducing a systematic bias in choice of law in certainly apt to affect the states' underlying substantive decisions about products liability.

The involvement of third, fourth, or fifth states in the transaction gives the plaintiff even more chances. If neither the plaintiff's nor the manufacturer's state allows liberal recovery, there is always the state where the injury took place or the state where the product was sold. The involvement of added plaintiffs and defendants complicates the issue enormously but without changing the bias. In short, although courts still occasionally apply the rules of a prodefendant state in conflicts, the current system of choice of law is heavily weighted in the other direction.

At the same time that a proplaintiff style of interest analysis was sweeping the field of choice of law, new modes of constitutional interpretation were eroding old constraints on plaintiffs' ability to shop for a favorable forum and on forum states' ability to apply a law favorable to plaintiffs.

The Supreme Court has acknowledged that forum-shopping has become less difficult: "The limits imposed on state jurisdiction by the Due Process Clause, in its role as a guarantor against inconvenient litigation, have been substantially relaxed over the years."[5] A dramatic illustration is *Keeton v. Hustler Magazine, Inc.*, in which a resident of New York alleged that she had been libeled by *Hustler* magazine, an Ohio corporation with its principal place of business in California.[6] By the time she filed her lawsuit, the statute of limitations had expired in New York, Ohio, and every other state except New Hampshire. And so she sued in New Hampshire, a state with which she had had no previous contact whatsoever and in which only a tiny percentage of *Hustler* magazines were sold. The Supreme Court upheld her suit, holding that a corporation can be sued in any state in which it distributes its products. And under New Hampshire law, she was entitled to collect damages for injury to her reputation in all fifty states, including the forty-nine whose statutes of limitations had already expired. (The court did not resolve the question whether the state could constitutionally apply its substantive law.)

For forum-shopping to work, not only must the plaintiff be entitled to sue in a state with a favorable law, but that state must also be entitled to apply its own law to the suit. This second step raises independent constitutional concerns of its own. Before 1981, the Supreme Court struck down as unconstitutional lower-court decisions that applied the law of a jurisdiction that did not have a substantial involvement with the events giving rise to the lawsuit, whether or not it was the forum state. This still allowed plaintiff-oriented courts to choose between the states where the plaintiff resided, the manufacturer was located, and the injury occurred to find the law most favorable for the plaintiff. Nonetheless, it did provide at least some constraint. But in 1981, with *Allstate Insurance Co. v. Hague*, even this constraint was effectively eviscerated.[7]

Allstate grew out of an accident in Wisconsin near the Minnesota border. A Wisconsin resident was killed while a passenger on a motorcycle driven by a second Wisconsin resident that collided with an automobile driven by a third Wisconsin resident. The crash victim had purchased an insurance policy in Wisconsin from Allstate, a nationwide insurer. Under Wisconsin law, the deceased was entitled to $15,000 in benefits under the uninsured-motorist provisions of the insurance. But the victim's estate sued Allstate in Minnesota for additional compensation under Minnesota law. In Minnesota, as in many other states, someone killed in similar circumstances would be entitled to $45,000 under the same policy.

The Supreme Court upheld the Minnesota state court's application of its own law for three reasons. First, after the accident, the victim's widow, who was executor of his estate, moved to Minnesota. Second, the victim had been employed in Minnesota and commuted to work from his home in Wisconsin. Third, Allstate does business in Minnesota.

If those three contacts between Minnesota and the litigation are sufficient, it is difficult to imagine what state's law a plaintiff would not be able to invoke before a sympathetic court, at least in a liability case involving a nationally distributed product. The first *Allstate* factor, the current residence of the plaintiff's executor in Minnesota, allows the litigation to be governed by the strategic behavior of the plaintiff. As Justice Lewis Powell commented in dissent: "If a plaintiff could choose the substantive rules to be applied to an action by moving to a hospitable forum, the invitation to forum shopping would be irresistible."[8] The second factor, the victim's employment in Minnesota, allows the case to be governed by an irrelevancy. The victim's employment in Minnesota surely increased the odds that he would come to some harm in Minnesota, but in fact the accident had nothing to do with his employment and occurred in Wisconsin. Had the case revolved around minimum wages, workers' compensation, or the terms of the employer's benefits package, the employment relation might have been significant. Under the circumstances, his employment in Minnesota was no more relevant to the lawsuit than his state of birth or the site of his alma mater.

The final *Allstate* factor, that the insurance company does business in Minnesota, is the most troubling. Under this theory, a manufacturer that distributes products nationwide can be sued under the country's most stringent state law — whether or not the plaintiff or the product at issue ever entered the state. To introduce this factor is to eliminate all constitutional constraint regarding choice of law for nationally distributed products.

The *Allstate* decision was not, to be sure, an abrupt departure from precedent. In actuality it had been decades since the Supreme Court last reversed a state court for applying its own law to an interstate conflict. In the intervening years the constitutional standard had seemingly relaxed. Nonetheless, *Allstate* was a signal that the relaxed standards had become formal doctrine. The extent of the change is not yet clear. Four years after *Allstate*, in *Phillips Petroleum Co.* v. *Shutts*,[9] the Court held that the forum state in a class action could not apply its substantive law to transactions with no relation to the state. It is too early to tell whether *Shutts* represents a retreat from the extremes of *Allstate* or merely shows that some applications of forum law are beyond the pale even under the relaxed standards of *Allstate*.

Even under the old rule in conflicts — place of the injury governs — any one state legislature would have little incentive to enact reforms that reduce the scope of liability, because the reforms would mostly benefit out-of-state manufacturers but would inflict most of their cost on plaintiffs within the state (and, not incidentally, on the plaintiffs' bar). If plaintiffs are forced to sue in other states, they will suffer some cost and inconvenience and will sacrifice the advantage of a jury predisposed to the local party. But the new approach to choice of law accelerates this trend. Even if a state is willing to say no to some of its own plaintiffs in order to help defendants nationwide, plaintiffs can sidestep the prodefendant law through a combination of forum-shopping and choice-of-law doctrine. Either they will sue elsewhere or they will obtain application of a more favorable law. Thus the most proplaintiff states will set the law for most of the country.

Under these conditions, states no longer serve as laboratories for social experimentation. The resultant law of products liability does not and cannot reflect actual judgments and experiences regarding the effect of liability on safety and compensation, on the one hand, or on innovation and wealth creation, on the other. Instead, states pursue a persistent and one-directional race toward ever-higher plaintiff recoveries, a race whose outcome does not necessarily represent the considered judgment of decision makers in the several states.

Full Faith and Credit Legislation

Article IV, section 1, of the United States Constitution provides: "Full Faith and Credit shall be given in each State to the public Acts, Records, and judicial Proceedings of every other State. And the Congress may by general Laws prescribe the Manner in which such Acts, Records and Proceedings shall be proved, and the Effect thereof." This explicit delegation of authority to Congress to prescribe the effect of the public acts or statutes of each state in the other states has never been exercised. The sole relevant federal statute, 28 U.S.C. 1738, provides only that state statutes "shall have the same full faith and credit . . . as they have by law or usage in the courts of [the] . . . State . . . from which they are taken." This statute is either meaningless or internally self-contradictory. If conflicting laws of two states appear to apply to a legal controversy, it is impossible for each state to give the other's law the "same full faith and credit." The statute has accordingly played no role in the development of choice-of-law principles.

Nonetheless, the federal power to adopt new choice-of-law rules is evident. Such rules would interfere far less with state sovereignty than would a federal products-liability code passed under the commerce power. What choice-of-law principle would best eliminate the bias in the system?

The sources of bias in the current system, as have been discussed, are two: (1) the proplaintiff orientation of interest analysis coupled with latitude for forum-shopping, and (2) the interest of the plaintiff's own state in allowing generous recovery, to be paid by consumers nationwide through higher prices. The solution to the first source of bias is to return to a choice-of-law principle under which the law governing a dispute is fixed at or before the time of injury. Plaintiffs should not be allowed to select the most favorable rule, and judges should not be allowed to weigh the "interests" of the various states retrospectively.

Among the various fixed rules for products-liability cases, some will create greater incentives for reform legislation and some less. Applying the law of the plaintiff's home state will create incentives for proplaintiff products-liability rules, since the price will be paid nationwide. Applying the law of the manufacturer's home state would have the opposite effect: most of the benefits of promanufacturer legislation under this choice-of-law regime would be enjoyed within the state, while much of the cost would be exported to injured consumers in other states, who would receive lower recoveries. Thus, while either of these fixed rules — the plaintiff's state governs or the manufacturer's state governs — would be preferable to the current system, both depart sharply from the autarkic result.

The traditional choice-of-law rule, the place of injury, is not much better. In most cases, the place of injury will also be the plaintiff's home state and will thus generate the same incentives for legislative strategic behavior. In the other instances, when the plaintiff is injured in a state other than his own, the place of injury will likely have no interest in favoring either party. This is an improvement, but it still does not create any incentive for reform.

Although further exploration of the incentive effects of choice-of-law rules on legislatures may lead to superior solutions, the best rule on the basis of current thinking is the law of the place of sale. "Place of sale," in this context, means the place of delivery of a product to the ultimate purchaser through ordinary commercial channels. If a Pennsylvania consumer drives to New York to buy a product, the place of sale is New York. If he calls a New York retailer, which mails the product to him in Pennsylvania, the place of sale is Pennsylvania. If a New Yorker buys a product in New York and resells the product years later in Pennsylvania to a Pennsylvania consumer, the place of sale remains in New York. Although there will be some difficult problems of proof, it will be feasible to determine the place of sale of most products involved in products-liability cases. The place of sale of drugs can be determined through prescription records; the place of sale of machine tools and automobiles is recorded on documents of sale; mail orders leave a paper trail. There will be relatively little opportunity for manipulation by the parties.

The incentive effects of this choice-of-law rule are likely to be modest, but positive. It will tend to discourage extreme liability rules. Manufacturers can refuse to distribute products in a state that adopts an unreasonable rule of damages. Consumers can, at least theoretically, avoid purchases in states with insufficient protection. State legislatures have an interest in increasing sales activity within their states, which is likely to give them a constructive interest in avoiding rules that repel either side of the transaction. One can imagine the consumer outrage if, for example, a New Jersey decision causes the producer of an important birth-control device to withdraw from sales in that state, when the device remains available across the border in New York. In theory, the effect of this choice-of-law rule would be to create an incentive for each legislature to strive for the optimal products-liability law: one that will attract the largest aggregate of producers willing to sell and consumers willing to buy.

Moreover, the proposal might make it possible for manufacturers to respond to different state products-liability laws by differential pricing—a response that is virtually impossible under the current regime. To the extent that differential pricing is now precluded by the ability of purchasers to buy a product in one state and use or resell it to users in another, the proposal would alleviate the problem. If it became possible for manufacturers to price the product in each state according to the liability exposure created by sales in that state, then the proposal would virtually replicate the autarkic result. The costs and benefits of products-liability law would be felt largely within the state: consumers would pay more for more generous products-liability protection.

Although the proposal would furnish a major impetus in theory for legislatures to design optimal products-liability laws, its effect in practice is likely to be less dramatic for three reasons. First, unless a state's products-liability law is far outside the mainstream, it is likely to prove a relatively minor factor in manufacturers' decisions to distribute products and consumers' decisions to purchase them. Manufacturers are unlikely to sacrifice sales in a state on account of small differences in liability exposure, however irksome. Consumers are unlikely to forgo a useful product, or travel to a distant state to purchase it, merely because the law of their own state provides for a somewhat lower recovery in the event of injury. Thus, while the proposal is likely to discourage the extremes, it may do little to advance the optimal solution. Second, though manufacturers would have more latitude to adjust price according to liability exposure in each state, the technical difficulty of doing so with any sort of exactness would remain, so price differentials are likely to be quite rough if they emerge at all. Third, the place of sale will commonly also be the consumer's home state, and many state legislatures are likely to continue responding to those constituent incentives rather than seek increased sales.

The proposal thus falls short of perfect neutrality in state incentives; nothing could achieve that in a system of nationwide distribution of products and state determination of products-liability laws. Nonetheless, it would be an improvement over the current system. It would discourage litigants from taking their lawsuits to the most proplaintiff forums in the country. It would also discourage them from manipulating the choice of law to their advantage, since that choice would hinge on fixed factors outside the litigants' control. It would bring greater certainty to private planning: producers would have a fair idea that the distribution of state laws they faced as defendants would roughly match the distribution of underlying complaints. It would create a modest incentive for state legislatures to promote sales within their states by passing rules that balance the interests of producer and consumer and would accordingly curb the tendency of every state to emulate the most proplaintiff law in the country.

The recent experience of liability reform shows the importance of getting both costs and benefits into the legislative trade-off. More than thirty states have passed liability-reform legislation since 1985. Certain reforms are by far the most common — limits on medical-malpractice claims, on municipal liability, and on the liability of taverns and social hosts for accidents caused by persons to whom they serve liquor. The common feature of these reforms is that defendants as well as plaintiffs reside in the state in question. Limitation on ski-resort liability is likewise very common; it is surely no coincidence that in those cases the defendants are in-staters and the plaintiffs are mostly from other places. By contrast, reform of products liability, in which defendants tend to be from out of state, is comparatively less common, even though the issue is more significant in dollar terms. This suggests that where both the cost and the benefit of a liability rule are felt within a state, legislatures are more disposed toward reform.

It is more difficult to compare the effects of this proposal with those of a possible federal products-liability code, since so much would depend on what the federal code would contain. There are at least three theoretical reasons to expect state legislation to be preferable to federal.

First, thinking about products liability is prone to dramatic shifts. Over the past twenty years the notion of basing liability on fault went out of fashion and was replaced by the notions of risk-spreading and enterprise liability. Then there was a swing back, as society came to see the ill effects of excessive liability and the tort system's inefficiencies in spreading risk. Legislative activity is thus taking many experimental forms around the state capitals. Some states are bucking the trend by continuing to expand the scope of liability in particular areas.

It is no accident that state legislatures in more than thirty states have passed liability-reform laws in recent years, while Congress has only debated. The Constitution was deliberately designed to slow the pace of change and guard against fads and fashions. It takes longer for Congress both to make and to correct a mistake. When the state of knowledge and opinion on an issue is in flux, it is generally sensible for the federal government to hold back. If a federal products-liability code is enacted in 1988, Americans may well be living with it for the next half century, much as they still live with New Deal throwbacks like the Agricultural Marketing Agreements Act of 1937 and with the energy-crisis package that was passed in 1978 and became obsolete by 1982.

Second, public preferences about products liability probably vary from region to region. Relying on state legislation allows more people to live under laws that suit them. A single national solution necessarily sacrifices the views of more people whose opinions differ from the norm.

Third, if incentives are properly structured so that states cannot succeed in benefiting their own citizens at the expense of others, they will have an extra reason to adopt policies more sensible than those the federal government would adopt. People and businesses can migrate far more freely from state to state in response to changes in law than from country to country. If New York enacted a liability law that manufacturers or consumers found harsh or threatening, they could move to New Jersey or Connecticut to escape it. Even gradual and marginal migrations of this sort influence state officials. If Congress enacted a harsh liability law, on the other hand, the dissidents would have to move abroad, which is a lot harder. Just as a competitive business has more incentive to give good service than a monopolist, state governments have a greater incentive to pass wealth-generating legislation than Congress does. The advantages of state over federal legislation should not be exaggerated. But given the poor prospects that comprehensive products-liability reform legislation will clear Congress, it is worth considering ways of working within federalism.

Conclusion

State law cannot be treated simply as a given. It is the result of a process of political deliberation, political power, and political negotiation. The outcome of the process is powerfully affected by the structure of decision making, just as the outcome of a contest of brawn or brain is affected by the rules of the game. The choice-of-law rules for products liability have been set without considering their effect on the substantive state laws themselves. A shorthand description of the rules — much oversimplified, to be sure, but basically accurate — is that plaintiffs in an interstate case can choose which state's law will apply to their lawsuit. If this is an accurate description, the prospects for products-liability reform at the state level are not promising. More precisely, individual states will be unable to enforce, and disinclined to enact, products-liability rules more favorable to manufacturers than the laws of other states.

In part, this bias is the result of changes in choice-of-law and personal-jurisdiction rules over the past thirty years. One possible avenue for reform is to modify the choice-of-law rules to eliminate proplaintiff bias without replacing it with prodefendant bias. Such reform would give each state an incentive to develop wealth-generating rules. And it would discourage the sort of strategic behavior by which states attempt to profit at the expense of their neighbors but succeed only in ensuring the disadvantage of all.

NOTES

1. *New State Ice Co.* v. *Liebmann*, 285 U.S. 262, 311 (1932).

2. Russell Weintraub, "A Defense of Interest Analysis in the Conflict of Laws and the Use of that Analysis in Products Liability Cases," *Ohio State Law Journal* 46 (1986): 493, 504.

3. See David Cavers, "The Proper Law of Producer's Liability," *International and Comparative Law Quarterly* 26 (1977): 703, 715.

4. Willis Reese, "Products Liability and Choice of Law: The United States Proposals to the Hague Conference," *Vanderbilt Law Review* 25 (1972): 34.

5. *World-Wide Volkswagen Corp.* v. *Woodson*, 444 U.S. 286, 292 (1980).

6. 465 U.S. 770 (1984).

7. 449 U.S. 302 (1981) (plurality opinion).

8. 449 U.S. at 337. Accord, *Reich* v. *Purcell*, 67 Cal. 2d 551, 63 Cal. Rptr. 31, 432 P. 2d 727 (1967) (Traynor, C.J.).

9. 472 U.S. 797 (1985).

Can Washington Repair the Tort System?

EDMUND W. KITCH

Observers who are distressed by current developments in American tort law find it tempting to look to the federal government for reform. Congress offers a single forum to address the issues and is supported by an elaborate and sophisticated staff. It would seem much easier to persuade Capitol Hill to act than to carry the issue to fifty state legislatures, each with its own idiosyncrasies. But in spite of the urging of those, including some in the Reagan administration's Department of Justice, who seek a national solution to the tort controversy, Congress is not the appropriate arena for reforming tort law. Its proper role is the limited one it has taken in the past: to address particular problems that directly affect the interests of the federal government.

Why is tort law best left to the states? First, most of the issues it deals with have no national implications; they exemplify the "local" issues that the framers of the Constitution intended to leave to the states. With some possible exceptions—chiefly products-liability law—the costs and benefits of any venture in tort liability law fall within the state that pursues it. No national interests intervene. Second, in practice, tort law is entangled with problems of court organization, administration, and procedure, which means that effective federal reform would either have to assign vast duties to federal courts or meddle in the most intimate details of state courts. Third, there is no consensus, expert or otherwise, on what the rules of tort law should be. Tort law is a confusing welter of competing objectives—accident deterrence and loss-shifting, to name the two most prominent examples—whose relative importance varies with the observer and the situation. Finally, individuals and businesses can move their activities in and out of states, and thus provide a nonpolitical check on overly costly choices by state governments, much more easily than they can move in and out of the country in response to errors at the federal level.

The arguments against federal intervention do not apply as strongly to the area of products liability, where states may have an incentive to help their own citizens by increasing liability at the expense of out-of-state producers. The concluding section of this paper suggests limited federal intervention that could address this problem.

Reasons for Limiting the Federal Role

The reservation of tort law to the states, with at most a limited federal role, was envisaged by the Constitution and has been traditionally respected by Congress. It reflects four prudent considerations of policy.

1. Tort law deals with local issues. Traffic accidents and barroom fights are events that affect only the immediate community. They need not be resolved on a uniform national (or even statewide) basis. That a citizen of one state can recover damages in a type of tort case where a citizen of another state could not do so in his state poses no difficulty for either of the two states or for the country.

An observer might consider the rules in a particular state biased for or against recovery. But absent constitutional concerns, such disapproval is no reason for federal intervention. Specific constitutional provisions constrain state tort law: for instance, a state may not make race a requirement for tort recovery. So long as no infringement of that sort is present and one accepts the legitimacy of a state's political process, there is no constitutionally appropriate reason for the federal government to insist that a state resolve conflicts among its citizens in any particular way. (The complexities of modern tort law and judicial procedure probably favor the well educated, but this bias has never been argued as a ground for invalidating state tort laws, nor does it seem likely that the federal government could do better in avoiding such a bias.)

The analysis remains much the same even when interstate movement is involved. When a person moves or travels from one state to another, the applicable rules may change, but to the extent that the change influences one's choices — and in the United States today the differences are not important enough to matter — one can learn about the differences and make adjustments, either by choosing not to enter a state (much as one might choose a route that avoids a state with a low speed limit) or by adjusting one's insurance coverage. The only problem would arise if a state could apply different and less favorable rules to nonresidents than to its own voting citizens. But this possibility is ruled out by the privileges and immunities clause and other provisions of the Constitution.

Nor, with exceptions to be discussed below, does the situation change when the decision makers are businesses. If a company operates a nationwide chain of motels and the rules of innkeepers' liability vary from state to state, it can take those differences in cost into account, along with variations in other costs, both in setting its prices and in deciding whether to enter and remain in a local market.

Spillover effects between states provide a traditional rationale for federal control of an area. If each state were expected to take steps against attack by foreign powers, some states might choose not to do so and instead take advantages of the security created by other states' investments. That is a reason for the Constitution to place sole responsibility for defense on the federal government. More recently it has been decided that the interstate movement of pollutants requires national intervention. But spillover effects are unimportant in the tort area.

Every actor is both a potential defendant and a potential plaintiff. A right to recover in tort offers benefits as well as costs to persons and businesses a state is trying to attract. A business can as rationally decide to avoid a jurisdiction that does not offer enough tort protection (and thus leaves the property and other interests of itself and its employees unprotected) as to avoid the jurisdiction with too-burdensome tort rules. So long as the pricing system permits sellers to set prices that reflect the costs of both the tort-liability risk and the risks of being deprived of tort recovery rights in the particular jurisdiction where the activity takes place, the costs and benefits of the tort rules chosen by the jurisdiction will be borne in that jurisdiction.

2. In practice, tort law is largely a law of procedure and court administration. Its substantive concepts — negligence, product defect, proximate cause, and so on — are embodied in generalized standards that are applied to a particular case by a "fact finder," usually a jury. More important than the substantive rules are questions about where and when a plaintiff can sue, how quickly the case will be heard, how the jury will be assembled, and in what environment the trial will take place. Indeed, more important differences in recovery prospects and amounts are often found between different courthouses in the same state than between courthouses in different states. For instance, it has long been common for plaintiffs to take claims arising out of rural railroad-crossing accidents to the city, where the corporate defendant is subject to suit and the jurors place a larger dollar value on such elements of recovery as lost wages and pain and suffering.

To the extent that trial by jury itself is seen as the problem, the federal government can be of little help, since the Sixth Amendment guarantees the right to such a trial in civil cases. The federal government has no institutional capacity to assume the task of hearing and deciding tort claims itself. The overburdened federal court system, barely one-tenth the size of all the state courts together, is a specialized system prepared to hear claims only in the larger cities. Requiring litigants to make their claim in Washington, D.C., might improve the convenience of administration; it is actually being tried in the new vaccine-compensation program. But it would provoke rightful indignation if applied to broad classes of claims.

As long as the states carry out the task of adjudicating tort claims, the federal government will have difficulty intervening in a meaningful way. A federal reform that imposed new substantive rules but left their administration in the hands of the states would probably have little impact. Such bifurcated responsibility, with the rules enacted in Washington but their implementation left to the states, could lead to results worse than any of the present system and also raise grave constitutional problems.

3. There is no national consensus that either rejects some state rules as clearly "wrong" or embraces other rules as "right" in any widely supported technical or political sense. Tort law is an uneasy balance of conflicting objectives, including

compensation for loss, deterrence of harmful conduct, social loss-spreading, procedural efficiency, and perceived fairness. The law itself sometimes follows principles of strict liability, other times those of negligence, and respectable academic opinion can be cited for either approach. Such widely advocated and sometimes enacted reforms as no-fault automobile insurance remain controversial after years of experience in particular jurisdictions.

If the states were carrying on or sanctioning some widespread and socially destructive practice that threatened the nation's continuing viability, the federal government would no doubt be justified in exercising the full sweep of its constitutional powers in attempting to stop it. This view of the situation was taken by those who favored the prohibition amendments and by many who advocate national no-fault automobile insurance legislation. But whatever the problems created by the rise of litigiousness and proceduralism in the United States, it is hard to sustain the case that it has imperiled society's ability to function.

That point could be reached if the share of the gross national product consumed by litigation continues to increase. But the states are, if anything, more likely than the federal government to arrest this trend. Certainly there is no reason to believe Congress has any necessary advantage over the state legislatures in achieving the correct balance between objectives. The important difference is that, if Congress blunders, everyone feels the effects. The states at least offer an opportunity for trying different approaches and learning about their costs and benefits.

4. State jurisdiction creates a political market for tort law. Given the confusion and complexity that surround the issues of tort reform, the limit to the geographic reach of each state operates as a useful escape valve to check wrong decisions. Individuals and businesses that find a rule or practice intolerable can credibly threaten to move out of the jurisdiction. Observing their responses may provide some measure of the costs and benefits of a particular rule. The states can thus function as "laboratories," not necessarily in the optimistic sense that their innovations will bring constant progress, but in the pragmatic sense that their mistakes can be corrected without first suffering national consequences.

The Constitutional Background

Private law—the legal rules determining the rights and duties of one person to another—is a paradigmatic example of the kind of power reserved to the states in the Tenth Amendment: "The powers not delegated to the United States by the Constitution, nor prohibited by it to the States, are reserved to the States respectively, or to the people." The delegated powers enumerated in article I, section 8, include no provision authorizing Congress to control the definition of rights as between persons within the states.

The original structure of the Constitution, however, has been altered by the Supreme Court's modern construction of the commerce clause. The Court's decisions declare that the federal government may control—and thus exclude states from controlling—any matter that "affects" commerce, no matter how tenuously.

The Court has extended the commerce clause to its furthest reach in upholding statutes aimed at reducing the evil of racial discrimination in public accommodation. It seems unlikely that it would strain as hard to uphold a national statute aimed at reducing the rights of injured citizens. But in theory the commerce power is available to furnish a rationale for wide-ranging federal control of the minutest details of state tort law. There is no doubt that the rules governing who has rights against whom in what situation will always have some effect on commerce, if only because a defendant who must pay damages cannot use the money it forfeits to buy goods in the national market. The considerations that animated the original scheme remain relevant, however, at least as a guide to congressional action, if not to Supreme Court jurisprudence.

An example of an older line of analysis consistent with the limited-powers view of the founders can be found in the "Trade-Mark Cases" of 1879 (100 U.S. 82). Congress had passed statutes overriding state law in the area of business torts by providing for national trademark protection. It did not, however, confine the law to trademarks used in interstate commerce, and the Court held that the statute went beyond the delegated power of Congress. "The property in trademarks," the Court ruled, "resting on the laws of the States in the same manner that other property does, and depending, like the great body of the rights of person and of property, for their security and protection on those laws, the power of Congress to legislate on the subject, to establish the conditions on which these rights shall depend, the period of the duration, and the legal remedies for their protection, if such power exists at all, must be found in some clause of the Constitution of the United States, the instrument which is the source of all the powers that Congress can lawfully exercise."[1]

Although the Constitution did not contemplate national control of private-law matters generally, it did enumerate some matters that fell within national power. A summary of the matters in which the Constitution either directly intruded on private law or empowered Congress to do so illustrates the contrast between the constitutional scheme and what would be involved in federal control of tort law.

One of the strongest constitutional provisions relating to private law is the "obligation of contracts" clause, which provides that "no State shall . . . pass any . . . law impairing the obligation of contracts." This provision establishes a nationally protected core of contractual obligation. It reflects the view that a society of free men and women cannot function effectively without a legal right to enforce the promises they make and that others make to them. The Constitution contains no similar clause for torts providing, for instance, that "no State shall . . . pass . . . any law impairing the right to recover damages for the wrongs of others." There was a consensus to support the norm that people should honor what courts find to be their promises, but not the norm that people should pay money damages for what courts find to be their wrongs. As the current state of tort law reveals, there is still no such consensus. A breach of promise is a breach of promise, but one man's wrong is another man's privilege.

Article I, section 8, does confer powers on Congress enabling it to regulate private-law rights. The commerce power, for instance, was plainly intended to confer on Congress the power to regulate legal relationships arising out of transactions in interstate commerce. The power to provide for uniform laws on bankruptcy permitted Congress to specify procedures and conditions for the avoidance of the very contractual obligations protected by the contracts clause, as well as obligations arising out of tort.

Where Congress Has Intervened

A review of the record shows that congressional enactments in the area of tort law have been consistent with the original constitutional scheme. Congress has legislated in areas that the Supreme Court has held to be beyond the power of the states and in areas affecting classic instrumentalities of interstate commerce or the operation of federal programs themselves. It has also set standards of care that assist, but in no way preempt, state courts. It has gone no further.

One area historically off-limits to state power has been the liability of the federal government itself. The doctrines of sovereign immunity and governmental immunity combined to protect the federal government, its subdivisions, and its agents from tort suits. Only Congress could provide a remedy for the wrongs suffered by those barred from suit by these doctrines.

The first such group to which Congress responded systematically were federal employees injured on the job, who could not sue their employer no matter what the circumstances of their injury. In 1908, Congress enacted the Federal Employees' Compensation Act, modeled on the state workmen's compensation statutes that applied to private employers. Well into the twentieth century, other injured persons went about making claims against the federal government by persuading a congressman to introduce a private bill appropriating funds in their behalf. As the federal government increased in size and complexity, the volume of this congressional business became oppressive, and the unfairness of basing outcomes on political influence became apparent. This system slowly evolved into one in which claimants presented their case to a tribunal, which adjudicated its merits much as in a private lawsuit. Congress then appropriated funds to pay the adjudicated claims in due course.

The system of special tribunals in turn matured into the Tort Claims Act of 1946, which subjects the federal government to direct suits by injured persons under the same tort rules as a private corporation would face. It provides that "the United States shall be liable, respecting the provisions of this title relating to tort claims, in the same manner and to the same extent as a private individual under like circumstances, but shall not be liable for interest prior to judgment or for punitive damages." Thus a private citizen injured on the road by a federal vehicle has much the same rights as if the errant vehicle had been that of a private company. The act extends the remedial expectations the citizens of a state would have when wronged by each other to their dealings with the federal government. To a major extent, then, it hands over a substantial chunk of tort law from federal to state control. The act's embrace of state tort law, however, is not complete. First, the suit must be brought in the federal courts, which are created and structured by Congress rather than the states. Second, claims are tried without a jury, thus reducing the influence of local self-interest. Finally, there can be no liability based on the exercise of a discretionary function, whether or not that discretion is abused.

The compensation of injured maritime workers became a matter of exclusive federal power in 1916 as a result of the Supreme Court's decision in *Southern Pacific Company* v. *Jensen* (244 U.S. 205). In that case the state of New York had awarded workmen's compensation under its statute to a stevedore injured in the course of his employment. The Court held that state workmen's compensation statutes could not be applied in the maritime context, because they conflicted with the liability rules established by federal courts applying decisions in admiralty law. (The decision, incidentally, was the occasion of Justice Oliver Wendell Holmes's famous remark: "The common law [meaning judicial decisional law] is not a brooding omnipresence in the sky but the articulate voice of some sovereign or quasi sovereign that can be identified."[2]) The ruling made it clear that, if maritime workers were to have a right to automatic compensation for injuries, it would have to be by federal statute. Congress responded with the Jones Act for merchant seamen in 1920 and the Federal Longshoremen's and Harbor Workers' Compensation Act in 1927.

Another set of congressional enactments has dealt with what are called federal instrumentalities. The classic example of a law of this type is the Federal Employers' Liability Act of 1908, which gave railroad workers a better chance to recover for injuries caused by other employees, by modifying various common-law employer defenses and permitting injured workers to sue in federal as well as state courts. The federal government already had a long history of close involvement with the organization and operations of the railroads, most notably in the Interstate Commerce Act of 1887. The 1908 statute was modeled on state employers' liability laws, which date back to the middle of the nineteenth century. It provided a uniform set of liability rules for railroads to their workers throughout the country. The statute covered only those employees engaged in interstate commerce; an earlier version had applied to all railroad workers, whether or not they engaged in interstate commerce, but in 1908 the Court held that statute unconstitutional in the *Employers' Liability Cases* (207 U.S. 463). The Jones Act of 1920, mentioned above, simply extended the coverage of this statute from railroad workers to merchant seamen.

A recent statute that fits in this category is the National Childhood Vaccine Injury Act of 1986. A spate of liability lawsuits has endangered the federal effort to maintain high rates of childhood immunization against various diseases, an effort that helps those who go unvaccinated as well. Under the statute, parents who can show that a child was injured by a vaccine are offered compensation as an alternative to pursuing a lawsuit against the company that made the vaccine or the personnel that administered it. The entire scheme applies only to seven childhood vaccines and is expected to produce few claims. Although some might view the statute as a precursor to some more general national reform of tort law, its highly focused nature suggests that it is best understood as an attempt to further the implementation of an important federal health program.

Finally, numerous federal laws and regulations are important for state tort law, not because they displace it in any way but because they provide a standard of care that can be incorporated into the generalized "reasonable care" standard of the common law. Plaintiffs who can show that a defendant violated a federal safety standard greatly strengthen their cases. Such standards date back at least as far as the Federal Safety Appliance Act of 1893, which requires safety devices on trains. They have multiplied vastly since then, increasing the importance of this type of federal-state interplay.

Significantly, Congress has not insisted on any controlling role for these standards. Although plaintiffs can prove negligence by showing defendants' violation of the federal standard, defendants cannot rely on compliance with the federal standard to defeat the claim that they were otherwise negligent. In other words, the federal government has provided standards of care but has not made them exclusive, allowing state tort law to impose different or additional requirements of due care.

Appropriate Federal Roles

Even if the federal government continues to follow its past practice and limits its involvement in the realm of tort law, it can play a constructive role in several areas. One such role is to collect and disseminate information on the costs and benefits of different approaches that are being tried by the states and by foreign countries. In an awkward way, recent bills in Congress have accomplished this to some extent by serving as the catalyst for hearings. But the national importance of tort law is such as to justify more methodical and sustained study. The national government is uniquely well situated to coordinate a sustained and nonduplicative study of different approaches to tort liability and their social and economic effects. Beyond that, the appropriate areas for federal action are those where the prudential arguments against national intervention break down. In those cases, the most effective form of federal intervention would be measures to shore up the competence of the states.

One problem area is products-liability law. Most national manufacturers cannot set different prices for a given product to reflect differences in liability risks between jurisdictions. If a product is sold at a significantly higher price in a high-liability state, middlemen will buy it in the low-price state and tranship it to the high-price state. Some consumers from the high-price state will visit the low-price state directly to do their shopping. In either case, the producer will face liability under the rules of the high-liability state. Under American law, it is nearly impossible for a seller to prevent buyers from reselling in this manner or to avoid liability to indirect purchasers under the laws of their states. The courts of Idaho, for example, have recently concluded that the diphtheria-tetanus-pertussis (DTP) vaccine now on the market is a defective product. The sale of the product in Idaho therefore invites products-liability claims. Yet the seller cannot legally restrict the sale of the vaccine in that state. By contrast, a fair degree of market segmentation is possible in international markets. Producers can suspend sales in the United States but continue to market their goods elsewhere, using the trademark and customs laws to prevent transhipment of the product into the United States by third parties. For instance, G.D. Searle & Co. recently suspended sale of its IUD contraceptive in the United States while continuing to offer the product abroad.

Because the seller must offer the product at the same price nationwide, courts that adopt prodefendant liability laws, while preventing their citizens from recovering for injury, do not succeed in securing significantly lower product prices for those citizens. Local prices will instead be determined by the national liability risk. Thus, prodefendant rules of products liability are a bad bargain for any state, whatever their actual balance of cases and benefits. The net economic winners are the liability leaders, those whose laws tilt most toward plaintiffs.

One solution to this problem would be for the federal government to impose its own standards of products liability, or set maximum permissible standards for the states, with all the difficulties that kind of intervention entails. Alternatively, federal legislators could attempt to correct the underlying market problem. One approach, suggested by Michael W. McConnell, would be to invoke the full-faith-and-credit clause of the Constitution to change the rules governing choice of law.[3] A suggestion along these lines by Harvey Perlman would make the law of the state of first sale controlling or let manufacturers (with appropriate labeling disclosure) choose the applicable law.[4] These proposals might be politically unattractive, however, because they give the power to choose the applicable law to the seller rather than to a neutral third party and permit the seller to continue benefiting, through transhipment, from sales in a market whose law he successfully avoids.

A more limited proposal would be for Congress to pass a statute permitting sellers, under specified conditions, to label products as not for sale in particular states and to provide that such labeled products could neither be sold legally in those states nor covered by their liability rules.[5] Under such a statute, sellers could withdraw their products from states whose courts are hostile without withdrawing them from the entire country. To prevent manufacturers from using the embargo power for purposes unrelated to products liability, the statute could be made to cover only products subject to a significant number of liability claims.

States with relatively prodefendant laws sometimes complain that insurance companies charge premiums that reflect the liability risks of average customers nationwide, not the differential risks faced by customers in that state. It is hard to imagine why insurers would do this deliberately, since it is clearly profitable for them to identify, and charge more to, customers in other states whose policie˙ are likelier to lead to big claims. But in any case, the states themselves hold the key to whatever reform may be needed in this area, since insurance rates and classifications are a matter of state regulation. If the states insist on rates that fall

CAN WASHINGTON REPAIR THE TORT SYSTEM? | 111

below the true risks faced by their consumers, however, they will find that insurance companies withdraw from their market.

A variant of these problems could arise in connection with the provision of federally subsidized services. For instance, if the federal government reimburses hospital care under Medicaid on a uniform or a cost-plus basis, and liability costs vary, then high-liability states can pass some of the cost of their medical-malpractice verdicts on to the federal treasury while their citizens enjoy the full benefits of recovery. In the vaccine area, Congress intervened in part because it was paying prices set to cover the national liability risk while distributing the vaccine to many jurisdictions where there had never been a single recovery. One reason that the Tort Claims Act of 1946 assigns cases to federal judges without juries is to prevent local citizens from helping themselves to the national treasury on behalf of their neighbors. As a general matter, however, there is no reason to think that problems of this type loom large on the overall liability scene.

Aside from these three areas, it is difficult to identify, even as a matter of theory, issues of tort law where Congress could make a constructive difference, and all too easy to identify dangers and complications in any such attempt. The repair of the tort system, in short, is not a job for the federal government.

NOTES

1. 100 U.S. 93.
2. 244 U.S. 222.
3. See Michael W. McConnell, "A Choice-of-Law Approach to Products-Liability Reform," in this volume, pp. 90–101.
4. Harvey S. Perlman, "Products Liability Reform in Congress: An Issue of Federalism," *Ohio State Law Journal* 48 (1987): 503, 508.
5. This proposal, advanced by the author, is discussed in an editorial in the *Wall Street Journal*, 15 Oct. 1986.

Where the Lines Have Held:
Tort Claims against the
Federal Government

JEREMY RABKIN

Critics often see contemporary tort law as a feverish scramble for the "deep pockets"—a mere effort to drop accident victims onto the doorstep of the holders of cash reserves, however remote from the injury they may be, in the misguided conviction that society somehow owes everyone a risk-free existence or full compensation for every serious injury. Defenders of expanded liability, on the other hand, see it as a logical mechanism for placing the costs of accidents on those best able to control risks or prevent accidents, notably the manufacturers of potentially hazardous products.

From either point of view, it might have been expected that the tort revolution would finally engulf the federal government. The same pressures that have worked such a dramatic expansion over the past decade in the tort liability of manufacturers and other private parties might have been expected to work a parallel expansion in the tort liability of the federal government.

The federal government's vast range of regulatory powers and responsibilities, after all, might seem to put it in the best position to manage the risks of modern industrial life and thus prevent injuries. Moreover, with its vast taxing and borrowing powers, the federal government is in a sense the deepest pocket of all. Manufacturers can go out of business, leaving tort claimants uncompensated; the government agency that sprayed the herbicide, approved the faulty medical therapy, or ordered the asbestos installed is still solvent and arguably was in at least as good a position to prevent injury.

But the fact is that this has not happened. Many kinds of private-sector tort liability clearly expanded far more rapidly between 1975 and 1985 than did the liability of the federal government. The figures are rough, but the overall trend is unmistakable. In that ten-year period, major tort filings against the federal government increased by an impressive 275 percent, but products-liability suits filed in federal courts increased by a much more impressive 785 percent. More important is the rate of success. Studies of selected litigation samples suggest that tort plaintiffs are winning a much higher share of their cases in certain fields than they were fifteen years ago. Between the early 1970s and the mid-1980s plaintiffs virtually doubled their rate of success in products-liability and medical-malpractice suits, from around one-quarter to almost one-half. The federal government, by contrast, continues to prevail in the overwhelming majority of tort claims filed against it.

It is not as if the tort plaintiffs' bar has overlooked the fiscal resources of the federal government. While "major" tort claims against the federal government nearly tripled in the years to 1985, the total damages sought by these claims skyrocketed from around $1 billion to $200 billion. Yet the increase in actual federal outlays for tort damages — while indeed reflecting a significant jump in both the number of claims and the average scale of damages — has not been of this magnitude. Overall outlays for tort awards or settlements against the federal government, which reached $137 million in 1976, stood at only double that figure ($277 million) in 1986, considerably down from a high of $502 million in 1981.

More striking than the absolute dollar figures are the trends in doctrine, in appellate courts' delineations of the areas in which the federal government may be held liable. Compared with the scope of private liability, which has grown radically, the scope of the federal government's liability has remained remarkably settled and restricted over the past forty years. In cases involving the federal government, landmark decisions of the 1940s that limited liability continue to be cited with emphasis and approval in the 1980s. For example, the doctrine that prevents servicemen from suing the government for injuries arising from their military service continues to be honored, as, by and large, does the parallel doctrine exempting government contractors from products liability for injuries caused by weapons or other products supplied to the military in accord with government specifications. Both doctrines have survived in the face of constant pressure for enlargement of liability, in an area where, in the nature of things, the potential for fatal accidents is obvious and considerable.

Even more revealing is that regulatory operations, like military operations, have continued to enjoy broad freedom from tort liability under traditional exemptions for "discretionary" functions and specifically governmental functions. A number of lower federal court decisions of the 1970s, it is true, suggested that regulatory officials could be held accountable for injuries they might have prevented by the exercise of greater care and caution in their duties. But in 1984, in *U.S. v. VARIG Airlines,* the Supreme Court emphatically reaffirmed the traditional doctrines and denied liability for the actions of federal airline-safety inspectors, even though, if the plaintiffs were correct, the inspectors might have averted an especially terrible crash by exercising greater care. Since then, some of the more liberal liability decisions of the 1970s have been repudiated by lower courts; for example, the Third Circuit Court of Appeals recently rejected a suit seeking damages against the Food and Drug Administration for approving a defective batch of antibiotics.

In sum, while the tort liability of private businesses — most emphatically including those subject to federal safety regulation — has greatly increased in recent years, the federal government's tort liability for its regulatory ventures has scarcely increased at all. This seems especially paradoxical, given that the litigation revolution of recent years has hit local government quite hard. Tort suits have forced tremendous increases in insurance payments to cover accidents incurred in local public facilities. At the same time, the U.S. Supreme Court has steadily extended the liability of state and local governments for tort claims charging violations of civil-rights guarantees.

The continued limiting of tort liability for federal agencies, then, cannot be explained by any judicial reverence for government in general. Nor does it reflect any special judicial inhibition about interfering with federal regulatory decisions. The larger trend in federal administrative law in recent decades, indeed, has been to expose federal regulatory agencies to more and more supervision by courts, and broader and broader challenges by public-interest groups and other advocates claiming to represent the intended beneficiaries of regulatory action. The crucial difference is that administrative-law plaintiffs seek declarative and injunctive remedies that alter future regulatory patterns, rather than compensation for past "negligence."

A number of recent commentators have criticized the intrusiveness of these administrative-law remedies, and the Supreme Court has shown some signs of concern that courts are intervening overmuch in regulatory decision making. The continuing limitations on the tort liability of regulatory agencies are thus all the more interesting, because they demonstrate a firm refusal to consider what might appear a particularly attractive (because less intrusive) alternative to the standard administrative-law remedies. On the face of things, the threat of tort liability might seem an appealing way to focus the attention of federal regulators on their work of averting injuries and accidents. By holding regulators accountable for the costs of their failures, tort liability might seem to provide them with incentives to improve their performance in ways that would be of deep concern to society; it might impose a "performance standard" on an otherwise unresponsive agency.

Why, then, have the lines held in this one area? Why has there been no systematic shift of liability for accidents to the ultimate insurer and risk controller in American society? Why has the movement in private tort law toward ascribing liability to more and more distant "causes" of accidents not been extended to the federal government, with its vast fiscal resources for compensation and its tremendous regulatory capacity to control risks? Why has the movement in administrative law toward bringing more and more aspects of regulatory discretion under judicial supervision not been extended to allow suits asking for compensation as well as future policy change?

There have been so many surprising and inexplicable departures in American law in recent decades that it is always hazardous to seek logical explanations for any emergent legal pattern. Nonetheless, there is a rational explanation for the seeming anomaly at hand. There are, at least, sound reasons for maintaining limits on regulatory liability, given the way such liability would probably operate in practice. But the reasons for preserving the limits on government liability may offer some useful reminders about the tolerable reach of private tort liability, which tort judges themselves might do well to keep in mind.

Sovereign Immunity and the Political Limits on Public Liability

The most direct explanation for the survival of limited federal tort liability might seem to be the most legalistic. It is the lingering presence of the ancient doctrine of "sovereign immunity"— the doctrine that government may not be sued without its consent. Congress refused to waive sovereign immunity for tort claims until 1946, and when it finally did so in the Federal Tort Claims Act (FTCA) of that year, it incorporated a number of exceptions to the waiver. Most notably, the FTCA limits liability to federal actions "for which a private person in like circumstances could be liable"— thus excluding liability for specifically governmental activities — and in particular excludes liability for "exercises of discretion."[1] The second exclusion would seem to reinforce the first where the act of alleged negligence is a discretionary regulatory decision. In VARIG and other cases, federal courts have simply invoked these statutory limitations to deny regulatory liability.

But the historical-accident explanation is not entirely convincing. The Administrative Procedure Act (APA), also enacted in 1946, imposes somewhat similar limitations on judicial authority, and courts had no trouble evading these limitations after the mid-1960s, when they sought to extend their control of agency behavior. The APA, for example, excludes judicial review when decisions are "committed to agency discretion," but the Supreme Court held in 1967 that this broad immunity would apply only in those "rare cases" in which statutes clearly and emphatically excluded review.[2] Similarly, the APA grants standing for judicial challenges to anyone suffering "legal wrong" (injury to a distinct private right) or to anyone "aggrieved within the meaning of a relevant statute," but the Supreme Court held in 1970 that anyone "aggrieved"— that is, disadvantaged — by an administrative decision should have standing to challenge it in court, even though, in the vast majority of cases, relevant statutes do not confer standing on those "aggrieved."[3] The generous readings applied to the APA to broaden access to the courts could have been applied to the FTCA for the same purpose.

A somewhat more satisfying explanation would have to start with the recognition that the Administrative Procedure Act and the Tort Claims Act were never entirely comparable. It has always been possible to seek injunctions against some federal administrative actions, and courts made such remedies more widely available in the decades before World War II. When the APA was enacted in 1946, therefore, it was regarded as little more than a codification of existing law, at least insofar as its provisions on judicial review were concerned. But before 1946 it had been impossible to seek tort damages from the federal treasury. Tort victims might sue for damages against the individual officials who had injured them; but if they did not secure full compensation that way, they could only appeal to Congress to pass a private bill appropriating what legislators judged to be adequate compensation.

The differential treatment of damage claims and injunctive remedies, then, has a long history, extending much further back than the adoption of particular statutory language in 1946. This difference can also be seen in the case of damage claims against government officials in their private capacities, which, though not directly constrained by the principle of sovereign immunity, have been generally harder to obtain than injunctive remedies since the nineteenth century. The reason for this particular discrepancy is obvious. In private litigation, common-law courts may have preferred retrospective damage claims as less intrusive than injunctive remedies. But for a government official, a damage claim paid personally would be far more onerous, and its threat far more intimidating, than an injunction governing his official conduct in the future. Both state courts and federal courts therefore sought to limit the liability of government officials at various levels to enable them to fulfill their responsibilities with some degree of confidence. When Congress enacted the FTCA in 1946, transferring liability from the pockets of federal officials to the coffers of the federal treasury, it essentially incorporated these earlier judicial constructions of personal liability to ensure that the federal government would not be accepting any wider liability than courts had thought proper to impose on governmental officials personally.

But the question remains why "sovereign immunity," which originally forced courts to improvise these limitations by restricting tort claims to government officials' own pockets, was so widely accepted by American courts in the first place. Commentators in recent decades have indeed regarded sovereign immunity as an inexplicable anomaly in American law, since it is usually traced to the medieval common-law principle that "the king can do no wrong," a curious maxim to retain in a republican constitution.

In fact, however, three practical, democratic concerns seem to account for the entrenchment of the principle of sovereign immunity in the course of the nineteenth century. The first and most evident reason is that legislatures were extremely jealous of their control over public spending. This jealousy seems to have been the principal concern that leading proponents of the Constitution were seeking to assuage when they endorsed the principle of sovereign immunity during the ratification debates. When the U.S. Supreme Court nonetheless ruled in 1795 that a state could be sued in federal court to enforce debts it owed to private creditors, the protests were so bitter that the Eleventh Amendment was quickly added to the Constitution, specifying that citizens of other states or of foreign countries could not sue state governments without their consent. Decades later, the Supreme Court was still mindful enough of this history that it refused to allow suits against state governments even by their own citizens, though the Eleventh Amendment did not specifically prohibit such suits.

Sovereign immunity never applied to municipalities, which were regarded as "corporations" rather than full-fledged sovereigns. In practice, an important reason for this exception was probably that state legislatures were more likely to resent judicial intervention when it infringed their own fiscal prerogatives than when it infringed those of municipalities. At any rate, courts never attempted to lay claims on the fiscal prerogatives of Congress, which was extremely jealous of those prerogatives from the outset. Probably Congress refused to authorize tort claims against the federal treasury before 1946 in large part because it wanted to retain responsibility—and credit—for doling out remunerations to appealing claimants one at a time. Thus, after the Civil War, Congress authorized suits by government contractors and a few others against the federal treasury—but expressly excluded pension claimants as well as tort claimants. As Congress continually widened eligibility standards, pension claims by Civil War veterans soared. By 1900 there were 635,000 pending claims, which generated twice as many related letters and inquiries to congressmen each year. Still, Congress continued to determine appeals on its own through "private bills" rather than delegate this "chore" to judicial tribunals. In short, sovereign immunity preserved legislative control over the flow of money—and money was the mother's milk of legislative politics then just as much as now.

A second rationale for sovereign immunity was that it safeguarded legislative control, or reduced occasions for judicial collisions with legislative pretensions, in regulatory matters. This point may seem less obvious if one considers compensation claims for bodily injury, but tort law was still in its infancy in the nineteenth century, and suits against government officials sought relief almost entirely from interferences with private property or commercial freedom. As courts became more insistent in imposing constitutional limitations on the expansion of government regulations toward the end of the nineteenth century, damage actions again might have seemed much more intrusive than injunctive remedies. Telling an official not to enforce a particular statute, because it was judged constitutionally invalid, was one thing; forcing the official to pay damages to those he had acted against would be quite another; forcing the government to shoulder the burden of compensation would be yet more intrusive. Ultimately, without sovereign immunity, courts might have ended up forcing governments to reimburse citizens for the costs of complying with regulation, as the most insistent defenders of property rights still urge. It is hardly surprising that courts shrank back from this extreme, even in the heyday of "laissez-faire" jurisprudence. In sum, sovereign immunity protected legislative power in regard to public regulation.

Finally, sovereign immunity bolstered the discretion of executive or administrative officials, thus preserving room for broad political influence on administrative operations. It is revealing that by the late nineteenth century, when sovereign immunity had become an entrenched principle in United States law, most governments in Western Europe had already accepted broad liability for the mistakes of their officials, with the exception of *actes du gouvernement* (high-level public-policy decisions). Such extensive government liability seems to act as a centralizing influence on administrative operations, and government administration was far more centralized in Western Europe than in America. Until the late nineteenth century, federal field services—like the post office, the customs service, and the United States attorneys—were extensively used for congressional patronage, and officials who owed their appointments to particular congressional patrons were not readily controlled by their superiors in the bureau. It was not until late in the nineteenth century, for example, that Congress confirmed the authority of the secretary of the treasury to overrule the decisions of federal customs officials in local ports—officials who invariably owed their positions to congressional sponsorship. It is hardly surprising that Congress did not welcome a system of government liability that would have allowed courts to impose closer controls on its minions. Nor is it surprising that courts did not dare to improvise such a system in the face of congressional resistance.

From this broader perspective, even the unprecedented development of administrative-law remedies in recent decades seems much less remarkable. Whatever else may be said of them, administrative-law remedies do not advance presidential control of agency decision making but the opposite, which might in itself suffice to recommend such remedies to Congress. In the environmental legislation of the early 1970s, for example, Congress authorized "any citizen" to bring suit against the Environmental Protection Agency to challenge inadequate performance of statutory duties. In fact, a number of factors make administrative-law remedies more serviceable than tort claims in a system that seeks to leave much room for political bargaining.

Even in the contemporary era of the "hard look" doctrine—which invites judges to give close scrutiny to the evidence and reasoning behind administrative decisions—respect for administrative discretion continues to be the central theme in administrative law. While tort claims are irreducibly specific (a named claimant either is or is not entitled to compensation), administrative-law litigation is characteristically murky and ambiguous. The most common "remedy" in the recent, more ambitious administrative-law cases is not a final order to administrators to do or not to do a particular thing. Instead, courts remand contested regulations or decisions for further explanations by the agency, the consideration of new evidence, or further processing in accord with tighter procedural standards. And as these outcomes by their nature directly affect many people other than the nominal plaintiffs, those plaintiffs are implicitly treated as representatives of many others with an interest in the outcome. Supreme Court decisions in the early 1970s that widened standing to challenge administrative decisions stipulated that standing should turn on a showing that "the interest sought to be protected" by the would-be plaintiffs was "arguably within the zone of interests" Congress had intended to benefit with the relevant regulatory statute.[4] The most insightful scholarly analysis could therefore plausibly describe the expanded system of administrative-law remedies that developed in the early 1970s as a "surrogate political process," furthering the balancing of interest-group claims that had traditionally been associated with congressional oversight.

Why not extend this system to provide compensation to intended "beneficiaries" who could show they had received direct injury from the agency's failure to regulate properly? The principal reason is no doubt that courts would then have to set standards of regulatory performance with much more detail and precision than they do now even in the most wide-ranging administrative lawsuits. This may not seem much of an obstacle in an era when federal judges can take over the management of local school systems, prisons, and hospitals and when the Supreme Court can ignore sovereign-immunity claims to order the broadening of welfare-benefit programs or the financing of court-ordered institutional reforms, such as extensive school-busing programs.

But much of the historic logic of sovereign immunity must still be reckoned with. Ingrained political tendencies of the contemporary system, similar to those that made courts reluctant to confront Congress with the costs of its programs in the nineteenth century, would probably frustrate the efficient workings of a system of regulatory tort liability. Today the danger for the courts is not that Congress would respond with indignation at moves in this direction but that it would not let them proceed as their architects might hope.

Practical Obstacles to a Regulatory Tort System

The logic of tort law as a system for reducing risks is to place the costs of accidents on those in the best position to control or avert them. Modern negligence cases do not inquire whether the tortfeasor intended to harm the victim. Where strict liability is applied, as in products-liability cases, courts do not even ask whether the tortfeasor acted "recklessly"— in the ordinary sense of the term — in failing to behave in a way that might have averted harm to the victim. The question is simply whether a feasible alternative course of conduct might have averted the harm. The hope is that the threat of liability will generate powerful economic incentives to avoid or reduce risk. In most cases, this threat gives insurance companies a powerful incentive to insist that businesses comply with specified safety precautions as a condition of getting insurance, and insurance specialists make it their business to gauge such risks with great care.

The heart of this system is the connecting incentive it maintains between compensation costs and efforts to limit accidents. If businesses — or insurers — limit the number or severity of accidents, they pay less. The central difficulty with a tort system for regulatory failure is that this connection could not be so readily maintained for a government agency.

To begin with, government is never dealing with its own money in the same sense as is a private business. Private tort defendants and their insurance companies have obvious incentives to resist fraudulent or questionable claims; they want to hold on to their money. The everyday business of many government officials is to dispense money, not to hold on to it. Lack of agency resistance to claims seems to be one reason why federal payments for Social Security disability claims soared from $9.4 billion in 1976 to $17 billion in 1981, a rise much in excess of cost-of-living increases and demographic changes in that five-year interval.

At issue is not the professionalism of government officials but their incentives.

There are few rewards for saving money in government service and often actual deterrents to trying too hard to do so. When, for example, the Department of Health and Human Services launched a program in the early 1980s – at the urging of Congress – to reduce fraud in disability claims, Congress soon changed its tune and, after excoriating the department at length for heartless and overzealous denial of benefits, moved quickly to cut back the program. Resistance to regulatory tort claims would almost certainly generate similar political pressure, particularly if large claims were involved. And many of the cases would surely be class actions involving large sums, since it would be easier to prove causality – to trace the plaintiffs' injuries to the action or inaction of regulators – when large classes could make a statistical case for the connection; and in any case the difficulty of documenting claims would encourage class actions as a way to pool research costs. As it is, the Justice Department receives continual inquiries and promptings from members of Congress whose constituents are involved in major tort cases against the government.

Members of Congress have strong incentives at present to press for out-of-court tort settlements favorable to their constituents for the same reason that agencies have few incentives to resist them: federal tort payouts do not come out of particular agency appropriations but from a general "judgment fund" that covers the entire government. Appropriations to cover such obligations, like those to cover entitlement programs, are regarded as "uncontrollable" spending, for which Congress cannot be blamed. Thus, in an era of budget limits, tort settlements can serve as a backdoor spending mechanism, a kind of entitlement program that allows appropriations subcommittees not only to escape the responsibility for voting new benefits but to finance these benefits outside the formal agency appropriation. Agency officials, for their part, have no incentive to devote time and energy to investigating and resisting claims settled with money that does not come out of their own appropriations.

Even if the Justice Department, which represents the agencies in the courts, can resist pressures from Congress and force the agencies to defend themselves, the fact remains that losing a tort claim will not force an agency to change its operating patterns, because the financial loss is not *its* loss. Peter Schuck, the leading advocate of expanding federal tort liability, has urged that the financing of tort settlements be linked to the affected agency's own budget so as to establish conventional tort incentives.[5] But there is doubt that Congress will ever allow such a system to operate for long if the dollar amounts become significant.

The Labor Department, for example, runs a program that compensates coal miners suffering from black lung (pneumoconiosis), a sometimes fatal lung disease attributable to overexposure to coal dust. The idea was that disabled coal miners or their survivors would be paid from a general fund when no "responsible mine owner" could be determined for ordinary liability purposes. The fund was to be financed by a special tax on the coal industry, making the industry as a whole responsible for the cost of such injuries when particular liability could not be fixed. In 1976, actual outlays for benefits under this program reached $13.8 million, and

Labor Department officials projected that outlays would more than double over the next several years. In fact, by 1980 annual payments had soared to $731 million. Although payment levels did decline somewhat in the mid-1980s, even a reorganized tax scheme adopted in 1981 proved inadequate to cover obligations. By 1987, some two-thirds of its payouts were being financed not through the special tax on the coal industry but by direct transfers from general revenues; the total amount transferred in this way in regular federal budget appropriations since 1981 had reached $3.7 billion. Having established a new entitlement program, Congress thought it more important to honor obligations to beneficiaries than to honor the original financing plan.

The same pressures that have shifted the financing of black-lung benefits over the years would almost certainly be felt when tort claims made a significant dent in an agency's budget. There would be irresistible political pressures to turn a tort-claims compensation program into a more or less free-standing insurance entitlements program. If tort compensation cuts too deeply into an agency's budget, other constituencies of the agency's programs would plausibly protest that it would be unfair to leave them with reduced levels of agency protection, merely because the agency's past mistakes had put it under heavy budget obligations to others. Congress would almost surely respond to such protests with new appropriations to ensure that tort claims could be paid without sacrificing other claims on the agency's resources.

To be sure, a tort system might be fine-tuned by providing outside funding to cushion against truly crippling claims while leaving enough of the obligations on the agency to provide continuing incentives for improvement. Even if political pressures to reimburse the agency for its losses could be kept in check, however, enormous difficulties would remain on the other side of the equation. An agency might be given definite incentives to respond to the pressure of tort claims, but it would still face enormous obstacles in trying to respond to these incentives.

Here again, government agencies are not in the same position as private businesses or insurers. Neither the ultimate consumer nor the business purchaser of insurance has much leverage to resist economic pressures for the improvement of safety standards. If one insurer finds it advisable to impose a condition in providing business coverage — say, the removal of diving boards from hotel pools — other insurers will be imposing similar conditions, and neither hotels nor consumers will find much chance to evade the new standard. By contrast, the constituencies of regulatory agencies have acquired many techniques for influencing the agency decisions that they will have to live with, and they are unlikely to relinquish these extra sources of leverage merely because a tort system has been superimposed on the agency as yet another competing influence.

On one side, then, business groups can be expected to press for less costly or less onerous safety standards, urging the agency, where it is uncertain about the effects of policy, to err on the side of tolerating more risk. And the more the tort system allows regulated businesses to shift their own liability back to the government — by attributing harms inflicted by their products to regulatory negligence, as the airline tried to do in the *VARIG* case—the more incentive the regulated businesses will have to resist tighter safety standards at earlier stages. On the opposite side, the various constituencies favoring tighter regulation (often including business interests alert to the relative effects of tighter controls on their competitors) are unlikely to refrain from pressing for the approaches they advocate, merely because the tort system points a government agency toward different priorities. On the contrary, to the extent that the pressure of tort liabilities pointed the agency away from addressing the concerns of particular constituencies, these groups could be expected to redouble their efforts to sway the agency's policy. Few constituencies, in short, are likely to defer respectfully to the promptings of the tort system; they will instead work overtime to convince the agency to ignore economic incentives.

The contending forces at work are amply illustrated by the regulatory experience of the Occupational Safety and Health Administration (OSHA) over the past decade. Policy analysts long ago pointed out that OSHA could prevent more casualties without increasing the overall burdens it puts on the economy if it promulgated a much larger number of new health-exposure standards but adopted a less demanding approach in each individual standard. Instead, the agency has identified dozens of dangerous substances slated for eventual regulation but has actually issued standards for only a few of them. Almost every time the agency does issue a new standard, it is immediately challenged by business groups as too severe and by labor (or consumer) groups as too lax; years of wrangling follow before a final standard is settled. So far it has been futile to appeal to business or labor to reach quick compromises in order to get on with a wider regulatory agenda; the burdens—or benefits—of each new standard are highly localized in particular industries, and the groups most affected have few incentives to compromise their positions for the sake of speedier progress on other issues that are likely to be of much less concern to them.

The current state of administrative-law litigation provides many opportunities for legal obstruction by all sides. Even if the courts could be persuaded to curtail those opportunities (and that is far from certain, given the entrenched precedents in this area), it seems unlikely that intensely interested groups would stop trying to resist OSHA's policy impulses in the political arena or that Congress or the White House would refuse to give them a hearing. Particular constituencies would still have few incentives to compromise for the sake of a more efficient overall program, and politicians would still have few incentives to ignore their pleas.

In sum, just as there would be powerful pressures to convert the compensation side of a regulatory tort system into a free-standing insurance or entitlements program, so there would be powerful pressures to deflect or nullify the deterrence side of such a system—pressures that would come from the political forces that already shape the program and have also helped shape the expanded administrative-law system in which the agency's acts will be reviewed. Arrangements geared to the claims of interest groups would not easily be dislodged by a separate government tort system geared to the claims of determinate, individual victims.

Conclusion

These obstacles to the efficient functioning of a regulatory tort system may help explain why the courts have resisted the development of tort claims against federal regulatory agencies. The obstacles may indeed seem so evident that it may be tempting to dismiss the whole notion of regulatory torts as no more than idle speculation. Throughout the twentieth century, after all, there has been no major move to link publicly provided injury insurance with public regulatory activity. When employer liability was superseded by workers' compensation programs at the beginning of the century, for example, the new compensation system was not closely coordinated with the early state ventures in direct workplace safety regulation. Dissatisfaction with the workings of the contemporary tort system has prompted renewed interest in governmental alternatives for both compensation and safety regulation. But the difficulties in meshing a tort system with governmental spending and regulatory systems should give us pause. The same factors that make it difficult to impose tort liability on public programs through a tort scheme make it difficult to design sensible or efficient public programs that substitute for the system.

There is obvious appeal in reducing the volume of litigation by creating or expanding programs such as workers' compensation. We ought to remember, however, that workers' compensation has worked relatively well precisely because it has traditionally succeeded in preserving a relatively strict definition of just what expenses it pays (medical costs and lost earnings) for just what injuries (those suffered on the work site). The more ambitious or generous a compensation plan is made to be and the wider the range of hazards and diseases it proposes to cover, the more difficult it will be to ensure proper controls in the processing of claims, and the greater the pressure will be to shift the costs to the taxpayer. Social-insurance programs that lack precisely controllable eligibility standards run into inevitable problems of fraud and abuse — and "abuse" may be a good deal more damaging than outright fraud. The black-lung program should stand as a general warning. To be sure, taxpayers are unlikely to tolerate many spending programs that cost twenty-five times more than their initial projections. But legislative efforts to limit or balance the costs of various public insurance programs may not operate in the end with much more logic or efficiency than the current private tort system.

Perhaps more important, displacing tort-based incentives with regulatory controls is bound to put new pressures on a regulatory system already under much strain. If compliance with regulatory standards were accepted as an automatic defense to tort claims, there would be tremendous additional pressure on government regulators to permit no risk at all in approving new products, a dismaying prospect for an agency like the Food and Drug Administration (FDA), which is already denying Americans access to many valuable drugs (including drugs for the treatment of heart disease and other life-threatening afflictions) available in Western Europe. One might also anticipate greater pressure to make exceptions to overly stringent standards, as the FDA is already doing in its approval of promising "breakthrough" treatments, like drugs for the treatment of acquired immune deficiency syndrome (AIDS). Such pressures will in turn exacerbate legal and procedural tangling as other claimants seek to exploit the loopholes open by exception-making.

It may still be worth while to broaden social-insurance coverage and substitute regulation for tort liability in a few areas, such as "toxic torts," in which responsibility for health effects is very difficult to pinpoint. But the advantages of a tort system should not be quickly abandoned when the source of injury is easier to trace. A well-functioning tort system can still, in principle, perform as a relatively efficient system for the control of risk by transferring the cost of injuries to those in the best position to control or reduce such injuries. The political system is not likely to sustain a program that functions as rationally, because it is bound to be distracted by many considerations other than the most efficient reduction of injuries. The impersonal, economically rational sorting of claims is not the strong point of the American political system.

The willfulness of this political system does not, however, indicate that the system will remain passive in the contemporary tort crisis. On the contrary, when the tort system generates politically intolerable results, some response is inevitable. Thus, to cite the leading example, when drug companies threatened to end the sale of highly effective vaccines in the face of prohibitively costly damage claims arising from occasional adverse reactions, Congress certainly responded. But its response took the form of a political "patch" on the tort system that managed to combine the worst features of contemporary tort litigation with the worst potentials for abuse in the governmental alternatives.

The National Childhood Vaccine Injury Act, enacted in the summer of 1986, limits the tort liability of manufacturers to an extent unclear until several more rounds of anticipated litigation have ended. In the place of that full liability, the measure establishes a public insurance program for victims of debilitating (or fatal) vaccine reactions and also seeks to strengthen public regulation of vaccines by the Department of Health and Human Services. Far from seeking to link accident compensation costs with this new regulatory scheme, however, Congress seemed eager to put as much distance as it could between the two sides of its response. Rather than attempt to build up administrative experience and expertise in the evaluation of accident claims in this technical area, Congress took the extraordinary step of bypassing administrative operations altogether and authorizing self-declared victims to appeal directly to the courts for compensation from a special new fund. The lawmakers seem to have feared that a specialized administrative agency would prove more skeptical or resistant to many claims than a system operating through nonspecialized judges. On the other hand, far from attempting to shelter the new regulatory controls on vaccine production from distortive political pressure, Congress authorized every citizen to bring suits protesting inadequate performance of duties by the new regulatory authority. This action assured advocacy groups of another channel to press their own priorities on the regulators.

Symptoms of social distress like the curtailment of vaccine production may have less to do with the legal principles of tort liability than with the freakish imposition of vastly inflated damage awards. If so, reform of private tort law may require less change in the law than some advocates have urged. If the tort system is imposing unpredictable — and uninsurable — costs, it is worth remembering that the political system may prove even less rational or predictable in its own operation. In most areas, the best forum for tort reform may still be in the courts.

NOTES

1. 28 U.S.C. §2680(a).
2. 551 U.S.C. §701(a)(2); *Abbott Labs* v. *Gardner*, 387 U.S. 136 (1967).
3. *Association of Data Processing Service Organizations* v. *Camp*, 397 U.S. 150 (1970). (Emphasis added.)
4. *Association of Data Processing Service Organizations* v. *Camp*, 397 U.S. 150 (1970); *Barlow* v. *Collins*, 397 U.S. 159 (1970).
5. Peter H. Schuck, *Suing Government: Citizen Remedies for Official Wrongs* (New Haven: Yale University Press, 1983), 106.

Compensating Workplace Toxic Torts

W. KIP VISCUSI

In recent years the focus of concern over workplace safety has shifted from the familiar problem of occupational injuries to the relatively unfamiliar problem of occupational disease. As science has found new links between toxic exposures on the job and illnesses that can crop up many years later, there has been a major wave of litigation; suits over deadly asbestos exposure have already bankrupted the leading producer of that mineral, the Manville Corporation. The lawsuits filed by Vietnam veterans against makers of the herbicide Agent Orange have brought the issue to an even wider public.

This essay analyzes why the current approaches to the occupational-disease problem are not working well and proposes a new response that might both provide fair compensation and promote efficient health-risk levels. Three key principles emerge from the analysis. First, proposals to compensate disease victims should be coordinated with direct regulation of workplace risk, because both influence employer decisions that affect worker health. Second, compensation plans should provide similar levels of income support to similarly situated victims. Third, policy initiatives should clearly distinguish between diseases that have already been contracted and those that will materialize in the future.

The Occupational-Disease Problem

Occupational disease is a problem of staggering proportions for both workers and industry. Approximately 162,000 occupational illnesses are documented annually by the U.S. Bureau of Labor Statistics. This figure probably understates the prevalence of occupational disease, however, since other Department of Labor statistics

This essay is an outgrowth of a report on toxic tort compensation policies prepared by the author for the Office of Management and Budget (OMB). The late Michael Mazur was the contract officer at OMB. Thomas Hopkins, Thomas Lenard, John Morrall, and Frederick Siskind provided helpful comments. Portions of the essay are drawn, with permission, from W. Kip Viscusi, "Structuring an Effective Occupational Disease Policy: Victim Compensation and Risk Regulation," *Yale Journal on Regulation* 2:1, 1984.

indicate that some 2 million people are severely or partially disabled by occupational diseases, of whom 700,000 suffer long-term total disability. Other estimates indicate that 85,000 of these are victims of asbestos-related diseases alone.

Several factors make it difficult to know the full scope of the occupational-disease problem or the exact number of victims. For one thing, symptoms of many occupational illnesses do not appear until years after the exposure to the hazard. When disease victims can be identified, it may be difficult or impossible to ascertain the causes of these diseases. Although there are some "signature" diseases, such as mesothelioma, whose relationship to a particular kind of exposure is well established, most chronic illnesses can be caused by exposure to any of several substances or by participation in any of several activities. Lung cancer, for example, may result from air pollution, cigarette smoke, asbestos, or many other carcinogens. Thus it may be quite difficult to disentangle the occupational contribution to someone's disease.

Workers' compensation systems insure workers against the financial risks of most sudden job injuries but place a number of restrictions on coverage of slow-acting workplace disease. The requirement that workers show the job-relatedness of their ailment is often a major difficulty. Damage to the nervous system from lead exposure and gradual loss of hearing due to excessive noise exposure, for example, can be linked to a job less readily than an acute injury, such as being maimed by a punchpress.

During the 1970s and 1980s, many workers began circumventing these restrictions and obtaining additional compensation by filing third-party suits against manufacturers of hazardous workplace products. The potential liability of manufacturers in such suits is enormous, and its rapid growth may threaten entire industries. For instance, the estimated value of valid claims against the asbestos industry generated by past exposures exceeds the combined financial resources of all asbestos producers and their insurers. The bankruptcies resulting from such claims, moreover, could mean that there is no money left to compensate workers who later discover that their illnesses are related to asbestos. Developing a national compensation plan is crucial if only for the sake of these late-arriving victims.

Why Markets May Fail

Theoretically, in a fully competitive employment market, market transactions between employers and employees could lead to efficient levels of health hazards and equitable compensation for diseased workers. Workers will not accept jobs posing known risks, unless the position offers some additional, attractive offsetting feature. Economists have sought to measure the additional wage compensation that these positions command, holding other attributes of the job constant. Overall evidence indicates that there are substantial risk premiums on the order of $3 million to $4 million per fatality and $30,000 per nonfatal injury. These risk premiums in turn establish a safety incentive for the firm. The firm can reduce its wage costs through an investment in greater workplace safety. When this market mechanism is fully effective, government intervention is unnecessary and should be avoided. For risk premiums to work properly, however, workers must be cognizant of the potential risks they face. This may be a particular problem in the case of occupational disease.

Because of the problems of multiple causation, the latency factor, and the difficulty of tracing environmental causes of disease, such risks are typically not as apparent as safety hazards, such as slippery staircases. In an extreme case, workers may know nothing of the particular toxic risk to which they are being exposed. Unlike accidental injury, health damage cannot always be observed by co-workers and employers even after it happens, so that experience will not necessarily give all sides some idea of the risks involved. When health hazards are hidden, workers fail to demand an adequate wage premium for risk, and employers provide too little control of health risks.

If, however, workers are warned of low-probability health risks, they may overreact. A series of studies has indicated that individuals systematically overassess low-probability risks of a magnitude comparable to that of workplace health risks. In particular, individuals display a systematic tendency to overestimate the fatality risks from botulism, tornadoes, floods, pregnancy, and other low-probability events. In addition, a recent study of consumer responses to risks suggests that biased perceptions of this sort lead to alarmist market responses.[1] Consumers who are apprised of annual product risks of around 1 in 100,000 (or less) acted as if these risks were considerably larger in deciding how much of a price cut was worth trading off for the risk.

The warning problem is thus double-edged. Unless workers are informed about the potential danger, risk levels will be too great. Employers have little incentive to provide this warning, since doing so would boost the wage rate they must pay, and this wage cost will often exceed any reduction in injury costs to the firm. Government regulations consequently must require that it be provided. On the other hand, any hazard-warning program must be designed to convey risk information without inducing undue alarm.

Current Regulatory and Compensation Policies

The information problem and other possible market failures create a potentially productive role for government action. The Occupational Safety and Health Administration (OSHA) enforces regulations designed to lower disease risk, and tort litigation also provides a major safety incentive. On the compensation front, workers' compensation and liability awards have aided many victims, though by no means all, and various legislative proposals would reach and compensate some additional victims. Unfortunately, these haphazard approaches do not add up to a coherent strategy for achieving either efficient levels of health risk or fair compensation for all disease victims.

OSHA, created in 1970, is responsible for ensuring that "so far as possible every working man and woman in the Nation [has] safe and healthful working conditions."[2] Although the agency has issued many regulations designed to reduce workplace exposure to hazardous substances, these rules have been overly costly for what they have achieved and largely ineffective.[3] Moreover, OSHA regulations are laid atop other programs that also influence the level of workplace health risks, so that the net impact of these efforts may be both unintended and undesirable.

OSHA has taken a number of steps to regulate workplace exposure to hazardous substances. For instance, it has regulated asbestos, the leading workplace carcinogen, since 1972. The agency has long been criticized for the rigid "command-and-control" format of its regulations, which reduces employers' flexibility and prevents them from meeting health goals in the most cost-effective manner. In many cases the agency would be better off issuing performance standards rather than mandating specific technological methods to reduce exposure. The best ways to reduce for employers the risk of byssinosis from cotton dust, for example, may be to issue disposable masks to workers and rotate workers who display early signs of the disease, rather than install dust-abatement machinery.

OSHA has also been castigated for its refusal to calculate whether the benefits of its regulations exceed the costs and for its dismal enforcement record. Not surprisingly, most studies show that it has had only marginal success in improving workplace health and safety. But its effectiveness seems to have improved since its early years, and in the health area it has had a notable success story in securing compliance with its cotton-dust standard.

Although the agency regulates a number of workplace carcinogens, it has set workplace standards for only a small fraction of the more than 2,000 such substances that have been identified. To fill this gap, it has begun to rely on the warning principle. Recently it started requiring worker-education programs and the labeling of hazardous chemicals. The original justification behind the rule requiring warning labels was entirely speculative, but it has been borne out by experimental studies. Well-designed warnings can alter workers' risk perceptions in the desired fashion, causing them to demand rationally higher wage premiums for risky work and influencing decisions to accept employment.[4] To be successful, however, a labeling effort must provide workers with new information they can use; it is much less successful if it advises workers to behave differently without providing them with a factual basis for doing so. For example, telling individuals that they should wear protective goggles will not be effective. However, an explanation that indicates the likely source of the eye injury and the role of goggles in reducing the risk will be much more influential.

OSHA's direct regulations and warning requirements can address only a part of the occupational-disease problem. The agency has no authority to compensate victims and cannot control the effects of the existing workers' compensation and tort systems on levels of health risk. A separate compensation system is clearly needed, one that will not interfere with attempts to regulate health hazards and that will provide an acceptable minimum of income support to disease victims.

Formal compensation for workplace injuries is supposed to be handled through the workers' compensation system. Before such programs were enacted, workers who were injured on the job or contracted a job-related disease could bring tort action against their employers. If the worker could prove that the employer was negligent, that this negligence caused the injury, and that the worker's own conduct had not contributed to the problem, the employee would have a good chance of winning a judgment. Because of the difficulties in proving all three steps, however, many workers went uncompensated.

Eventually, all states established workers' compensation programs to replace tort suits against employers. Under the programs, an injured worker does not normally have the right to bring a tort suit against the employer for negligence. Instead he files a claim against a central fund. This claim need not allege employer negligence, which makes it easier and less costly to obtain an award. However, unlike a successful tort recovery, a workers' compensation award makes no attempt to restore to the claimant the full value of the loss. It does not compensate for pain and suffering, and it compensates for physical losses like the loss of an arm at significantly lower rates than juries usually do.

Two other features of workers' compensation systems impede adequate recovery for toxic exposures. First, to qualify for workers' compensation, a claimant must show that he suffered an injury arising from and in the course of employment. This causation requirement is fairly straightforward in most work-related injuries but much more problematic in many occupational-disease cases. Most workers' compensation–system statutes will not pay for a disease unless it is "peculiar to the worker's occupation"[5] and not simply one of the "ordinary diseases of life."[6] Proving the workplace link may be extremely difficult, especially since records on the worker's history of exposure to hazardous substances may never have been kept or may have been lost during the period of the disease.

The second impediment to adequate recovery is the requirement that the worker report the injury and file a claim within a specified period. Even if evidence on the other points is readily available, a worker may still fail to collect because the statute of limitations has expired before his condition is diagnosed. Courts in some states have sought to get around this problem by ruling that the "accident" that starts the statute-of-limitations clock ticking may be defined as the onset of the worker's disability or his discovery of its cause, rather than the original exposure to the hazard.

Statistics on actual compensation show that these limitations lead to inequities in the treatment of equally deserving claimants. Victims of occupational injuries are more successful in securing benefits than victims of occupational disease. One report found that employers are six times more likely to contest a disease claim than an accident claim. Furthermore, a worker disabled by an occupational disease waits an average of a year before receiving benefits, while a worker bringing an injury claim waits only two months. Statistics also show that victims of occupational illnesses receive lower benefits, on average, than victims of occupational accidents. This discrepancy occurs in part because it is hard to demonstrate that a disease is job-related and in part because disease victims are more likely to accept negotiated settlements.

In addition, these statistics record only the outcomes of claims actually filed.

The difficulty of proving that a disease is job-related keeps many workers from ever filing compensation claims. When job-relatedness is easier to prove, the success rate for compensation increases dramatically. The asbestos situation provides a good example: 61 percent of the workers' compensation claims filed for asbestos-related deaths have been fully awarded, 25 percent have led to less compensation than was sought, 3 percent have been denied, and 1 percent have been dropped.

The job-relatedness requirement also results in dramatic disparities between the levels of compensation that equally deserving disease victims get. Some receive full workers' compensation awards, while others go away empty-handed. And, of course, persons who contract similar diseases from nonoccupational sources cannot obtain workers' compensation at all. They may have either less or more recourse than diseased workers, depending on whether there is anyone for them to sue.

Aside from these inequities, workers' compensation programs also fail to promote efficient levels of health risk. The plans are funded by employer premiums that are often based only loosely on workplace health and safety conditions. The premiums therefore provide relatively little incentive for companies to provide a healthful work environment—far less than, for example, direct taxes on hazardous conditions would.

Although workers' compensation programs forbid most suits against employers, they do not prevent workers from bringing products-liability claims against the manufacturers of the hazardous materials and technology to which they were exposed in the workplace. Manufacturers of motor vehicles and construction equipment, for example, are often sued after such accidents as the overturning of a vehicle, on the grounds that they should have provided better warnings or installed the sort of safety seat that protects the driver if the vehicle is tipped over. Depending on where the lawsuit is filed, they can seek relief under negligence or strict-liability theory. Even under strict-liability theory, which is more favorable to plaintiffs, a victim must establish that the product was defective, that the defect proximately caused the injury, and that the defendant was the manufacturer of the defective product. Each of these elements can be unusually hard to prove in an occupational-disease case.

Under strict-liability doctrine, a product is defective if it is unreasonably dangerous. Consumer products are typically judged to be so because of a manufacturing flaw or an inherently unsafe product design, which may not be the problem with a chemical. However, a product may also be judged unreasonably dangerous if the manufacturer fails to warn of its dangers or instruct users how to use it safely. Failure to warn has been the basis for most cases in which manufacturers have been held liable for occupational disease caused by their products. The victim must thus establish that the manufacturer knew or should have known about the hazards at the time of the failure to warn—a difficult task, since the link between many products and occupational diseases has been established only recently. A manufacturer can also defend against a warning theory by presenting evidence that the victim was aware of the risk and accepted it voluntarily.

Under the second proof requirement, a plaintiff must show that the hazardous product was the proximate cause of his illness. As we have seen, proving what caused an occupational disease can be extremely difficult. Finally, under the third proof requirement, the plaintiff must show that the defendant was the one who manufactured the hazardous product. This burden is easy to meet in some cases but very difficult in others. Consider, for example, a worker who has been exposed to asbestos while working for several different employers, each of whom had bought asbestos from several different suppliers. Some courts allow the worker to sue all the suppliers; others do not.

Other impediments can also prevent recovery. The statute of limitations may have expired, as in the workers' compensation case, before the victim realized the extent or the cause of his illness. Recovery may also be thwarted if the defendant is no longer in business or has been driven bankrupt by unanticipated tort claims, and insurance policies have been exhausted. Finally, workers may be out of luck if their own employer was the one who manufactured the hazardous product, since workers' compensation is the exclusive remedy in such cases. Despite these limits on recovery, products-liability suits have become the major source of compensation for occupational-disease victims.

A policy relying on such lawsuits is inherently inequitable. First, suits by workers with comparable work-related diseases may have different outcomes because of such unpredictable factors as the length of the latency period or the availability of evidence showing whose products caused the illness. Second, recovery in successful suits may vary widely among equally deserving victims. Third, because the products-liability system is not coordinated with other forms of compensation, a successful plaintiff may receive not only a substantial tort judgment but also workers' compensation and Social Security payments. Such multiple awards waste resources that could be distributed to victims who now go empty-handed.

Products liability also fails to establish efficient incentives for many workplace-health decisions, because the judgment occurs long after the tort. Tort liability has the strongest incentive effect when the judgment follows closely upon the tortious behavior. It then provides immediate feedback that allows the manufacturer to consider all costs in reaching product-safety decisions. But over a period of decades there is no assurance that a company will remain in business, and if it does the present managers are likely to have long since departed. Performance evaluations are seldom based on remote legal obligations.

In short, products-liability law is striving both to compensate disease victims and to deter workplace health risks — and not doing either well. A better way would be to address each goal separately.

One possibility is to extend workers' compensation and to establish a comparable system for health risks. The appeal of such an approach stems from the many attractive features of workers' compensation. First, the program is generally viewed as an efficient way to get resources to accident victims. At present, firms pay premiums in excess of $20 billion, 80 percent of which is paid to accident victims — a much better record than that of tort liability, for which the court costs and lawyers' fees are considerable. Second, workers know about and clearly value the benefits of workers' compensation, leading them to demand less of a wage premium for hazardous work. Indeed, recent studies done by this writer with Michael Moore indicate that on average workers' compensation more than pays for itself from the employer's point of view, although recent increases in benefits have not been self-financing on the margin. Third, workers' compensation premiums are linked to a firm's safety and thus function as a form of injury tax. Indeed, the author's recent study with Moore indicates that worker fatality rates would be 72 percent higher in the absence of workers' compensation. These safety incentives dwarf the estimates of OSHA's contribution to safety improvement.

The desire to reap similar benefits no doubt has contributed to the pressure to extend workers' compensation to provide greater coverage of health risks. But none of the system's three major advantages are likely to translate easily from the accident to the health case. The relative efficiency of workers' compensation in transferring income stems from the comparative ease of showing a link between an acute injury and the job. For diseases with multiple causation, the link is more tenuous. Indeed, where the present workers' compensation system covers illnesses at all it tends to take much longer to process illness claims than injury claims. Even in the case of potent carcinogens, such as asbestos, other sources of lung cancer may cause three to four times as many illnesses among affected workers as the job exposure. Any program targeted to health risks related to the job would run into enormous problems of determining causality.

The second advantage of workers' compensation — it is highly valued by employees — would also hold for the health risks, at least after the fact. There would not, however, be a wage offset if workers do not perceive the health risk while on the job and thus anticipate being covered by an insurance program that is particularly relevant to their situation. To the extent that market levels of health risks are seen as less than ideal because workers do not perceive health risks, there will be a similar weakness in the mechanism that leads to a wage offset.

The third advantage of workers' compensation — the safety-incentive effect — also assumes that there will be an opportunity for experience rating of employers. If instead the assignment of causality is by industry group, there will be no targeted incentives for individual firms; when a hazard leads to claims, the incentive will simply be for the whole industry to lower its output. These are not the mere conjectures of economic theory. All three disappointments have been realized in the case of the compensation effort for one narrowly defined ailment — black-lung disease in coal miners.

The Black Lung Benefits Act of 1969 provides benefits to coal miners struck with the disease and their survivors. The program compensates victims of pneumoconiosis, "a chronic dust disease of the lung . . . arising out of coal mine employment."[7] To receive benefits, the miner must show that he is totally disabled, that the disability is caused by pneumoconiosis, and that the pneumoconiosis resulted from exposure to coal dust. The benefit provided is an annuity that is independent of the particular claimant's wages.

In contrast to state workers' compensation plans, the black-lung program eases claimants' burden of proof by incorporating rebuttable presumptions in their favor. In the original act, black lung was presumed to be the cause of death if a diseased miner had worked in a coal mine for at least ten years. Furthermore, a worker was presumed to be totally disabled by black-lung disease if he presented medical evidence of lesions in the lung and he had worked in mines for ten years. In 1972, the law was expanded so that all respiratory and pulmonary impairments in workers with fifteen years of coal-mining employment were considered to be pneumoconiosis.

The black-lung experience shows how hard it is to estimate accurately the cost of a compensation scheme. Its annual outlays mushroomed from $150 million in 1970 to more than $1 billion by the late 1970s, in part because of unexpectedly rapid growth in the number of claims filed. Significantly, the possibility of such cost overruns should be much smaller in coal mining, where there is good information about miners and black-lung risks, than in wider programs that attempt to track large, mobile populations of workers exposed to minute but harmful amounts of hazardous substances in many different workplaces.

The black-lung program is funded by a tax on coal production: $1 a ton for underground mines and 50 cents a ton for surface mines. The tax is ineffective at reducing hazards, because it is not explicitly linked either to workplace conditions or to the incidence of disease. Instead of providing direct incentives for mining companies to improve workplace health standards, the production tax tends merely to reduce their overall output.

The nature of black-lung compensation, moreover, raises equity concerns. Although it has eliminated many of the inequities between black-lung victims arising from the difficulty of proving causation, it has probably compensated many victims of diseases other than black lung, and it creates an undesirable new disparity between program beneficiaries and victims of equally severe illnesses that cannot plausibly be ascribed to black lung.

Perhaps because of the disappointing record of black-lung compensation, Congress has not yet enacted any of several proposals that would extend its model into new areas of compensation. One such proposal is H.R. 3175, introduced in 1983 by Representative George Miller (D-Calif.), which would provide money for disease victims and exempt manufacturers of hazardous substances from products-liability suits. Unfortunately, proposals of this sort have an enormous cost, and because they fail to separate the objectives of fair compensation and efficient risk control, they may achieve neither.

The eligibility standards for compensation under the Miller bill are relatively liberal. It would establish a series of presumptions for asbestos-related diseases that would make proof of causation much easier than it is under workers' compensation or products liability. It would grant workers an irrebuttable presumption that conditions in asbestos workers that are diagnosed as asbestosis or mesothelioma were caused by exposure to workplace asbestos. The bill would also presume that lung cancer in asbestos workers was caused by exposure to the mineral, but this presumption would be irrebuttable only if there were evidence showing that asbestos had caused changes in the lung or pleura.

The liberal presumptions could have an enormous economic effect. Under H.R. 3175, the total cost of compensating fatalities resulting from asbestos exposure is estimated at between $16 billion and $30 billion (in present-value terms). It may be impossible, however, to determine which cases of lung cancer in asbestos workers are caused by asbestos and which by other factors. As a result, all cases of lung cancer in asbestos workers could be compensable, raising the total cost of the program to between $54 billion and $108 billion. By comparison, estimates of the cost of asbestos products-liability suits (again in present-value terms) range between $8 billion and $91 billion under comparable assumptions. Thus, if its presumptions were applied liberally, H.R. 3175 might inflict greater costs on manufacturers than the current products-liability systems, forcing many more of them out of business.

The effect the proposal would have on reducing health risks remains uncertain, because the details of the funding mechanism are not specified. In all likelihood, the approach would take the form of an output tax, as in the black-lung and "Superfund" programs. Such a tax would reduce total work hazards somewhat by reducing the output of the affected companies. However, it would have little direct influence on the health risks of remaining workers, because it would not vary with workplace health conditions; employers who invested heavily in worker protection would pay just as much into the fund as employers that neglected to do so.

A Proposed Strategy

Past proposals have tended to ignore the effect of compensation schemes on employer incentives. Yet such effects are one of the major policy variables at work. For example, suppose the present combination of market transactions and OSHA regulations is thought to provide too little health protection to workers. Then a compensation scheme should not only compensate workers but also encourage employers to take additional health precautions, by tying the tax to the riskiness of present operations. For instance, the hazards involved in the construction procedures used for different building designs may not be fully known to the workers but can be captured in the workers' compensation premium levels, thus generating a safety incentive. Conversely, if market transactions and OSHA health regulations already provide the optimal level of exposure to a given risk, funding an additional compensation program through a risk-based tax would lead employers to provide excessive precautions, in the sense that their cost would exceed their value to workers in health terms. In that case, compensation taxes should not be designed to influence employer behavior. In short, occupational-disease policy should take into account the incentive effects of compensation plans on risk levels and coordinate these effects with the incentives created by regulatory programs.

Some hazardous substances at present may already be the target of not simply adequate regulation but substantial overregulation. Consider the case of asbestos itself. After a long period of regulatory inaction when thousands of lives could have been saved inexpensively, the government has now overreacted by trying to cut exposure virtually to zero. OSHA's asbestos rules cost on average $89.3 million for every life saved, and the Environmental Protection Agency (EPA) has proposed regulations that would impose a cost on average of $104.2 million for every life saved.

Meanwhile, having been identified as a highly risky substance, asbestos is now being targeted by many other societal institutions as well, including market forces and insurance pressures, both of which create important incentives for safety. Today's widespread awareness of asbestos means that workers demand substantial risk premiums to work with it and often refuse to be exposed at any price. Workers' compensation insurance premiums for workers in asbestos-related industries have also skyrocketed, bolstering the incentive for safety. A legislative compensation scheme linked to current asbestos exposures would add entirely superfluous safety incentives while discouraging those uses that are still prudent and justified.

This pattern of excessively stringent regulation may not be unique to asbestos. Other workplace hazards, such as arsenic exposures in glass manufacturing, are stringently regulated by OSHA ($92.5 million per life saved), and the EPA has proposed additional regulation. Unfortunately, there is no coordinating mechanism to ensure that the risk level that results from these diverse efforts is appropriate or to keep society from responding excessively to a few targeted hazards while ignoring others.

The goal of a coordinated compensation policy should be to ensure that all victims are receiving at least acceptable minimum payments and that comparable groups of victims are compensated similarly. Neither objective is currently met. Perhaps the fundamental issue is whether society should compensate victims of occupational diseases more generously than victims of nonoccupational diseases. If not, then the focus should be on appropriate social insurance for all disease victims rather than on particularly generous coverage for victims fortunate enough to be targeted for special coverage.

Finally, decision makers should aim to help not only victims who have already contracted diseases but also those who will contract them in the future. A penalty tax linked to past exposures may punish sins, but it will not create an incentive to reduce current and future risk levels, except indirectly by lowering an industry's output. By contrast, a penalty tax linked to present exposure levels will encourage employers to reduce workplace health risks to the point that the marginal cost of additional precautions equals the tax. The latter method is far more efficient at optimizing risk-reduction investments, encouraging employers to clean up their operations rather than just close them down.

A strategy for achieving both fair compensation and efficient levels of health risk would combine two types of financing: a targeted tax to help victims of current hazards and a broad-based program to help victims of past exposures, who would be compensated through the Social Security system or some other social-insurance fund financed by a general payroll tax.

Relying on a broad-based fund to compensate past victims would have several advantages. First, if a disease has already been set in motion, the only remaining issue is how to compensate victims; risk-based taxes do not change incentives and are therefore irrelevant from an efficiency standpoint. In addition, the Social Security program already exists and, unlike workers' compensation, does not require a showing of causality. Social Security disability insurance provides income support for workers with long-term disabilities, whatever the cause. Since benefits would be generally available, inequitable distinctions could be avoided. Victims of occupational disease would be treated the same as victims of diseases caused by, say, contact with hazardous wastes, or those of unknown origin — which is as it should be. In general, compensation should depend on how a disease affects its victim, not on how it was contracted.

A program funded through a broad-based payroll tax like the Social Security disability program is in one sense unfair, compared with a program funded through a targeted tax: companies that were not responsible for a worker's disease will pay into the fund the same as those that were responsible. On the other hand, this perceived inequity arises only when responsible companies can be identified. That is generally impossible because of the difficulties mentioned earlier in making causal connections in the realm of occupational disease. And under this proposal, moreover, manufacturers that could be identified would still face products-liability suits from workers. The only difference would be that the amount of coverage already received would be deducted from the amount of any award.

Workplace conditions should be regulated through a combination of minimum standards and penalty taxes based on the current hazards in the workplace. To improve the operation of a workplace market for risk, OSHA should strictly enforce its hazard-communication regulation and extend it to other industries (such as construction). OSHA should also adopt a system of direct regulation that integrates minimum performance standards with graduated hazard penalties so that companies can forgo safety improvements that are inordinately expensive, given the benefits that will arise. Thus, the objective of regulatory enforcement should be not to compel compliance with an arbitrary standard but to induce firms to make whichever safety investments are most feasible to attain the level of safety society seeks. Beneficiaries of this plan would still be able to bring products-liability suits against companies, providing further deterrent force, although the level of such awards would be reduced by any disability payments. The compensation scheme itself, however, would not penalize companies for conditions that no longer exist.

The strategy set forth here is not a cure-all; the problem is too complex to be solved that easily. But by separating compensation from deterrence, it provides a framework to begin addressing occupational disease in a manner that looks forward rather than backward. Unlike the current reliance on liability suits or the various compensation schemes being advanced in Congress, it offers the hope of compensating victims without the specter of randomness or ruinous expense and encouraging safety without distorting the operation of those workplaces that are already optimally safe.

Notes

1. W. Kip Viscusi and Wesley A. Magat, *Learning about Risk: Consumer and Worker Responses to Hazard Information* (Cambridge: Harvard University Press, 1987).

2. Occupational Safety and Health Act of 1970, Pub. Law No. 91–596, SS. 2, 84 Stat. 1590 (1070) (codified at 29 U.S.C. SS. 651 [1983]).

3. W. Kip Viscusi, *Risk by Choice: Regulating Health and Safety in the Workplace* (Cambridge: Harvard University Press, 1983).

4. Viscusi and Magat.

5. See, e.g., *Alabama Code* SS. 25–5-111 (1975); *Michigan Comp. Laws Ann.* SS. 418.401 (6) (West. Supp. 1984).

6. See, e.g., *Georgia Code Ann.* SS. 34–9-280 (3) (1982); *Virginia Code* SS. 34–9-280 (3) (1982); *Virginia Code* SS. 65.1–46 (1980).

7. 30 U.S.C. SS. 902(b).

Forum-Shopping, Forum-Skipping, and the Problem of International Competitiveness

DOUGLAS J. BESHAROV

Two important issues facing Congress are trade reform and tort reform. The two interact in a way that has been largely overlooked. American courts apply more stringent liability standards than courts in other countries. By "forum-shopping," persons injured abroad can increasingly resort to the American courts to sue United States-based corporations under more generous liability rules than they would find at home. At the same time, because of antiquated jurisdictional rules, foreign exporters whose products injure United States consumers can often escape the full force of American liability laws. As a result, United States corporations face a double handicap, losing market share in both domestic and foreign markets, while American consumers are less well protected from dangerously defective foreign products.

Forum Follows Function

Following the Bhopal, India, disaster in December 1984, there was intense legal maneuvering over whether the case would be tried in the United States. The Indian government, which claims to represent the victims, and the victims themselves, as represented by American lawyers, have sought to have the case heard in the United States. Union Carbide, for its part, has fought to have the case heard in Indian courts. The irony is central and revealing: the Indian government sought to keep the case in American courts even though one would have thought its persuasive powers there would be less than in its own courts, while Union Carbide,

The first part of this essay draws heavily from two articles by the author and Peter Reuter, senior economist at the Rand Corporation, in *Wall Street Journal*, 16 May 1985 and 28 October 1985. The essay was prepared with the assistance of Harvetta M. Asamoah.

much vilified in India, was unwilling to leave its fate in the hands of its own countrymen.

Bhopal plaintiffs could sue Union Carbide in almost any United States court they choose, because a company can be sued "wherever it can be found," that is, in any jurisdiction in which it does business or with which it has "sufficient contacts." But judges need not accept a lawsuit just because it falls under their formal jurisdiction if in their view it should be heard elsewhere. They can invoke the legal doctrine of *forum non conveniens*, which as its name suggests is a doctrine based largely on convenience: in which country is it more convenient, given the witnesses and documents, to have the cases heard? Union Carbide emphasized the failure of local plant operators; the plaintiffs emphasized the role of United States designers and Union Carbide's overall corporate responsibility.

The stakes are immense for both sides. First, litigating the claim in American courts would increase the chance that the *substantive* law of an American state would be applied. If it appeared that key management and design decisions were made in the United States, an American court might apply American rules of strict liability in product manufacture and extended liability for construction or design defects. In India, however, the application of strict liability is much in doubt, even though both tort systems share a common English ancestry.

In this case, the application of American substantive law is unlikely. But substantive law is only a secondary reason for wanting the cases heard in the United States. The real attraction is American procedural rules — which would be applied in this case. (The term *procedural rules*, as used in this essay, encompasses all the nonsubstantive rules that govern litigation, a somewhat broader definition than is often used in "choice-of-law" analysis.)

Foreign plaintiffs enjoy a number of major procedural advantages when a case is tried in the United States. In addition to much more liberal rules on discovery (that is, access to Union Carbide records and officials), the plaintiffs would have enjoyed far more generous rules on damages. Noneconomic awards for "pain and suffering" and a broad definition of "consequential" damages are among the kinds of damages that are given much greater recognition in American courts than elsewhere. The availability of punitive damages as well as compensation is another procedural advantage that plaintiffs enjoy in the United States but not in most other countries.

Contingent-fee rules are likewise procedural. These arrangements provide an important public service by allowing plaintiffs' lawyers to advance the costs of litigation, thus permitting major suits on behalf of plaintiffs who are not wealthy. Although contingent fees are illegal in most countries, they are permitted in the United States.

Raising the Value of a Claim

Most lawsuits are settled before trial. The most provocative issue of the Bhopal case is how large the settlement will be. Here we see the impact of the forum issue.

If ordinary Indian court practices are followed, a large award against Union Carbide is unlikely. The consensus of informed observers is that by the most "liberal calculation" the total award would be less than $75 million.[1] (There has been some suggestion that the Indian government is changing its tort laws to permit a larger award.)

An award from an American court, however, would be much larger. A rough calculation of the likely award, derived from data on claims compiled by the Rand Institute of Civil Justice, found that compensatory damages could be as much as $235 million.[2] Possible punitive damages dwarf even this figure. If Union Carbide had been found to have acted with reckless disregard of the welfare of those around the Bhopal plants, possible damages would be limited only by the net worth of the company.

It was the specter of punitive damages that probably led Union Carbide to offer a settlement of $350 million, a figure approximating the likely compensatory award of an American court but many times higher than that likely from an Indian court.[3] (The company apparently offered a "structured settlement," with an initial payment followed by installments to be paid over a number of years. Thus the present discounted cash value of the offer was substantially lower.) For the plaintiffs, it was probably also the possibility of punitive damages that led them to reject an otherwise plausible offer. As the resolution of the forum issue became clearer, the American plaintiffs' lawyers apparently grew willing to accept the Union Carbide offer, but the Indian government held out for more money—its suit in India sought $3.12 billion. The Bhopal victims' attempt to persuade American courts to accept jurisdiction over their claims is the prototypical example, albeit the largest, of a growing class of cases. Numerous aircraft and drug companies, for example, have been sued in the United States for products sold abroad and, in some instances, even manufactured and licensed there.

The majority of foreign claims in American courts are ultimately dismissed, as it appears the Bhopal claims will be. But "majority" and "ultimately" are important qualifications. Although most attempts to bring United States lawsuits for foreign injuries fail, some succeed—some because of their facts, some because of the law of the particular state in which the claim is brought. In *Corrigan* v. *Shiley*, for example, California courts exercised jurisdiction over a wrongful-death and products-liability claim involving a heart valve surgically implanted in the chest of an Australian citizen in an Australian hospital. The courts also permitted the application of California's substantive law of strict liability for product defects, not Australia's negligence standard. The courts observed that even though the valve was sold only abroad and, in fact, was subject to a Food and Drug Administration license that permitted international (but not domestic) sales, it had been manufactured in California by an American company.

Furthermore, "ultimately" means that it can take years of litigation, often to the U.S. Supreme Court, before a case is dismissed. Plaintiffs' lawyers know that uncertainty and delay can raise the value of a claim; that is one reason such cases continue to be filed.

The lesson to American companies doing business abroad is clear: assume that American levels of liability can be imposed on goods and services sold anywhere — and act accordingly.

Exporting Safety

Many Americans will welcome this higher level of corporate accountability. The United States does not want to export dangerous products and manufacturing processes that exploit unprotected foreigners. But such high-minded attitudes ignore two unpleasant realities of the international marketplace. First, stringent liability standards inexorably raise the price of United States–produced goods, services, and investments. Other countries do not want to pay the price for the higher level of citizen protection that the United States provides. They will reject our attempts to sell them this protection by buying fewer American goods and services, and the United States's share of international trade will continue to erode.

Other developed countries, even those with higher per-capita wealth, have not adopted a liability regime like that of the United States. They rely on a combination of government regulation and social insurance to protect their consumers, and they have many rules that discourage products-liability litigation. They are doubly unwilling to accept foreign claims: if Union Carbide were a Japanese company, no Japanese court would have seriously considered hearing the Bhopal claims.

Conversely, less-developed countries cannot afford an American-style liability scheme. The per capita gross national product (GNP) of the United States is $15,000; India's is a mere $256. Third World peoples tolerate more product and workplace hazards than we do, because they want to encourage economic development just as we once did. As the federal district court stated in dismissing the Bhopal claims: "It would be sadly paternalistic, if not misguided, of this Court to attempt to evaluate the regulations and standards imposed in a foreign country."[4]

Placing higher levels of liability on American companies doing business abroad handicaps them as they compete against foreign companies that need not carry a similar burden. In 1985 the McDonnell Douglas Corporation, trying to sell aircraft to the government of China, felt obliged to incorporate possible American liability costs in the price. The Chinese protested that there was no such liability in China and denounced the company's explanation as "American flim-flam." McDonnell Douglas explained that, although such a suit might be unlikely in China, it was possible for Chinese citizens and foreign nationals to sue in American courts. The sale was made anyway, but at the higher price. Salespeople for the European Airbus consortium certainly labor under no such burden.

Products differ, of course, in the amount of damage they can cause and thus in the extent to which their price must be raised to cover potential lawsuits. In the case of a bar of soap, the degree of risk is negligible and the concomitant rise in price trivial. But for other products, the cost of liability can be high enough to inflict substantial market-share losses. Liability insurance constitutes about 10 percent of the cost of general-aviation aircraft manufactured in the United States; for certain machine tools, as much as 15 percent.

Recently, some United States companies have considered creating undercapitalized foreign subsidiaries to market their products abroad. That sort of protection would probably be illusory, since American courts would likely bypass such a sham and hold the parent company liable.

Foreign Producers' Home-Court Advantage

At the same time that the United States is exporting high levels of tort liability to countries that do not want it, American consumers ironically do not enjoy full tort liability protection on United States imports. The problem is not the applicability of American laws — all goods sold in the United States are subject to state products-liability laws — but the enforceability of those laws against foreign manufacturers.

Many foreign companies do not have an actual business presence in the United States and instead operate through independent export agents or wholly owned subsidiaries that take title before the products are exported. If it is difficult to collect against companies like A.H. Robins (the maker of the Dalkon Shield), collecting against an elusive export agent can be impossible. Although these middlemen are subject to American jurisdiction, they are often small operations with few assets, making them all but judgment-proof. The parent company may decide to let such a subsidiary fail rather than pay a large claim. Successful recovery often requires gaining jurisdiction over the foreign producer itself. There are two ways to accomplish that goal, but neither works very well.

One way to gain jurisdiction is to "pierce the corporate veil." The legal test for doing this is one of control and capitalization: Did the parent company control the actions of the subsidiary? And was the subsidiary left undercapitalized in order to protect the parent? Both questions require the kind of evidence often available only through discovery. Unfortunately, foreign courts are unlikely to allow the degree of discovery needed. Many countries refuse to compel the disclosure of the relevant corporate records. In some countries, disclosure is actually a crime.

The second way to gain jurisdiction over a foreign company is through a "long-arm statute" that extends to parties who, though never in the United States, are legitimately subject to suit here. The judicial test is whether the party had at least "minimum contacts" with the jurisdiction. The U.S. Supreme Court has ruled that the test is met if "a corporation delivers its products into the stream of commerce with the expectation that they will be purchased by consumers in the forum State."[5]

In February 1987 the Supreme Court ruled unanimously in *Asahi Metal Industry v. Superior Court of California* that California had been wrong to assert jurisdiction over Asahi, a Japanese manufacturer, even though it sold 100,000 tire-valve assemblies annually to a Taiwanese company that used them in tire tubes for export. Although five justices suggested that they might take a more expansive view of personal jurisdiction under different conditions, most observers agree with David O. Stewart, a Washington lawyer, who, writing in the *Journal of the American Bar Association*, concluded that the decision "eased the risk of suit" for foreign firms.[6]

Even jurisdiction over the parent company, however, may not be enough. The plaintiff must still prove that the product was defectively designed or manufactured or that the defendant failed to give adequate warning of the product's dangerous characteristics. On these points, discovery in the country of manufacture can again be crucial—and difficult to obtain.

As usual, Japanese companies add a further twist of their own: many of them use wholly owned subsidiaries to conduct research and development. A "shell game" is how Miami lawyer Gary D. Fox describes what can happen: "In the past, Honda Motor has objected to discovery requests on the grounds that it did not have the information—Honda R&D had it. . . . In another case, the defendant, American Honda Motor Co., Inc., the wholly owned subsidiary responsible for importing Honda vehicles into the United States, objected to discovery requests on the grounds that the parent company, Honda Motor, had the data."[7]

Faced with this lack of cooperation, some American courts will award judgment for the plaintiff as a sanction; others will not. But enforcing the award is another matter. Unless the foreign company has assets in the United States, the assistance of the courts in the home country is again needed. Since these courts were hostile to the discovery claim on which the award was based, they often refuse to enforce the award or impose numerous obstacles to its enforcement. (This, by the way, is not unreasonable. American courts also reserve the right to refuse to enforce a foreign judgment that violates due process or public policy.)

It can take years of costly litigation before there is any prospect of even partial compensation from foreign defendants. This uncertainty and delay mean that smaller claims (under, say, $100,000) are all but uncollectible. They are simply not worth pursuing, even under contingent-fee arrangements. Larger claims are worth pursuing, but their settlement value is much reduced.

In one case, a partnership between the wholly owned subsidiary of a European multinational corporation and an American company went bankrupt. An American multinational corporation with a $40 million claim against the partnership was forced to settle for 10 cents on the dollar. The prospect of an endless argument in a European court over the discovery needed to pierce the joint venture did not seem worth while.

A Free Ride for Importers

A major purpose of American tort law is to remove dangerously defective products from commerce. When foreign producers avoid the force of the tort law, some American consumers will go without this intended protection. Moreover, the relative freedom of foreign producers from United States tort claims gives them a substantial cost advantage over companies that must price their goods to include American levels of liability. For some products, the difference is a substantial one that can clearly affect United States competitiveness. According to Howard J. Bruns, president of the Sporting Goods Manufacturers' Association, products liability costs his American member companies over eight times what it costs Japanese companies (4.2 percent of the price compared with 0.5 percent).[8]

In principle, the tendency of foreign producers to escape liability should reduce the attractiveness of their products, compensating for their lower price. Or, by putting retailers and other middlemen at greater risk, it should cause them to insist on a higher price markup. However, not many consumers realize that the level of liability protection differs from one good to the next, and many consumers do not value the added protection anyway. Moreover, many sophisticated buyers expect their insurance to cover their economic losses in any case and know that premiums do not go up when they purchase foreign goods. One Fortune 500 executive, when asked whether the lack of recourse against a foreign producer might lead his company to purchase a more expensive American product, answered no — because the company's insurance would cover any accidents. Middlemen, for the same reason, may find that their liability insurance premiums do not vary according to the proportion of goods they import. Perhaps there is a message for insurance carriers here.

Unlike the forum-shopping issue, which came to widespread notice after the Bhopal tragedy, the forum-skipping issue has not yet captured the public's attention; there has yet been no one large case of inadequate relief for injured Americans, partly because when claims against foreign defendants fail an American defendant is usually available to pay the entire claim under the doctrine of joint and several liability. The cumulative impact of hundreds of small cases, however, is clear: for many American claimants, the full enforceability of products-liability laws stops at the shoreline.

The situation worsens every year as imports fill more and more of the United States market. Between 1970 and 1986, merchandise imports as a percentage of goods production have risen from 8.8 percent to 22.1 percent. Of course, there comes a point when a foreign company's sales have grown so far that it is likely to maintain a substantial business presence in the United States, which then makes full products liability enforceable. Until it reaches that point, however, its artificial price advantage will help it to build market share, at the expense of United States consumers and insurers as well as its competitors.

There are many reasons to be concerned that the level of tort liability in the United States is too high. Nevertheless, sound consumer policy and sound trade policy alike would seem to require that foreign producers be brought under the full ambit of whatever such law prevails. Likewise, both equity and national interest call for American companies selling abroad to face the same liability standards as their local competitors, not a special and extra-strict standard applicable only to them. And the inconsistency between the two phenomena — which has led American courts to police the quality of goods sold and used abroad but not goods sold and used in this country — should be apparent.

Limiting Forum-Shopping

American interests can be protected without closing the courts to foreigners bringing action against United States companies and without making major changes in American tort law. Recall that the legal doctrine of *forum non conveniens* allows a court to decline jurisdiction when it determines that the litigants' private interests and the public interest would be better served in another forum. Significantly, the avoiding of artificial handicaps to United States trade competitiveness is not one of the "public-interest factors" that the Supreme Court has instructed federal courts to consider in deciding forum issues.

Rather than simply prohibiting the bringing of such cases, a better approach would be to remove the incentives for bringing the litigation to the United States. The law already recognizes the dangers of forum-shopping and seeks to deter it by applying the "substantive" law of the country in which the tort occurred. What it does not recognize is that procedural rules can be an equally strong attraction.

Recognizing that procedural rules can determine outcomes just as surely as substantive rules, the United States should try to see that when a case arising overseas is tried in an American court, it follows the procedural as well as the substantive law of the country where the injury took place. (Possible exceptions include cases where a good is also sold in the United States and where the foreign injury is to a United States citizen.) No one would suggest that American courts use the protocols of a foreign court right down to the filing deadlines and forms. But it is possible to aim legislation at the heart of the problem: liberal discovery, expansive damages, and contingent fees. Under its constitutional powers to regulate commerce and foreign policy, Congress has ample authority to pass remedial measures.

Congress should consider limiting the availability of all three—discovery, damages, and contingent fees—to the same degree as they would be available in the country where the injury occurred. If liberal discovery, expansive damages, and contingent fees are important to other countries, their governments should make them available against all firms—not just American corporations sued in the United States. (Congress may find it politically impossible to change discovery and contingent-fee rules, but it could probably achieve agreement to amend the law of damages, the strongest incentive for importing cases.) There is already a precedent for such a law. Many states have adopted "borrowing statutes" that apply another state's shorter statute of limitations to cut off claims that are filed in their courts after the clock has run out in the state where the dispute arose.

Congress should impose these reciprocal limitations on both state and federal courts. Under current liberal rules of state court jurisdiction, most large American companies can be sued in almost any state (since jurisdiction can be based on minimal business contacts). This is why Union Carbide could be sued in California, Connecticut, Florida, and Texas for what happened in faraway Bhopal. The forum law of the most liberal state becomes, in effect, a national law applicable to all large United States corporations.[9]

Making American Laws More Enforceable

Congress should also consider legislation ensuring that American courts have jurisdiction to enforce state products-liability laws against defective foreign products. To prevent the misuse of undercapitalized middlemen and subsidiaries, it could enact a more far-reaching long-arm statute granting American courts jurisdiction over companies whose products are likely to reach the United States or a statute requiring the producer of any good entering the country to consent to being sued in the United States. To facilitate the enforcement of judgments, Congress might require goods entering the country to carry a certificate of insurance or a letter of credit sufficient to cover probable injuries caused by them. (Since this might be a difficult calculation, a simple formula might be established, proportioned to the exporter's annual sales.) Such remedial legislation would have to be carefully drafted to reflect the legitimate requirements of the American tort system — for example, the riskiness of the product — and to avoid erecting a nontariff trade barrier. To avoid disproportionate burdens on smaller and poorer producers, Congress might want to legislate an exemption for producers below some minimum level of annual sales.

No matter how carefully drafted, such legislation might antagonize the United States's trading partners. Few of them have adopted anything like the American tort system and its goals, whether because they do not understand its merits, because they understand it but do not like it, or simply because they cannot afford it. While unilateral congressional action could go a long way to remedy present difficulties, the United States should also consider an international agreement or a series of agreements addressing this and other pressing issues in international trade law that would help put American business on an equal footing with its competitors.

Other countries have recognized a national interest in reforming private international law, and over the past twenty-plus years many have reached agreements to regularize the handling of lawsuits between the nationals of different countries. For many reasons, the United States has signed few of these agreements. Some clearly do not meet American needs, in part because we did not participate in the drafting. Some have been endorsed or in part drafted by successive administrations but were not ratified because various domestic interest groups have opposed them. This relative isolation from international law reform should end; if existing treaties and conventions do not meet American needs, the United States should work with its major trading partners to develop ones that do.

Conclusion

Clearly, the suggestions of this essay would intrude on state tort law and court procedure, domains that Congress has been reluctant to enter for various political and policy reasons. There is an unusually broad coalition, however, that might be mustered to support rules to facilitate the free — and fair — exchange of goods and investments. Corporations lose both ways from the present system and would presumably welcome reform. Trial lawyers profit from the chance to seek extra damages in Bhopal-type cases but lose much more from the difficulty of suing foreign companies here; they would benefit overall from a compromise. American consumers gain nothing from giving foreign citizens the right to sue in domestic courts and lose when foreign producers escape tort responsibility. Insurers and miscellaneous tort defendants lose when they are left holding the bag for injuries caused by fugitive foreign producers, and insurers lose again when they pay inflated damages for torts that occur abroad. That such diverse and antagonistic groups all have a stake in reform is a sign that broad national interests — as well as the cause of fairness — are ill-served by the imbalances in the present system.

NOTES

1. Stephen Adler, "Bhopal Journal: The Voiceless Victims," *American Lawyer* 7 (April 1985): 1, 128-36.

2. Douglas Besharov and Peter Reuter, "Averting a Bhopal Legal Disaster," *Wall Street Journal*, 16 May 1985, 32.

3. *Corrigan* v. *Shiley, rev. denied*, Calif. Sup. Ct., No., B015387 (1986), *cert. denied sub nom.*, *Shiley* v. *Corrigan*, U.S. Sup. Ct., No. 86-842 (1987).

4. *In Re: Union Carbide Corporation Gas Plant Disaster at Bhopal, India in December, 1984*, 634 F. Supp. 842, 864 (S.D.N.Y. 1986).

5. *World-Wide Volkswagen Corp.* v. *Woodson*, 444 U.S. 286, 297-98 (1980) (citation omitted).

6. David Stewart, "Shortening California's Long Arm Statute," *American Bar Association Journal* 73 (April 1987): 45-46.

7. Gary Fox, "Discovery from Japanese Companies," *Trial* 22 (August 1986): 18-20.

8. Letter to the president of the United States, 23 April 1982.

9. See generally Peter Huber, "Courts of Convenience: or Have Lawsuit, Will Travel," *Regulation*, September/October 1985, 18.

Knowledge of the Law Is No Excuse

PETER HUBER

In "The Objection to Being Stepped On," Robert Frost recounts how he accidentally "stepped on the toe of an unemployed hoe." The implement instantly "rose in offense" and struck Frost a blow "in the seat of [his] sense." The Bible had foretold the day when weapons would be turned into tools. "And what do we see? / The first tool I step on / Turns into a weap-on."

There is a great insight here. The line between tools and weapons is exceedingly fine. Knives cut, irons scorch, dynamite explodes, poison kills. In the wrong hands, or under the wrong foot, the most innocuous domestic object quickly becomes an instrument of assault and battery.

Until the 1950s, the law on these matters was fairly simple. Whenever possible the old tort law left it up to the consumer to distinguish between weapons and tools in his own private universe. If someone wanted to buy a fast horse, lightweight canoe, sharp knife, or strong medicine, that was his business and his risk, or, more precisely, it was a risk that he and his seller could allocate between themselves as they chose.

The new tort jurisprudence that developed in the 1960s was quite different. Tort law advanced; contract principles receded. A new tort system gradually stepped in to preempt and rewrite a vast number of allocations of risk and responsibility that had once been decided by contract. The new system was much busier than the old. And having made product "defects" the center of its attention, it had a much more technocratic function.

How does one go about locating a defect in a complex product? "Manufacturing defects" are often easy to find. The jury compares the product as it reached the plaintiff with hundreds of others that came off the same assembly line. In effect, the mass manufacturer establishes his own standard by which any one of his own products can be gauged. Manufacturing-defect cases are easy. They are also comparatively rare.

Far more common today, and also far more difficult, are cases in which the product is said to be defective in design. The search for design defects often requires a jury to compare real with hypothetical products. What is a jury to do, for example, when a lawyer for a sick child claims that a whooping-cough vaccine was defective in that it was based on a whole virus rather than a virus extract? That formulation of the vaccine in question is the only one sold in this country. An alternative formulation has indeed been tested in Japan, but the U.S. Food and Drug Administration (FDA) does not approve its use.

And how is a jury to decide whether a whole class of products — say, the intrauterine device (IUD) contraceptive — is inherently defective? The new tort system has apparently reached that conclusion, having driven from the market not only the notorious Dalkon Shield but also its far safer substitutes, the Copper-7 and the Lippes Loop IUDs. The FDA, Planned Parenthood, and the vast majority of doctors do not endorse the verdict, but the verdict stands, nonetheless.

It is not enough to identify a safety failing; the jury must also weigh the cost of remedying it. In the early 1970s, the Ford Pinto was to automobile "crashworthiness" cases what the Dalkon Shield later became to contraceptives. The Pinto weighed under 2,000 pounds and cost less than $2,000. Ford's own tests revealed that its gasoline tank was vulnerable to rear-end collisions, but the company decided not to spend an extra $10 per car to reinforce the structure — a calculation on which plaintiffs' lawyers subsequently grew very rich. Ten dollars is not much, but full-force rear-end collisions are not common either, and there are innumerable other equally rare hazards that could also be averted for $10 or less. Protecting against all of them would cost thousands. And people with thousands to spare do not buy a Pinto in the first place; they buy a Mercedes. What about other cars in Pinto's class? Some certainly had safer gasoline tanks — which is not to say they were safer cars. A jury later fined Honda $5 million for its "reckless" act of using lighter gauge materials than some other manufacturers in a 1971-model vehicle. (The driver of that vehicle admitted he had bought it for its economy.) Toyota lost a $3 million judgment on similar grounds. The subtle message here may be that all economy cars are inherently defective for tort purposes. But the National Highway Traffic Safety Administration (NHTSA), millions of consumers, and all major automobile companies view the matter quite differently.

With lawnmowers, kitchen appliances, airplanes, and safety valves, the conclusion is almost always the same: safety is no exception to the rule that buyers can always pay more and get more. Design is an infinitely variable and subtle process. It is always possible to strengthen an airplane wing or a building column; it is always possible to reduce the dosage of a drug or change the method or timing of its administration. But the follow-up questions are the difficult ones. There are questions of function: Will the airplane still fly? Will it fly as fast? There are questions of cost: At what point is an incremental benefit in safety no longer worth the price increase it would entail? There are questions of safety itself: Has the product really been improved, or has one risk just been traded off for another, possibly a more serious one?

The rule of thumb for American engineers is that the perfect device will be too late, too heavy, or too expensive. "We make do with the third best," the British said in World War II, "because the second best is always too late, and the first best never gets built." The perfectly safe vaccine, birth-control pill, or airplane is also perfectly ineffectual or impossible to use. Whether the objective is to cure disease, to alter the body's chemistry, or to travel at 600 miles an hour, some trade-off between safety and functionality is always in order. Disquieting though these judgments may be, they are a fact of real-world design. Indeed, they are the full-time business of countless design experts in both industry and government.

The more honest supporters of the new tort law recognized the problem and struggled to develop rational guidelines. A blueprint evolved that has since been widely quoted in jury instructions and appellate decisions.[1] A jury is to consider first the utility of the product, including "the needs, wants and desires served by the product," "the technological and economic feasibility of serving the same needs with alternative designs," and "the technological and economic feasibility of making the product safer." Next, it must weigh "the usefulness and desirability of the product — its utility to the user and to the public as a whole, the safety aspects of the product." It should then assess "the likelihood that [the product] will cause injury and the probable seriousness of the injury," considering, 'of course, "the user's ability to avoid danger by the exercise of care in the use of the product." Here the jury should also take into account "the user's anticipated awareness of the dangers inherent in the product and their avoidability, because of general public knowledge of the obvious condition of the product, or of the existence of suitable warnings or instructions." Also relevant are "the availability of a substitute product which would meet the same need and not be as unsafe, [and] the manufacturer's ability to eliminate the unsafe character of the product without impairing its usefulness or making it too expensive to maintain its utility." Finally, the never-tiring jurors must determine "the feasibility, on the part of the manufacturer, of spreading the loss by setting the price of the product or carrying liability insurance."

Perhaps this numbing profusion of words conveys a sound message, but could any jury really follow its subtle and complicated directive? In the attempt, trials would have to become advanced seminars in industrial design. And they did. Experts on both sides now line up to educate juries, for example, on the finer points of designing a morning-sickness drug, a crashworthy car, or a safe playground swing. The old tort law refused to hear this kind of testimony in all but the most exceptional cases. But relaxed federal rules of evidence were introduced in 1975, just in time for the new tort system's purposes. Today, one referral service in Pennsylvania maintains a nationwide list of about 10,000 experts grouped in 4,000 categories and reports an annual growth rate of about 15 percent. Classified advertisements in legal journals offer counsel on bicycle mishaps, lawn-mower accidents, beer-barrel incidents, hot-air balloon calamities, and so forth. Automobile-crashworthiness cases now routinely inquire into the relative frequency and severity of the different sorts of accidents and injuries that occur with a given model, the type of precautions that might have been taken, how those precautions might have impaired overall design and performance of the automobile, and how they might have affected the vehicle's price and the protection it affords against other types of accident hazards.

By the late 1970s, the technical and economic questions being raised in design-defect cases were triggering titanic courtroom struggles. But these struggles remained mere parodies of the actual process of real-world design. The original design of an automobile, drug, or pesticide takes years, as does its review by a government agency like the FDA. With or without the help of two camps of experts, a jury typically has only a few days and rarely more than a few weeks. As George Bernard Shaw caustically observed, "the theory of the adversary system is that if you set two liars to exposing each other, eventually the truth will come out." The paid experts have multiplied the number far beyond two, but there are few signs that any new truth has emerged.

The Matrix of Existing Standards

Since the Industrial Revolution, professional associations and government agencies have set safety standards that embody their expert judgments. In the early days of steam technology, for example, boilers exploded with appalling regularity, killing and maiming thousands of stokers and firemen and many bystanders. Engineering societies eventually settled on standards of proper design and operation for boiler manufacturers and users. Today these standards are well established and universally recognized. Boiler explosions are extremely rare.

Devising or endorsing such standards was the mission of many of the regulatory agencies that proliferated in the 1960s and early 1970s. The Environmental Protection Agency (EPA) and the National Highway Traffic Safety Administration have joined the FDA and similar bodies in setting thousands of safety standards for foods, drugs, cars, heart pacemakers, aircraft, pesticides, and so forth. When no government agency issues licenses or sets standards, nonprofit trade associations or professional societies like the National Underwriters Laboratories usually fill the gap.

Experts in pharmacology, engineering, medicine, and chemistry must constantly draw the boundary between the dangerous weapon and the useful tool, but only after years of careful work. Good design is subtle and difficult. Tort lawyers know that an error in one direction can lead to carnage. What they often forget is that error in the other direction can be equally harmful, if it deprives people of valuable medicines or major technological advances that make life safer.

The founders of the modern tort system might well have used the existing matrix of public or quasi-public standards to structure their new jurisprudence. The crux of their philosophy of accident law, after all, was that the protection of health and safety is part of a larger social contract that must supersede bilateral private agreement. Individual judgments about safety matters were to yield to publicly prescribed standards. The most obvious candidate standards were those established by professional agencies and associations.

As it happened, the courts had long accepted that view, at least in a negative context. At least by the 1870s, the violation of a regulatory standard was treated as conclusive evidence of "negligence." One of the clearest statements of the rule was supplied in 1920. Elizabeth and William Martin, driving their buggy near Tarrytown, New York, were hit by a car coming from the opposite direction, driven by Samuel Herzog. A jury found Herzog at fault, even though the Martins had been traveling that evening without buggy lights, in violation of a local statute. But the court of appeals overturned the jury's decision and ruled against the Martins. "We think the unexcused omission of the statutory signals is more than some evidence of negligence," wrote Benjamin Cardozo for the court. "It *is* negligence in itself. . . . To omit, willfully or heedlessly, the safeguards prescribed by law . . . is to fall short of the standard of diligence to which those who live in organized society are under a duty to conform."[2]

The idea that safety standards are made to be obeyed is sensible enough. Modern courts, like their predecessors, will simply not permit a jury to reexamine, after a poisoning, for example, whether it really *was* negligent for a company to sell a drug the FDA had not approved. Of course, the FDA could have made a mistake — perhaps its rule was overly strict and thus a menace to potential consumers who needed the drug. But an inexpert jury is unlikely to provide important insights on the safety question that the FDA had missed, and it might well approve a product that should not be on the market. Nor will the drug company be permitted to argue that it was unaware of the FDA regulation — ignorance of the law is no excuse.

But knowledge of the law, surprisingly enough, is no excuse, either. The rule still applied in every jurisdiction in the United States is that even the most complete conformity with applicable regulation will not shield a defendant from tort liability. This rule, too, has a venerable ancestry. On the twenty-first of October 1928, the Hotel Berry in Athens, Ohio, caught fire. Ray Mitchell, a guest, injured herself jumping from her window, and she sued the hotel, claiming that it had not provided convenient fire exits. The trial court ruled for the hotel on the ground that it had fully complied with applicable fire-exit laws. A court of appeals immediately overruled. "Although it be shown that the defendant had all the exits required," the court declared, "it is not acquitted of a charge of common-law negligence by proof of its compliance with the statutes."[3]

The logic was uncomplicated, at least in the context of its time. Most products and activities were so sparsely regulated that full compliance with applicable rules meant little. That a driver was not intoxicated and had obeyed the speed limit hardly proved that he had driven prudently. Perhaps icy roads dictated a speed slower than the posted one, or maybe the driver had rashly stayed at the wheel all night and dozed off. The driver might have done all sorts of technically legal things that prudent drivers nevertheless do not do. In a lightly regulated world, full compliance with the regulations meant only that a defendant had done the minimum necessary and not that he had necessarily behaved prudently.

As regulation intensified in the 1960s and 1970s, however, the array of health and safety rules began to cover much more of the canvas. The FDA began spelling out exactly how drugs could be composed, packaged, labeled, and prescribed. Significantly, since 1962 the FDA has had to judge not only the safety but also the efficacy of products, a task that requires the agency to reach an *affirmative* conclusion that an approved drug is actually beneficial, not merely harmless. The Federal Aviation Administration and the Nuclear Regulatory Commission developed equally exhaustive standards for the design and use of aircraft and nuclear-power plants, again under a mandate to ensure not merely safety but also advancement of the public good. New agencies like the NHTSA and EPA took as their mission not just *ad hoc* rectifying of cases of flagrant defect in cars or pesticides but also reexamining overall composition and design.

Many of these developments favored plaintiffs. When regulations proliferate, so do the opportunities to violate them. And when rules were violated, the courts continued to apply the old rule of incontestable negligence quite strictly. Whether a regulatory standard had been transgressed in a manner that was wanton and momentous or merely inadvertent and technical, any violation constituted virtually conclusive evidence of negligence. Significantly, the corollary implications about defendants' compliance did not change in the slightest. Time and again defendants attempted to raise prior regulatory approval as a shield; time and again they failed.

So the Piper Aircraft Company discovered in a fairly typical case involving a crash of one of its Cherokee aircraft. The surviving spouses of two passengers sued the company, claiming that the airplane's engine failed because the carburetor had iced. A better-designed engine, they argued, would have used a fuel injector. Piper pointed out that the airplane's design had been fully approved by the Federal Aviation Administration; more than 80 percent of airplanes of similar size, in fact, had carburetors instead of fuel injectors. A jury nevertheless returned large verdicts for the plaintiffs.

In a lengthy opinion, the Oregon Supreme Court conceded at the outset "special problems in the nature, and necessary proof, of a 'defect' in a product which reaches the consumer in precisely the condition intended by the designer/manufacturer." The court also sympathetically noted Piper's objection that "a lay jury is not qualified to determine technical questions of aeronautical design." The court went even further: it reexamined all the evidence presented at the trial and concluded that it was not "sufficient to permit the jury to find that the airplane was dangerously defective." But "we have found no cases," the court finally ruled, "holding that compliance [with FAA regulations] is a complete defense. We hold that it is not." Thus, it sent the carburetor-injector debate back for a second jury to weigh anew.

The law today can be simply stated: No matter how thorough, careful, and complete, advance regulatory approval counts for little in the subsequent lawsuit. One month the FDA may conclude that the Sabin polio vaccine is as safe as is technically feasible, vital for the public health, and preferable to the Salk vaccine, which is less effective in conferring mass immunity. The next month a jury may conclude that the Sabin vaccine is dangerously "defective" and that the Salk vaccine is to be preferred. The jury may carry *that* conclusion through to a multimillion dollar verdict, perhaps including punitive damages. Standards written by regulatory agencies, industry associations, insurance laboratories, or even Congress itself are given polite but only nominal attention. Juries alone are the final arbiters of "defective design."

Examples abound of the independence of juries. At the time of the lawsuit, ophthalmologists almost uniformly agreed that routine glaucoma tests were inappropriate, but an under-forty plaintiff who lost his sight to glaucoma prevailed on the theory that a doctor should have administered the test anyway. The Dayton Hudson Corporation paid $1 million in punitive damages to a girl burned after her cotton flannelette pajamas caught fire; the pajamas complied fully with the Federal Flammable Fabrics Act of 1982, but the victim's lawyer persuaded the jury that the government test was not reliable and that Dayton Hudson knew it. A lawsuit brought by Karen Silkwood's family against the Kerr-McGee Corporation established that a reprocessor of nuclear materials could be held liable to its employees, despite essentially complete compliance with all federal safety regulations. The manufacturer of a birth-control pill paid $2.75 million in punitive damages for an allegedly defective chemical formulation, despite complete compliance with FDA regulations.

Similar logic has meant that the defendant's care and good faith are irrelevant when the plaintiff alleges a defect in the warning rather than in the product itself. If compliance with the substantive rules of behavior addressing hotel fire exits or aircraft carburetors made no difference in liability cases, compliance with government-prescribed labels would not protect a defendant either—as the Chevron Corporation discovered in connection with the herbicide paraquat.

Richard Ferebee worked at a U.S. Department of Agriculture research center in Beltsville, Maryland. He claimed he had contracted pulmonary fibrosis, a serious lung disease, as a result of long-term exposure to diluted solutions of paraquat and that Chevron had not adequately warned of the risk. The EPA had long regulated the sale and labeling of paraquat under the Federal Insecticide, Fungicide, and Rodenticide Act of 1976, and had spelled out the warning label to be used. Chevron had followed the EPA requirements to the letter. The warning stated, in large, bold type, "DANGER. CAN KILL IF SWALLOWED. HARMFUL TO THE EYES AND SKIN." It went on to direct that any skin exposed to the chemical should be washed immediately and contaminated clothing removed. "Prolonged contact," the warning label concluded, would cause "severe irritation."

This warning was insufficient, concluded a jury and then a federal court of appeals. The label inexcusably failed to mention "the specter of long-term lung disease culminating, perhaps, in death." The decision conceded that Chevron had no legal right to add to or to depart from the EPA-prescribed warning in even the slightest detail. But "even if Chevron could not alter the label . . . the manufacturer ought to bear the cost of compensating for those injuries that could have been prevented with a more detailed label than that approved by the EPA." Chevron could comply both with EPA rules and with state tort judgments, the appellate court was happy to conclude, by simply "continuing to use the EPA-approved label and by simultaneously paying damages to successful tort plaintiffs."

Why does a showing of good-faith compliance not count for more? The usual explanation is that safety regulation is intended only to set a floor—a minimum standard that is necessary but often insufficient. Regulation may address only particular aspects of conduct, manufacture, or design. The regulators may never have contemplated the specific type of hazard involved in a given accident. What if they clearly did contemplate a particular hazard but nevertheless judged it to be unavoidable? In court, agencies and legislators themselves are not to be trusted; they may have tailored their regulations or statues to suit producers rather than consumers. Industry standards deserve even less deference, having been written by the very sort of people whose conduct must be scrutinized at trial. To favor relaxing standards of tort liability, according to defenders of the legal status quo, is to be against safety and hostile to consumers.

Is it really? Neither tenet of the new tort law — that safety is an unconditional good and that more liability leads to more safety — will bear examination. Difficult safety choices have always existed in a world of finite resources. What is new under modern tort law is not the need for choice, but who is choosing. The courts have assumed the overwhelmingly dominant role as final arbiters on matters of safety.

What is wrong with that? Somebody has to direct the world in progressive, safer directions. Why not the courts? Judges, for the most part, are well educated and well intentioned. And juries serve as a sort of populist minilegislature drawn from the public. The courts are there to watch for things that the individual might not understand, or a regulatory agency might not consider, or a legislature might find politically expedient to ignore. Somebody has to choose between activities and products that are acceptably safe and those that are unacceptably dangerous: Why not the courts?

There is a simple reason why not. Having the courts make safety choices is a certain path to a more dangerous world. The tort system can only say no, equivocally and after the fact. But prudent promotion of safety ultimately depends on knowing when and how to say yes, decisively and in time to make a difference.

Safety in the Affirmative

Perfect safety, like perpetual motion, will always be elusive. The challenge, then, is not so much to deter risky activities as to choose intelligently among them — to distinguish risks that are part of a problem from those that are part of the solution. Making positive safety choices is vital, whether the issue is essentially private or entirely public.

Most risks, except those of highway accidents, arise in a fairly narrow, largely private context. Catastrophes like nuclear meltdowns are less likely to injure people than smoking, improper diets, unsafe sexual habits, or mishaps involving a consumer product, a doctor's services, or a hazard on the job. In all these cases, of course, prudent choice involves many negatives. The consumer spurns the compact car, rejects the cheap lawn mower, and avoids the substandard hospital. The "just-say-no" philosophy of safety regulation has much to commend it.

But knowing when to make affirmative responses is equally vital to safety—buying appliances from the reputable manufacturer, accepting the specialized services of the large hospital, and favoring the safer car, cosmetic, or child's toy. Without these responses, the consumer lives in a very spare world, devoid of countless goods and services that make life not only more convenient but also safer and healthier. The austere life of the hermit is infinitely more dangerous than life amid the products of modern affluence.

It has been understood for some time that some safety choices cannot be left to private control. Electric-power plants, chemical factories, mass immunization programs, waste disposal, and countless other activities of modern industrial society create both risks and benefits that are broadly shared by the public. Public risks necessarily require public choice. Individuals may lack the information or incentive to deal prudently with risks of this kind. Even with a legal right not to be exposed to the factory's smoke, they may singly lack the motivation to sue the polluter. They may each hope that someone else will attend to the problem and be inclined to understate their own concern in the hope of free-riding on someone else's lawsuit. Contrariwise, when it is in the communal interest to *agree* to a publicly risky activity—the construction, say, of a needed power plant, waste dump, or factory—the selfish individual may be tempted to overstate an aversion to it in the hope of extorting a buy-out price from the community reflecting the large collective benefit at stake. Finally, it is sometimes merely convenient to make safety choices collectively. All sorts of important decisions are delegated to experts like lawyers, bankers, and physicians; and sometimes it makes sense to delegate safety choices to government bodies.

Whether public or private, safety regulation inescapably involves a negative and a positive side. The negative side is familiar enough—the federal regulator refuses to license an unduly hazardous pesticide or power plant or shuts down an excessively dirty smokestack. But the positive side of the safety coin is no less important. Of the available ways to generate electricity, control a crop pest, or fight an infection, some will be better under given circumstances. Regardless of whether the individual or the government makes the decision, safety lies in intelligent, positive choices. The assumption that life is made safer by hostility to all risk is wrong. Safety lies as much in embracing good risks as in spurning bad ones.

Until the new-tort revolution of the 1960s, the two-sided nature of safety regulation was understood and reflected in the most important elements of the law. Safety choices in the individual's domain were made largely by private contract. The consumer who did not want to take a risk refused to buy the good or service. But accepting a risk was equally straightforward. A private contract is essentially an affirmation. Contract law is what two parties depend on to affirm a service, a sale, or a mutual venture or adventure, risky or otherwise.

Safety choices in the public domain had a similar, two-sided character. If a business was of a type that the government had chosen to regulate comprehensively, it was conducted under license or not at all. A "license" is the equivalent of a contract for a government agency—the official assent by which the acceptably safe is distinguished from the unacceptably dangerous. For licensing agencies, the function of regulation is approving practices and products — selectively, of course — on the basis of a critical comparison of the full range of options available.

The courts can never make effective positive choices about safety, because they are decentralized, uncoordinated, dispersed, and operated locally. Judges as a group do not constitute a coordinated management team. There are thousands of lower state courts, fifty state supreme courts, and several hundred federal district courts. Each is an individual fiefdom, and each jury is a new authority.

This independence makes systematic affirmative choice impossible in court. No positive safety judgment is ever final under tort law. Today's plaintiff may lose, but the next day's plaintiff files a new lawsuit and is entitled to a new decision. Even in class actions, individual litigants often opt out and fight their own, private crusades. The results, especially with products marketed nationwide, compare with the progress of a bus steered by a fractious committee of its passengers.

Is Bendectin a safe and valuable morning-sickness therapy, as the FDA has concluded, or a teratogenic poison responsible for countless birth defects, as several juries have declared, with a conviction measured in the hundreds of millions of dollars? The mainstream scientific community has agreed with the FDA. So have most juries, but not all, and the courthouse door is always open for the issue to be relitigated anew. Bendectin is off the market as a result.

Are all contraceptives defective? There have been several multimillion-dollar judgments against birth-control pills (which very occasionally cause kidney failure or strokes) and against the spermicides used with condoms and diaphragms (blamed for birth defects). In all of these cases the products reached the end user precisely as the manufacturer and the FDA intended.

The same story has been repeated time and again with other products in a "heads-you-lose, tails-we-flip-again" process that guarantees full employment for lawyers on all sides. A company cannot gain an effective go-ahead on a new product before committing itself to actual production and marketing. It must stake huge sums on what might be called liability futures — which even in the best of circumstances are a highly speculative venture. Worst of all, it is possible to win most tort cases and still "lose" the overall battle. The litigation process itself becomes the punishment.

If the judicial process is one of fragmentation, it is also one of polarization. Decision making in the courts is inescapably bilateral; what one side wins the other necessarily loses, and the bystanders whose interests may also be affected (though only indirectly) do not appear in the decision at all. But bilateral decision making is exactly what will not work in managing matters of public (as opposed to strictly private) safety and welfare. Such matters require public management and are removed from the domain of private contract precisely because a bilateral approach will not yield a desirable outcome. The courts' dominance of the most far-reaching issues of public safety has undone everything that was originally accomplished in transferring such matters out of the control of the individual to an administrative government forum in the first place.

These problems are sharpest when the stakes are the highest. How will the modern tort system handle a mass-immunization program against acquired immune deficiency syndrome (AIDS) or the genetic engineering of crops and animals, with its far-ranging risks and benefits? What coherent message can tort liability convey for the still novel and unfamiliar technologies of gas-cooled nuclear reactors, fetal surgery, hepatitis vaccines, bullet trains, and countless other innovations that promise enormous benefits, including advancements in safety, but may also entail some unfamiliar new risks? Other branches of government can weigh these technologies and select among them, denying one and approving another. The courts can only remain brooding on the sidelines, holding out the threat of hostile intervention, never able to offer a reliable go-ahead or any definite promise of acceptance or approval.

Whether they decide private safety matters through multiple identical lawsuits or public safety matters throughout the polarized framework of bilateral litigation, the courts are ill-equipped to make positive safety choices. Piecemeal adjudications, orchestrated by self-interested lawyers on both sides and crafted according to each jury's limited preconceptions of what is acceptably safe, do not magically coalesce into a coherent program for advancing either individual or public safety. The power to punish and avenge is not equivalent to the power to encourage and protect. A blackball system is not the ideal way for a club to recruit promising new members.

Promoting Positive Safety Choices

The biggest irony in tort liability concerns the simple question of jury competence. The new-tort edifice of products liability was founded on the assumption that members of the general public were unqualified to make intelligent and therefore binding choices about the safety of complex products and services. Thus the legal system abandoned the doctrine of caveat emptor, disclaimers of liability are no longer binding, and even the most explicit and detailed product warnings are often dismissed out of hand in litigation. Now, however, the inexpert member of the public is summoned to make choices in the jury box that he has already been judged incompetent to make in the marketplace.

It is unrealistic to suppose that the product of a thirty-year legal crusade that is the law today can be replaced overnight with sweeping reforms proposed by a new generation of academics. But change at the margins is possible — and urgently needed. The key is to promote positive, consensual safety choices outside the courts and to downplay the importance of the negative, adversarial decision making inside.

One may start through the use of warnings. A strong link between tort liability and warning makes a great deal of sense. It is also compatible with venerable legal tradition and long-standing core principles of contract and individual control. The physician or drug manufacturer often knows of risks that the consumer does not. Full disclosure should be an ordinary and essential part of fair dealing in the modern commercial world. And detailed warnings have indeed long been the commercial and regulatory norm for such things as therapeutic drugs, vaccines, medical care, consumer appliances, pesticides, and cigarettes — partly because of commendably persistent pressure from the tort system. Warning and disclosure enhance individual autonomy, and accurate information, when sensibly conveyed and intelligently used, is an unconditional good. A tort jurisprudence founded on warning could serve society much better than one built around erratic judicial attempts to ferret out "defective designs" in products or "negligence" in services. Informed consumer choices would not always be wise, but such a system would at least encourage the positive choice that offers the only real road to greater safety.

The most urgently needed correction here concerns warnings crafted by federal agencies like the FDA and EPA. Such agencies write, rewrite, and refine the warnings that must accompany drugs, vaccines, medical devices, food additives, pesticides, and toxic chemicals. The agency-prescribed warning is mandatory, and no substitutions or elaborations are allowed. The objective, of course, is to provide just enough warning, neither too little nor too much, the risk of the latter being to deter the use of safety-enhancing — perhaps even life-saving — products. At the very least, an officially approved warning label should be exempt from liability attack. If the agency has weighed the question of warning in detail and specified the language to be used, there should be no debate over warnings for tort purposes.

Some safety matters will always remain too complex or far-reaching to be resolved through private agreement, with or without full warning. Informed consent by the individual is never going to take care of such things as chemical-waste disposal, mass vaccination, and central power generation. These matters must obviously continue to be delegated to agents representing the collective good.

An agent in legal terms is someone who acts on behalf of a principal. The agent negotiates, buys, and sells; if properly vested with authority, the agent can make fully binding decisions for the principal, as if the latter were present. In safety matters, the government agency fits comfortably into the standard mold. Its responsibility is to make good choices for the public, just as individuals would do for themselves if they were in a position to do so. To represent a principal effectively, a broker must be able to buy as well as sell. In other words, the broker must have power not only to reject bad safety choices but also to embrace good ones.

The key, again, is to restore some balance to the tort law. It would certainly be appalling if tort law allowed judges to order a nuclear-power plant into operation after the NRC had refused a license on safety grounds. In the reverse case, however, the modern law does not hesitate to intervene by inviting a lay jury to second-guess the agency that had approved the product or activity. This asymmetry is senseless, except on the premise that nuclear power is so awful that any way of stopping it is justified. The licensing of a nuclear plant, after all, reflects a conscious decision that its total risks, in terms of accidents, pollution, and security of supply, are worth bearing compared with those of alternative energy sources.

It may be politically unrealistic to propose that a company conducting activities with the express approval of qualified regulatory agencies be immune from liability. But at a minimum, complete compliance with a comprehensive licensing order should provide protection against punitive damages. The courts should be required or at least strongly encouraged to respect the risk and safety choices made by expert agencies. The formal federal licensing of a new drug, medical device, vaccine, aircraft, or nuclear-power plant should be far more than a routine and irrelevant pleasantry that is forgotten as soon as the first tort plaintiff enters the courthouse. This simple prescription sounds radical only in the context of a tort law that is itself radically expansionist. It has always been true that ignorance of the law is no excuse. At present, knowledge of the law is no excuse either. But it should be.

NOTES

1. John Wade, "On the Nature of Strict Tort Liability for Products," *Mississippi Law Journal 44* (1973): 825; David G. Owen, "Rethinking the Policies of Strict Products Liability," *Vanderbilt Law Review 33* (1980): 681; Robert Keeton, "The Meaning of Defect in Products Liability Law: A Review of Basic Principles," *Missouri Law Review 45* (1980): 579.
2. *Martin v. Herzog*, 126 N.E. 814 (1920); Restatement (Second) of Torts 288B (1), Comment a.
3. *Mitchell v. Hotel Berry Co.*, 34 Ohio App. 259, 171 N.E. 39 (Ohio 1929).

Alternative Dispute Resolution: Wrong Solution, Wrong Problem

AUSTIN SARAT

The widespread view that the United States is suffering from a "liability crisis" that is part of a more general breakdown in the justice system has helped fuel an influential movement to reform and improve the courts. One favorite goal of reformers is to create methods of alternative dispute resolution (ADR) to settle conflicts outside the judicial system. This essay traces how claims of a liability crisis have encouraged this enthusiasm for ADR, how ADR is intended to improve on the performance of the courts, and why it is a misconceived program that would likely create new problems if fully enacted.

The idea that there is a liability crisis is based on several separate yet related stories, or narratives. The first is a story of how American legal culture has changed; the second recounts the rise and the baneful effects of judicial activism; the third tells of alleged declines in economic productivity, efficiency, and innovativeness; and the fourth describes the eventual decline of the courts to a state of congestion, overload, and crisis. While the fourth narrative provides the link to ADR, the first three must be sketched in as background.

The narration of change in American legal culture juxtaposes a memory and a fear. The memory is of a golden age in America, a time when the legal culture allegedly embodied a happy combination of individual self-reliance on the one hand and widespread consensus, agreement on fundamental values, and interpersonal trust on the other. The fear is that this ethic of self-reliance has disappeared along with the consensus and trust that supposedly marked the earlier age. The result is a culture of contention — searching for "causes and culprits" and eagerly embracing an ethic of redress. Americans, it is feared, have come to believe that wherever there is injury, illness, or disappointment there must be blame, responsibility, and compensation. Fatalism, endurance, and self-reliance have given way to a belief that destiny can be controlled, that accidents are preventable, that progress can and should mean the reduction of human suffering. No longer do "the injuries that befall us, caused indirectly, if not prompted by other people," appear to be "part of the natural order."[1] Consequently, it is argued, Americans are quick to sue.

A cultural change of this sort, however unwelcome it might be to some, could not plausibly be labeled a "crisis." As a result, a second narrative is required to create a crisis, a narrative about courts and judges. According to this story, courts today are receptive to a wide variety of claims that would have been unthinkable in the past. These claims range from the frivolous to the gargantuan, from those that try patience to those that strain capacity. This tale blames judges and the courts for acquiescing to, indeed encouraging, the culture of contention. The story typically contains an indictment of judicial activism as a theory of judicial decision. On the level of particular decisions, those especially criticized include cases in which judges have expanded the reach of existing duties or composed new affirmative obligations, have assigned or expanded liability even when individual culpability could not be established, or have undertaken the management of complex institutions like prisons and schools in an effort to vindicate claims brought under the Fourteenth Amendment. This story line also links the alleged liability crisis to the irresponsibility of juries in imposing outrageous punitive-damage awards.

The third narrative strand in the tale of the liability crisis details how the expansion of litigation and liability has reduced economic productivity and efficiency, incentives for innovation and risk-taking, and the competitiveness of American products in international markets. When tort law shifted its emphasis from self-reliance to compensation, it was said, the result was the overdeterrence of socially valuable activities. Skyrocketing insurance rates prompted doctors to leave high-risk specialties and municipalities to lock children out of playgrounds and swimming pools.

The fourth narrative focuses on how the liability crisis has allegedly brought on the courts an insuperable problem of judicial administration. This story tells of rising caseloads, increased backlog and delay, abuse of procedures like discovery, escalating costs, and frustrated and dissatisfied litigants. The American public is said to be litigating more and liking it less. Clogged dockets and interminable delays are an inequitable way to ration justice, because they discourage many litigants with meritorious claims. Paradoxically, then, overly accessible justice threatens access to justice. The excess of litigiousness threatens to weaken both the capacity and the legitimacy of the same courts that are said to be among the causes of the problem.

This last subplot of the liability-crisis story has played a significant role in spurring the ADR movement. Proponents of ADR want to ease some of the increased demand for court services by creating substitute forms of dispute resolution. They argue that ADR can be cheaper and more effective than conventional litigation and adjudication. In addition, they say that ADR is especially well suited for some types of claims that the courts lack the resources, capability, and flexibility to redress properly. ADR is said to be one important way for both courts and claimants to cope with the consequences of the liability crisis.

ADR: A Program of Reform

Proponents of ADR often present it as a "retail" rather than a "wholesale" response to the problems of judicial administration associated with the liability crisis. Their hope is not to divert a large number of cases but to redirect those that are allegedly ill-suited for adjudication. They expect ADR not only to reduce caseload and capacity problems but also to provide a superior alternative for the kinds of cases that the courts allegedly handle poorly. ADR proponents thus want to "reserve the courts for those activities for which they are best suited and to avoid swamping and paralyzing them with cases that do not require their unique capabilities."[2] This critique of judicial competence, or capacity, which is central to the ADR program, is based on notions of what courts can and cannot do well, notions that supposedly derive from the courts' institutional characteristics, procedures, and resources. Among the courts' salient limitations are said to be the following:

Reactivity. Possibly the most distinctive aspect of courts is that they are reactive institutions. They do not set their own agendas; they respond to cases brought to them by outside parties. This does not mean they are obliged to accept every case. They can invoke prudential doctrines like mootness, standing, and the political-question doctrine to weed out cases that appear inappropriate for adjudication.

Dependence. Courts cannot employ independent investigatory capabilities; they "know" only what they are told by the parties in the forms prescribed by law. In framing their cases, the parties provide only a partial and artificial view of the whole truth, so courts often miss the real point of disputes.

Limited resources. Courts have limited staff resources. Judges are legally trained generalists, and their activities and expertise are rarely supplemented on an outgoing basis.

Lack of enforcement power. Finally, courts have no built-in enforcement powers. After they render a decree, they rely on the parties to report any failures of compliance. In the rare decisions requiring ongoing supervision or performance, the courts must make ad hoc and often unsatisfactory arrangements to monitor that performance.

Given these characteristics, proponents of ADR ask, what can we expect the courts to do well? What kinds of disputes could be handled more efficiently and effectively elsewhere? One possible group of candidates for ADR is cases with no real disputes. When courts must process cases like uncontested divorces, judges and resources are diverted from contested cases, and the parties must bear the expense of a court proceeding. Perhaps dignitary or symbolic values may properly be satisfied only if a judge officially certifies the termination of a marriage, but these values, it is argued, must be weighed against the equally compelling need to conserve court resources and minimize expenses and inconvenience to litigants.

Another group of potential ADR cases involve complex and ongoing relations between the litigants. Cases involving disputes between parents and children, between spouses or lovers, and sometimes between neighbors or between businesses raise important social questions that may not be best handled through the formal adversarial proceedings of courts. Such cases may require the courts to review a long, complex series of grievances, of which the formal cause of action may be the least important or relevant.

Proponents of ADR speak as if such cases come to the courts only because other institutions or norms that once regulated private relationships have been weakened or dissolved. They say that families, churches, and schools no longer help resolve problems in ongoing relationships. Judges cannot be expected to be social workers, and yet they cannot ignore real problems that can be framed as questions of legal rights. Adjudication narrows disputes, and it intensifies them. It is argued that parties who need to rely on each other in the future are poorly served by a process that almost inevitably brands one "right" and the other "wrong."

Cases like these, ADR proponents argue, could best be managed by nonjudicial institutions. Alternative forums could be efficient, less costly, and less adversarial than the courts. Moreover, such diversions would alleviate the problems of gaining access to the courts for everyone while serving the real interests of the judiciary by reducing its workload and reserving it for the most appropriate cases.

Advocates of ADR also believe that it is possible and desirable to classify all dispute-processing techniques into discrete clusters (e.g., mediation, arbitration, adjudication) by identifying the essential attributes of the techniques in each cluster. This essentialism informs the ways in which proponents of ADR think about the capacities of all dispute-processing techniques. They attempt to deduce from the essential attributes of each technique an understanding of its distinctive capacities and limits, an understanding of the kinds of disputes or problems each different form of dispute processing is best equipped to handle. In the following description, for example, mediation is particularly appropriate in family disputes:

> [First,] mediation . . . looks to the future and has as its principal goal the repair of the frayed relationship. Second, mediated solutions are more flexible than those brought about by adjudication because they are created by the parties themselves, albeit with the help of a mediator. Third, mediation avoids the winner-loser syndrome, a consideration that assumes special importance where an ongoing relationship is involved. Fourth, the mediation process involves wide ranging inquiry into what the interested parties want to talk about. . . . Finally, mediation gives an enhancing sense of participation to the disputants.[3]

This description defines mediation by its advertised advantages. If a disputing process fails to display these appealing attributes, it cannot claim to be mediation; it must be something else. In the ensuing discussion, of course, mediation is bound to sound promising, since its actual contexts and practices are not given much attention. The language of description masks the basically prescriptive nature of the argument.

There have been numerous efforts to define the essential characteristics of dispute-processing techniques, but the most influential effort remains that of Lon Fuller.

His "Forms and Limits of Adjudication" is an effort to refine the essence of adjudication, the method courts allegedly use in resolving disputes, from the different ways it has been carried out historically. Fuller sought to "define 'true adjudication' or adjudication as it might be if the ideals that support it were fully realized." As he saw it, "the 'essence' of adjudication lies in the mode of participation it accords to the affected party," in which parties present arguments to an impartial decision maker.[4] Fuller's work on adjudication has its parallels for mediation, arbitration, and other dispute-processing techniques. In each the effort is to abstract from history and context to see through, or ignore, variations in local practices. The dispute (as presented for resolution) is taken as given, with fixed dimensions and relatively stable characteristics that can be cataloged in the approved manner and matched to the various dispute-processing mechanisms.

The capstone of the ADR program involves an effort to develop a theory of allocation. How can disputes and dispute-processing techniques be matched up, how can an understanding of the essential attributes of different forms of dispute processing "be utilized so that, given the variety of disputes that presently arise we can begin to develop some rational criteria for allocating various types of disputes to different dispute resolution processes?"[5] Proponents of ADR approach the subject of disputing and dispute processing with a desire to find a way to channel disputes and match dispute-processing techniques. For those who advocate dispute processing as a response to the alleged liability crisis and as a response to problems of judicial administration, "one consequence of . . . [a theory of allocation] is that we will have a better sense of what cases ought to be left in the courts for resolution, and which should be 'processed' in some other way."[6] Thus the ADR program would employ dispute processing as one aspect of a strategy designed to respond to the difficulties of courts caused by the liability crisis.

In order rationally to allocate disputes between courts and ADR, proponents advance, at least implicitly, a set of standards that might be employed in making choices about what types of problems can best be handled by what types of procedures. The standards most often suggested include:

The magnitude of the rights at issue. It is argued that, as a rule, cases involving alleged violations of fundamental constitutional rights should be dealt with through formal, usually judicial, procedures. When individual liberty is the issue, courts are always the appropriate forum. The amount of money claimed in a dispute is not in itself, however, a clear indicator of the magnitude of the rights involved.

The probability of error. Disputes that raise highly complex technical matters, proponents of ADR suggest, should be channeled to institutions or procedures that can call on experts. Because medical malpractice cases sometimes require judges and juries to evaluate detailed medical procedures, for instance, some states have created screening panels of doctors and lawyers to review malpractice claims. This standard requires that someone be empowered to decide whether the issues in a dispute are technically complex enough to warrant diversion.

Another criterion meant to reduce the probability of error holds that when clear and relevant guidelines are available for deciding particular types of cases, the cases should be heard by individuals with expertise in interpreting and applying those guidelines. In addition, the best procedures will be those that ensure that the decision maker actually follows the guidelines in resolving the disputes; unlimited discretion is intolerable.

Finality. Court judgments may end lawsuits, but they do not often end disputes. Social disruption may continue and engender further litigation, especially if the legal cause of action did not derive from the real or underlying conflict or problem. If a dispute arises between intimates, for example, no award of money damages to compensate an alleged tort or breach of contract may end the real trouble. To the extent that prudent social policy requires finality, allocation theories attempt to direct these cases to forums that can provide lasting as well as binding decisions.

Cost-benefit balance. Though acknowledging that cheaper may not be better, in the realm of dispute resolution reformers try to channel disputes to the least costly alternative. Disputes should not be allocated, they argue, to forums in which costs are unduly disproportionate to the injury incurred and the expected result.

Public demand and user satisfaction. Some reformers have framed the question as one of giving disputants what they want from institutional facilities. Why create elaborate new mechanisms if no one would like or could afford them? Although not everyone will be pleased with every decision, users should generally feel that the results are just and satisfactory, compared with the alternatives.

While this list is by no means exhaustive, it does indicate the range of standards that reformers have established. It also suggests the difficulty of the challenge they face: reconciling the criteria with one another or striking a balance when they conflict, identifying the nature and magnitude of the rights at stake in a particular dispute, and predicting the success of particular techniques in resolving disputes. Yet these difficulties are too often glossed over as if they were easily handled in practice.

The Inadequacies of the ADR Program

Whatever one's position on the so-called liability crisis, the evidence suggests that the ADR program is an inadequate response. The desire rationally to allocate disputes to appropriate dispute-processing forums raises several difficult questions for proponents of ADR: Who is to be responsible for allocation decisions? How much attention will be paid to the wishes of the parties? At what point in the life history of disputes would, and should, such allocation decisions be made? How would allocation decisions be monitored to determine whether they are made correctly?

In order for a theory of allocation of the type envisioned by the ADR program to work, at least two things would have to be true. First, the nature and characteristics of disputes would have to be fixed before their assignment to a particular forum of dispute processing. Second, dispute-processing techniques would have to be sufficiently different in their capacities and operations to allow for clear choices to be made. Available research suggests, however, that neither of these conditions is likely to be realized, and that the ADR program is based on an inadequate portrait of the way the disputing process works and on an inadequate understanding of the actual operations of dispute-processing alternatives.

To begin with, at what point in the history of a dispute would an ADR system intervene? Presumably the answer is well before the matter went to a jury, indeed before a trial began. But would it be before the "discovery" process in which each side learns how strong its case is? Would it be before a suit is filed?

This demonstrates one of the hidden weaknesses of the ADR program: it takes as its starting point the already articulated dispute. Yet it is clear that in practice potential disputes evolve in complex ways. At each stage many potential disputes are satisfied, abandoned, or repressed. Against the backdrop of all injurious events and questionable conduct, the rate at which disputes emerge, even in this allegedly litigious society, is quite low.

The first step in the development of a dispute is the recognition of a problem, when a victim realizes that an event or transaction has been injurious in some way. Often this step occurs directly or immediately; the classic case is the automobile accident in which the injury is apparent as soon as it happens. Many other problems, however, elicit no such immediate recognition. As society is now beginning to realize, the apparent benefits of new technology are often immediate and attractive, while its associated side effects and injurious consequences may appear only years later. The most important barriers to the emergence of disputes may be the difficulty in recognizing injury or the reluctance of people with legitimate claims to acknowledge their problem or admit that they have had an injurious experience.

The next step in the process is the transition from a perceived problem to a grievance. At this stage, the injured person begins to feel wronged and also begins to believe that the wrong can be remedied. A grievance is more than a generalized complaint; it is the attribution of fault for an injury to another individual or institution.

After blame has been fixed or alleged, the next step in the dispute process is reached when someone musters the courage to raise a claim, that is, to voice grievances to the party or entity believed to be responsible. *Claim* is used here in the sociological sense of confronting an adversary rather than in the legal sense of filing a lawsuit. Disputes develop only if the adversary resists the claim and the plaintiff decides to press it anyway.

A grievance ripens into a claim and then a full dispute only if people overcome substantial social and cultural obstacles to disputing. Going public with a dispute, whatever its outcome, may create more trouble for both parties than if they had kept their claim to themselves.

To enter a claim for redress involves a social declaration of trouble, a declaration that may lead to social disruption and disorientation for the party entering the claim as well as for the other party. For the worker who perceives herself to be the victim of discrimination on the job, to take one example, the declaration of trouble is really just the beginning of more trouble; that helps explain why many discrimination victims make no complaint. Most claimants feel a sense of foreboding about what a wrongdoer may do in return.

Notions of civility and tact also encourage people to ignore trouble; disputing can seem like a breach of cultural order. In addition, people are reluctant to acknowledge publicly that their life is troubled, even if they have acknowledged it to themselves. People who seize on any social opportunity to register dissatisfaction are considered neurotic or obnoxious.

Along with the risks that go with breaching public presumptions of civility and decorum, those who experience trouble are often held causally or morally responsible for having caused the trouble or having failed to avoid it. Blaming the victim is all too common a cultural tendency. When, for example, parents perceive their children as being disturbed and seek therapy for them, psychiatrists often assume and even allege that the parents themselves are at fault.

In short, disputing is an uncomfortable, dirty business that poses risks of loss of face, reputation, or status. No wonder many potential claimants are deterred. Claimants pay for disturbing the peace and for their inability or unwillingness to put up with grievances. As a result, one or both parties in a social interaction may believe that something is wrong in the relationship but will not say so for fear of engendering hostility or being labeled a troublemaker. Hence the attractiveness of private endurance.

Endurance might be unbearable without catharsis. One copes with trouble by discussing it with others who are not involved, in a kind of social displacement. At the dinner table people may talk about their experiences at work, complaining about their fellow workers, business associates, students, or anyone else. Returning to work, however, they often complain about their insensitive spouses who never understand them. They complain to the same co-workers who were earlier criticized. In these ways, public allegiance to definitions of civility and order may be maintained while trouble is endured or rendered manageable.

ADR proponents underestimate the social pressure to repress grievances or claims, that is, the social pressure not to dispute. Trouble complained of privately is always less severe than trouble aired publicly. In the long run the revelation of grievance or long suffering always has the potential to restore harmony and order, but its immediate effect is to open up the floodgates of recrimination and retribution. Society is held together by the implicit promise *not* to tell the entire truth about grievances, angers, or resentments. The boundaries of the disputing process are very hard to manage: the burden of raising a claim is the fear of creating more trouble.

These social and cultural barriers are not, of course, impossible to overcome, nor do they operate equally in all types of disputes. But they demonstrate why the ADR program is impoverished by its preoccupation with processing and resolving already articulated disputes. This deficiency might be less important if the disputes that emerged were, at the end, stable and fixed. This, however, is not the case.

Disputes, even after they emerge as articulated disputes, do not exist in fixed form independent of the techniques used to process them. They change shape as they are processed. As Lynn Mather and Barbara Yngvesson have said, "A dispute is not a static event which simply 'happens.' . . . What a dispute is about, whether it is even a dispute or not, and whether it is properly a 'legal' dispute, may be central issues for negotiation in the dispute process."[7]

Disputes are transformed more than even this quotation suggests. The objectives of the parties may change dramatically as disputes are processed. New information becomes available, each party's needs change, and costs are incurred. Delays, frustration, and disappointment raise or lower the stakes. For example, victims of job discrimination frequently start by wanting the job or promotion they were unjustifiably denied but later, stymied by the difficulties in proving discrimination or more aware of the work environment from which they have been excluded, are much more willing to accept a monetary settlement.

The substantive scope of a dispute is also not fixed. Some types of dispute processing narrow the disputes they encounter in order to produce a construction of events that appears manageable. Others expand context and circumstance; they encourage a full rendering of events and exploration of interactions. The identity and number of parties are not fixed when the dispute processing begins. As information about the disputed issues is clarified, a bipolar dispute may become multipolar, and parties may change their view about appropriate adversaries or desirable allies.

Consistent with the ADR program's urge to classify the bounds of disputes is its ideal of effective resolution. Proponents of ADR think that matching the right disputes with the right processing techniques can restore harmony and resolve problems in ways that satisfy the disputants. They tend to speak of dispute resolution rather than dispute processing. This emphasis reflects an image of social life in which order naturally prevails and in which conflict is an exception to be remedied through mediation, arbitration, and other dispute-resolution mechanisms. In practice, loose ends and nagging discontents are all too likely to linger.

The ADR program, with its interest in neatly tagging disputes and rationally allocating them to the proper dispute-processing modes, is thus likely to be frustrated by the fluidity of disputes and their life cycle. The assignment of a dispute to one ADR mechanism or another undermines the entire scheme. What happens when the dispute changes character? What looks like a suitable case for mediation may become suitable for arbitration and then adjudication. Those who favor ADR because they think there is now too much disputing may be surprised to find that many disputes that would never result in suits will be submitted to alternative dispute tribunals. Furthermore, these disputes are likely to involve more parties and more wide-ranging issues than do lawsuits. By raising these issues, ADR mechanisms may educe grievances that plaintiffs had not known about, for which mediation is not the answer, and that may create actual lawsuits.

As Sally Merry has pointed out, another problem for ADR proponents is why such services are rarely sought voluntarily. The ADR approach, after all, "assumes that dispute resolution is a rational and instrumental process in which actors seek to maximize their self-interest. They make calculated choices about dispute resolution techniques based on their cost, speed, and anticipated outcomes. Under this model, actors are expected to flock to more efficient fora."[8] Yet they do not.

ADR proponents do not address this discrepancy. They will hardly want to embrace the view that ADR mechanisms are cumbersome or inefficient. More likely, as Merry suggested, ADR proponents have simply been mistaken about what disputants want out of disputes. According to research that she reported, people prefer to handle most disputes through direct negotiations; they are, in most situations, reluctant to involve third parties or make their claim in a public forum. The commitment to direct negotiation wavers only when disputes involve issues of rights and principles. At the point when disputants seek outside aid, however, they are least likely to be attracted by processes like mediation and arbitration, whose primary advertised advantage is their refusal to traffic in the language of rights and principles. Thus the theory of allocation is likely to fail or require coercion to work, precisely because it assumes that disputants simply want their dispute resolved efficiently and do not care how. It incorrectly posits that they are indifferent to the forms and symbols of the processes that deal with their disputes.

Along with its static and unrealistic view of the disputing process, the ADR program suffers from an overly formalistic view of dispute processing itself. Much of the discussion of alternative dispute processing revolves around the efforts of ADR proponents to pigeonhole dispute-processing techniques under the labels "adjudication," "arbitration," and "mediation," each label allegedly corresponding to determinate and identifiable procedures. The supposed distinction between negotiation and adjudication, one might observe, roughly parallels the way nineteenth-century legal formalists distinguished the legal categories of contract from those of tort. Negotiation, as well as mediation, resembles contract with its emphasis on will, voluntariness, and agreement; adjudication resembles tort in its emphasis on imposing external standards when private bargaining seems inappropriate or impossible.

Just as legal realism deconstructed the abstract legal categories that dominated nineteenth-century legal thinking, contemporary sociological research suggests the inadequacy of the nominalism and conceptualism that characterize the ADR allocation scheme. Dispute-processing techniques are internally inconsistent, and they change form as they adapt to the problems that are brought to them. They are no more set in their operation than disputes are fixed in their form and content.

For example, mediation is evidently practiced in different ways in different places and by different mediators. Some mediators have a therapeutic orientation and attempt to facilitate communication in hopes of encouraging a party to recognize the other's perspective. Other mediators emphasize agreement between parties; as a result, they narrow issues and close off avenues of inquiry that would likely escalate conflict. Mediation practices differ greatly in different contexts; the mediation of environmental disputes and the mediation of divorce may share nothing more than the same abstract label. At the extreme, the practices of mediators may have less in common with each other than they do with dispute processors employing techniques of negotiation or arbitration.

Dispute-processing techniques are not only internally diverse; they also reflect a cultural background. "The ideological definition of the process, springing from its social and cultural context, exerts a powerful influence on the behavior of those who carry it out," Merry noted. "For example, a third party who believes that she is balancing demands based on contradictory rights will define the dispute resolution project differently than one who thinks that she is overcoming misunderstandings. A person who views her task as one of restoring peace, or 'making the balance' will have a different vision of the job than one who defines it as punishing a rulebreaker."[9]

Depending on the case at hand, supposedly distinct techniques may be similar in practice; their adaptiveness and fluidity blurs the boundaries between them. If one compares the ideal type of mediation with the ideal type of court litigation, the differences are stark. But in practice most court cases culminate in plea bargains or negotiated settlements that are not so different from the expected outcomes of mediation. Similarities in form and function exist between processes with antithetical abstract descriptions. It is worth quoting at length the conclusions of Susan Silbey and Sally Merry from their study of the mediation and adjudication of minor disputes:

> After three years of observation in court and mediation, however, we were struck by the ways, despite clear differences, in which these processes were the same. We found that in both arenas third parties develop techniques to manage and contain troubles which come to them as cases. Yet in neither court nor mediation are disputing parties passive recipients or an institutionally defined process, but active participants who struggle to control the situations in which they find themselves. Here, citizens' demands for public intervention in their private conflicts exert an influence on the institutions.
>
> Moreover, we found the distinctions used in the dispute resolution literature between formal and informal, between adjudication and mediation, between coercion and conciliation, inadequate to describe the handling of minor disputes in both the lower courts and mediation alternatives. Instead we found a blending of formal and informal decision making in both settings, sometimes a strict adherence to set procedures irrespective of the parties or the case, while at other times a self-conscious responsiveness to the particularities of individual circumstances. Neither could we describe lower court processes as the imposition of decisions by authoritative third parties and mediation as a two party negotiation aided by a non-authoritative third party. In court, most cases were disposed of through collaborative decision making by a wide array of participants including social workers, police personnel, prosecutors, probation officers and attorneys as well as defendants, victims and judges. In mediation, although third party interveners lack legal authority to impose solutions, they nevertheless generally rely upon claims of authority or manipulation, two distinct forms of power, to forge agreements between disputing parties.[10]

Conclusion

The ADR program makes sense only if one accepts the idea that nonjudicial dispute-processing mechanisms are distinct from judicial ones, that some of these methods are clearly preferable (by some standard) in resolving some types of dispute, and that these disputes can be identified in practice and allocated to the alternative mechanisms. It seems that each assumption is critically deficient. Dispute processes are too flexible and adaptive, boundaries are too blurred, and capacities are too uncertain to be effective in a theory of allocation. There is no real agreement on standards by which an ADR technique would be "preferable," and those that have been proposed — avoidance of the language of right and wrong — are specifically rejected by many disputants.

Some might argue that this account has taken too literally the idea of rationally distributing disputes among processing mechanisms and that it is unlikely that actual ADR reforms would attempt such allocation. But whether or not this allocation is ever likely to be attempted, it provides the theoretical fulcrum of the ADR program, and some ADR proponents do take the idea seriously, at least on a small scale. Once the idea of rational allocation of disputes is discarded, however, the remaining ADR program amounts to little more than a pious wish that disputes would be less acrimonious, complex, and lingering than they are or a coercive urge to force disputants to accept dispute mechanisms that they find less desirable than the present legal system.

NOTES

1. Jethro Lieberman, *The Litigious Society* (New York: Basic Books, 1981), 187.
2. Frank Sander, "Varieties of Dispute Processing," in *Neighborhood Justice*, ed. Roman Tomasic and Malcolm Feeley (New York: Longman, 1982), 37-38.
3. Stephen Goldberg, Eric Green, and Frank Sander, *Dispute Resolution* (Boston: Little, Brown, 1985), 314.
4. Lon Fuller, "The Forms and Limits of Adjudication," *Harvard Law Review* 92 (1978): 365.
5. Sander, "Varieties of Dispute Processing," 26.
6. Ibid.
7. Lynn Mather and Barbara Yngvesson, "Language, Audience and the Transformation of Disputes," *Law and Society Review* 15 (1980-81): 776-77.
8. Sally Merry, "Disputing Without Culture," *Harvard Law Review* 100 (1987): 2062.
9. Ibid., 2064-65.
10. Susan Silbey and Sally Merry, "Interpretive Processes in Mediation and Courts" (manuscript, 1986), 3-4.

A Regulated Market in
Unmatured Tort Claims:
Tort Reform by Contract

ROBERT COOTER
STEPHEN D. SUGARMAN

At any given time, potential and actual accident victims have rights that are determined by the contours of tort law. These rights create bargaining chips that are normally played by a claimant following an accident in return for a financial payment from the injurer or the injurer's insurer. The settlement, of course, exhausts the victim's tort rights. By contrast, only a few victims actually see their tort claims through to a trial in which a court determines their worth.

Potential victims do not ordinarily do anything with their rights; they simply hold onto them until an accident occurs. Indeed, in unusual situations where potential victims have already waived their rights through a preaccident exchange, many courts have been hostile to such deals and have refused to enforce the contract against the victim.[1]

This issue, of course, arises only after an injury has occurred and the injurer seeks to rely on the preaccident release from future tort liability that had been obtained from the victim. Judges rationalize setting aside those private agreements on the ground that they are protecting potential victims from their own ignorance and weakness in bargaining with parties who are better informed and stronger. Such protection is often necessary. But judicial intervention in private arrangements is misguided when it blocks exchanges that improve the position of both victims and injurers.

This essay discusses a potential market in unmatured tort claims that could correct many shortcomings of existing tort law. In brief, it envisions a market in which people who are otherwise adequately insured against accidents will sell their preaccident bargaining chips. This market would function mainly through transactions in which workers with good employee-benefit packages would sell their future tort claims to their employers, who in turn would sell them to (i.e., presettle them with) liability insurers.

Suppose, for example, that an employee misses several weeks of work and requires additional medical attention, because her physician carelessly failed to diagnose a broken arm. When such malpractice occurs today, she can sue the doctor for her lost income, her medical and other expenses, and her pain and suffering. If, however, the employee already has adequate health and temporary disability insurance, she would probably not consider her tort rights all that important to her well-being. For one thing, most of what she stands to recover in a lawsuit would result in double payment, would have to be repaid to her other insurance sources, or would be spent in the costs of litigation. Employees in her position with adequate first-party benefits might be eager to sell their tort rights for an appropriate price before the malpractice case arises.

Suppose that such transactions were respected and that this employee had previously elected to sell her tort rights to her employer. Although she could not sue the doctor, she would be assured of compensation for the medical costs and lost income from this injury (since the validity of the sale would depend on that protection). Because the sale is to the employer, her compensation would almost surely be provided through the regular employee-benefit package. The payment received for the sale of her tort rights would likely take the form of an employee-benefit package that is better or more generous than the benefit packages of fellow employees who retain their tort claims. If employees could dispose of their tort rights in this way, they would consider themselves better off and would not be candidates for judicial paternalism if they became victims of malpractice.

The market in tort claims ought not to end there, however. Assume that the employer, in turn, sells this victim's potential malpractice claims to the doctor's insurer (using the proceeds, at least in part, to fund a better employee-benefit package). When the accident occurs, there is no tort claim, because the doctor's insurer has already settled it in advance. The amount it pays the employer helps determine the amount of the doctor's malpractice insurance premiums.

Many deficiencies of current tort law could be corrected by such a market. If such a socially desirable market could be developed, surely it ought not to be hampered in a misguided attempt to protect the very people who could benefit by it.

The Potential for a Market in Unmatured Tort Claims

At least three deficiencies in current law provide the basis for a market in unmatured tort claims. First, when viewed as a system for compensating accident victims, tort law has many gaps. For example, drivers who suffer identical injuries have similar financial needs, whether the accident was caused by an icy road or by the negligence of another driver; yet the tort system permits recovery in only one of these cases. Most potential victims would prefer to close the gaps in their coverage and be protected against losses of both types. As a practical matter, however, it can be cumbersome to arrange for protection that merely fills in where tort law does not apply. Therefore, many people arrange for first-party protection (through their employer or private insurance). Once they have done so, tort law becomes superfluous in paying their out-of-pocket losses, as it was with the adequately insured employee in the medical-malpractice example described above. Many potential victims with adequate first-party protection would be happy to sell their tort rights to redundant awards for less than the amount that injurers now spend settling lawsuits.

Second, tort damages awarded by courts (or arranged through settlements) are capricious, especially in providing for pain and suffering. This unpredictability is unattractive to potential victims. Few of them seek to buy first-party insurance against pain and suffering. Again, it is reasonable to assume that potential injurers place a higher value on being rid of claims than most potential accident victims place on their rights to sue for such losses and that there is room for the two sides to strike a mutually beneficial deal.

Finally, the legal and related costs of tort disputes account for a high proportion of the stakes. The plaintiff's attorney alone routinely takes a third of the damage award. If these costs could be reduced or avoided, both injurers and victims could benefit.

Together these three deficiencies of the tort system afford considerable potential for a mutually beneficial exchange. A properly regulated market in such exchanges could reallocate legal rights to the advantage of both injurers and victims.

The Proposed Market

The primary participants in such a regulated market, although not necessarily the only participants, would be employers and insurance companies. The employers would buy up the preaccident bargaining chips of their employees, who are all potential tort victims. The only reason for them to want to buy their employees' tort rights against third parties would be to resell them to potential injurers and their insurance companies. Such a cash sale would effectively leave tort claims "presettled." (Since employers would probably not want to wind up with leftover claims, which would be inconvenient to press in court, their purchases from employees might be made contingent on resale. In this sense, the employer would be, in effect, the employee's agent.)

If a victim were certain to be adequately insured, courts would have no reason to invalidate bargains in which he waived his tort rights, any more than other kinds of bargains that are routinely enforced. The major "regulation" of this market, therefore, would be making the sale of unmatured tort claims conditional on the availability of other adequate compensation arrangements of a sort described below. To facilitate such exchanges, it must be clear that courts will enforce such contracts, so judicial cooperation is necessary if the market is to get off the ground.

Here is how this market might work. An employer could offer its employees a choice between two options. One plan would leave tort rights in place as they are, along with whatever health and income-replacement insurance the employer provides. In the other option, the employee would cede unmatured tort claims to the employer in exchange for either cash (in the form of higher wages or lower employee contributions to the benefit plan) or benefits, such as a higher income-replacement rate, lower health-plan deductibles or coinsurance obligations, and added health-care benefits like outpatient mental-health treatment and dental care. Details of the two plans would be worked out, as usual, by unions or other employee representatives.

Why involve employers in such a market? Why not have consumers negotiate directly with insurers? There are several reasons. First, employers have more bargaining power with liability insurers than individual employees would. Second, employers could dispose of the bargaining chips in mass quantities, and so more efficiently. Not only could employers get more money for those rights than employees acting alone, but they might also be better able to demand that insurers police the safety efforts of the potential injurers who are their clients. Third, employers already provide packages of health and disability benefits, and augmenting those benefits is the most sensible way to compensate employees for waiving their rights to sue. By integrating the added benefits into existing packages, employers could better approximate the kind of coverage their particular workers preferred.

The interests of employees would be protected in this system in several ways. First, the contemplated transfer of tort rights would be voluntary; courts would disallow arrangements in which the waiver of future tort claims against third parties is a requisite of employment. Second, the employers' bargaining power, together with potential competition in the market for tort rights, should help ensure that employees' tort rights fetch their full market value when sold. For example, if the injurer's insurance company refused to offer full value for the tort rights of potential victims, some other buyer (perhaps a law firm) might purchase them instead and press the claims as they mature. Indeed, the fear that tort rights will be snapped up at auction by successful plaintiffs' lawyers should help convince insurers to bid generously for the rights. In addition, employers would be motivated by self-interest to make the plan work well. They would be allowed to take a profit by selling the rights for more than they had invested. The wish to maximize the number of employees who chose the sale option, as well as ordinary concern for employee satisfaction, would give employers reason to make sure workers wind up better off. Finally, employers are themselves defendants in tort cases involving other companies' employees. By participating in the grand scheme, they could foresee a reduction in the cost of their own liability-insurance premiums and the burdens of defending against tort claims. Their own insurers would be presettling their tort liability by buying up other people's unmatured tort claims.

The advantage to liability-insurance companies would be considerable. By presettling claims, insurers would reduce the uncertainty of their obligations and save the transaction costs that they would have incurred from handling claims. Both factors would give liability insurers an incentive to buy up as many claims as they could.

Injurers would still pay for the harm they cause, and, as they do when they buy insurance today, they would continue to pay in advance. But they would pay less under the proposed market plan because of the savings in transactions costs.

Handling Less Serious Injuries

Personal-injury claimants can be classified into two groups — the 10 percent with serious injuries and the other 90 percent. Serious injuries may be defined as those in which the victim is disabled for more than six months, permanently impaired, or seriously disfigured.[2]

It seems that if people could be assured reasonable protection against the income loss and medical expenses caused by these less serious injuries, most of them would be prepared to dispose fully of their right to bring a tort suit for such harm. By selling their tort rights in such cases, people would mainly be surrendering compensation for pain and suffering. There are several reasons people would likely be willing to trade away such rights. First, people do not ordinarily seek to buy direct "first-party" insurance against pain and suffering from nonserious injuries. Second, while this suffering is very real for a time, it is generally a distant memory by the time compensation arrives. Third, much of what is presently paid ends up not in the victim's hands but in those of his lawyer. Under the proposed arrangements, money for a lawyer will no longer be necessary. Fourth, the right to claim such losses under today's tort system generates many nuisance claims and exaggerated charges that are ultimately demoralizing and costly to those who file genuine claims and ultimately demeaning to those who do not.

In less serious injury cases, moreover, there should be little trouble showing that the employee's insurance is adequate to cover the health and disability loss, the precondition for upholding tort claim sale. A rule of thumb might be to require that a victim have substantially complete coverage for at least six months of out-of-pocket losses. Were the details simply left to common-law development, courts might inquire as to what employee-benefit and insurance-company experts agreed were quality benefit packages and uphold tort-rights sales when the victim had at least that level of coverage. Legislative or regulatory participation in the definition of "adequate insurance" could, of course, lead to quicker agreement on the precise minimum.

Plans with reasonable deductibles and coinsurance provisions would presumably be allowed. For income replacement, these plans might mean, for example, that employees could be asked to use their accumulated sick leave for the first week of their disability; that wages (after taxes) need be replaced only at, say, an 85 percent basis; and that wages need be replaced up to only, say, twice the state average. For medical expenses, employees could be responsible for a $100 deductible or 10 to 20 percent coinsurance payments. In short, as long as employees receive high quality first-party protection, courts would be justified in validating the sale of their tort rights, even if some small portion of those out-of-pocket losses, which would have been compensated by tort-damages law, is left uncovered.

In fact, most employers (especially those of large and medium size) already guarantee their employees medical coverage for less serious injuries and, similarly, already have well-developed sick-leave and temporary-disability insurance plans. In such cases, employees do not need to be brought up to a higher standard of protection as part of their payment for waiving their tort rights. Rather, they might be free to take more direct compensation by lowered employee contributions to the employee-benefit package, outright cash payments (possibly as higher wages), or new benefits beyond the legal minimum.

Once the market is functioning, employers should not have too much trouble reselling employee tort rights for less serious injuries. The appropriate buyers in the case of medical-malpractice claims would be easy to identify, since in any single locale there are typically few active liability insurers of doctors and hospitals. Indeed, where employees belong to health maintenance organizations through their workplace, the employer already has a direct contractual arrangement with potential medical-malpractice defendants. In such situations the health-care provider could, in effect, reduce the premiums it charged the employer for its health plan in exchange for waivers of tort liability from the participating employees. Other exchanges might create a new class of intermediaries who, for example, might form enterprises to purchase employees' unmatured tort claims for resale to manufacturers or, more likely, their insurers.

In the case of automobile accidents, employers might also deal directly with the liability-insurance carriers on behalf of their employees. Once again, in most locales relatively few automobile-liability insurers dominate the market. Another possibility would be for employees with adequate work-based protection to deal directly with their own automobile-insurance company. They could choose between an insurance policy that left their own tort rights intact and a policy that charged less in exchange for transferring to their own insurer their tort rights in less serious automobile accidents. For the latter policy, the insurer would in turn presettle future claims against other drivers' insurance companies. Once the system was set in motion, two insurance companies could trade the future claims of their policyholders against each other. By this method, private agreement could largely dispense with the tort system for less serious automobile accidents. For victims of such accidents a no-fault automobile-insurance scheme would, in effect, be put into place by private contract.

Some people may want to have their first-party protection for accidents attached to their automobile-insurance policy rather than their employment package. This seems an unlikely choice for anyone covered by adequate employee benefits. Hence, one would expect this to be a residual route to be taken primarily by those who do not have either adequate employee benefits or government benefits (such as Medicare) but who do own automobiles.

Serious Injuries

Separate consideration is required for the remaining 10 percent of injuries defined as serious. A traditional, otherwise generous employee-benefit package may not provide enough first-party protection for injuries that seriously disfigure, impair, or disable someone for more than six months. Therefore, a new and higher level of "adequate insurance" would be needed before sales of tort rights would be enforceable. There are two issues here. First, when employees suffer long-term disabilities, their health- and disability-insurance plans may not provide a high degree of out-of-pocket protection. Many employers that provide income protection against short-term employee disability do not provide protection against long-term disability. Furthermore, the person with a serious disability may stop working and thereby cease to participate in the health plan routinely provided to continuing employees. Without such protection, courts might not see it as sensible for workers to waive tort compensation and might refuse to uphold the sale of unmatured tort claims.

It is less clear, however, whether or not most employers would be willing to make the necessary insurance benefits available to their employees. Some currently do offer, or make available for purchase, both long-term disability income protection and continued access to the enterprise's group health plan for disabled former employees; they could thus satisfy the "adequate insurance" condition with little or no change in their existing program. These employers might be likely candidates to buy and resell the tort claims of employees for serious, as well as transient, injuries. An alternative arrangement might develop, however. While employers might be the ones to buy up less serious injury claims from their employees, insurers themselves (possibly working through unions or other employee groups) might organize efforts to buy up prospective serious-injury tort claims.

The second issue raises another complication. In serious-injury cases, many more people might insist on compensation that goes beyond out-of-pocket expenses before consenting to sell their tort rights. Therefore, at least at the outset, reasonable coverage for serious injury itself should probably be part of the "adequate insurance" definition for serious-injury cases. People would probably not, however, insist on an individualized, after-the-fact benefit determination of the kind that tort law now makes. Most would likely be content with some predictable, predetermined, generous but not extravagant schedule of benefits. One place to look for a comparison is in the accidental death and dismemberment policies that many employers sell or provide to their employees, which provide so much for loss of a finger, so much for loss of a hand, and the like. Another place to look is to workers' compensation; most states insist that benefits, in cases of permanent or partial disability, be provided for the impairment itself. In general, therefore, an insurance policy (or other arrangement) with payoff schedules similar to these examples ought to be deemed adequate to support the sale of unmatured serious tort claims.

Will Markets in Tort Claims Actually Work?

Once functioning, the market for unmatured tort claims could be even broader, extending perhaps to such torts as defamation or invasion of privacy. On the other hand, the market might be less active than its supporters may hope. At least in the beginning, many people might be reluctant to presell their tort rights or might wish to sell only the rights to relatively minor claims.

A full market in unmatured tort claims for serious injuries might be considerably slower to take off. Meanwhile, people might begin to sell portions of their stake in such cases as part of the same transaction in which they sell rights concerning less serious injuries. For example, people might agree not to claim damages for losses covered by other sources of payment, not to seek pain and suffering damages of more than $150,000, and to waive their jury trial rights with respect to punitive damages. Since giving up these rights would enhance the worth of what employees were otherwise selling, they should realize more value for them. But unlike the complete sale of unmatured tort claims for serious injuries, the sale of such partial rights would not have to be linked to any guaranteed level of first-party protection. For even after such a sale, seriously injured victims could still sue in tort for uncompensated income losses and out-of-pocket expenses and for substantial general damages; judges would reasonably consider this to be adequate protection. At the same time, the ability to buy up partial claims, especially of the most unpredictable portions of liability, could appeal to liability insurers.

This essay has thus far concentrated on personal injury problems, but property damage is plainly another area ready for a market in unmatured tort rights. That market might operate best, however, through enterprises that now provide homeowners' and automobile insurance. Individually sold insurance policies are currently the main source of property-damage protection, unlike protection against physical injury, which is covered mainly by employee-benefit plans and social insurance. Such markets might operate similarly to the market previously described.

The goal of this essay is not to anticipate fully this imagined market's operation but to suggest how it might improve on the current allocation of tort rights. If officials were convinced of the case for such improvement, they might overcome their hostility to the waiver of tort claims and instead direct their energies to determining what level of insurance should be required of those who sell such claims. Although various definitions of "adequate insurance" have been suggested, many subtleties might eventually be taken into account in setting such standards, whether through legislative, administrative, or judicial decisions.

Another matter deserving brief mention is the quality of information that potential victims must be given about the tort rights that they sell. It is widely thought that consumers today do not have enough information to evaluate limitations on liability and waivers of tort rights that might appear in standard-form contracts for the purchase of consumer goods. The failure of the market to inform consumers is so severe that courts quite rightly will not generally enforce such limits. The proposals described here would not involve allowing manufacturers to include such waivers in most consumer contracts, since consumers could not be expected, in their direct dealings with manufacturers, to be made aware of the value of what they are giving up. Such contracts would still not generally be enforceable. A market organized through employers, however, would largely avoid these problems. Employees have a much better chance to look over a single plan for injury coverage rationally, the better to understand what they are gaining and forfeiting by the sale of their tort claims.

Liability insurers might find it appealing to band together to buy claims collectively and save on negotiating costs. If the market develops into what economists call a monopsony — one powerful buyer, many weak sellers — antitrust principles would be invoked to restrain market power. In any event, smaller insurers may find that they can compete only by pooling their buying efforts; such group activity would presumably be permitted.

Another problem involves "moral hazard" — the tendency of people to change their behavior when they are relieved of liability. At least two issues of moral hazard arise in the sort of market proposed here. First, after an injury victim sells his tort claims, he no longer has an incentive to participate in pressing them. The buyer of an employee's tort rights would not find them worth much if the employee was unwilling to help the buyer press a matured claim in court. This kind of problem, however, will not scuttle the proposal, because there are good ways to obtain cooperation were it needed. Buyers could come up with financial inducements or contractual clauses that would lead injury victims to participate in suits brought to enforce rights they have sold. Besides, when claims are finally sold to liability insurers, there is no longer the need for a lawsuit for the victim to assist.

A more serious problem could be that the presettlement of tort claims would erode incentives for injurers to take precautions. The reduction of precautionary effort is, of course, a cost of virtually any insurance system. There are a number of devices that counter this tendency, including coinsurance, deductibles, and experience rating. All of these devices would be available in the market proposed here. The value of an unmatured tort claim depends both on the probability that an accident will happen and on its severity. If a manufacturer relaxed its quality control in response to the presettlement of its tort claims so that more hazardous products found their way into the marketplace, it would soon find that the value of unmatured tort claims against it had increased. When those claims were presettled, insurers would have to pay more and in turn would demand higher premiums from the manufacturer in future years. This feedback mechanism would give a manufacturer a continuing incentive to maintain quality control.

A brisk market depends on the parties' ability to determine the value of the rights that are being exchanged. What should the insurers be willing to pay to presettle tort claims? And how should they allocate those costs to their insureds? Determining how much a large group of employees could gain from matured pressed tort claims would enable an employer to establish what insurers would have to pay to avoid that liability. Presumably, statistics and the market would combine to allocate that burden among the insurers and defendants. Once this market began, and as long as a significant part of the tort system were still functioning, there would be adequate information available on the likelihood and worth of any large group of employees' tort claims.

Since some people are more likely than others to be tort victims, their rights are worth more, in principle. Yet highly individualized compensation between employers and employees is unlikely. Faced with standardized alternatives, the employees whose tort rights are most valuable will be the least inclined to sell them. Although eager sellers have less valuable rights to sell, and the buyer cannot set prices individually, the problem of adverse selection seems no more severe here than in other insurance markets.

Precedents

The idea of selling unmatured tort claims through employers to liability insurers may seem strange, but the notion of trading in tort rights has been advanced in many creative ways in recent years.

Most prominently, over the past fifteen years Professor Jeffrey O'Connell has proposed a great variety of elective no-fault schemes in which victims would trade their tort rights for a package of no-fault benefits that covered their out-of-pocket losses. Although some of O'Connell's proposals focus on deals that might be made *after* an accident,[3] others foresee exchanges beforehand. Among his proposals, for example, is one for a series of direct, voluntary, preaccident exchanges between potential victims and potential injurers, such as product sellers and physicians; in return for agreeing in advance not to sue, the victim would be entitled to specified no-fault compensation from the injurer if he is later hurt in ways covered by the contract.[4] The most important difference between this idea and the proposal of this essay is that the proposal here does not call for postaccident payment from injurer to victim.

Another O'Connell proposal calls for potential victims to sell broad tort rights to first-party insurers in exchange for a guarantee of income and medical-expense protection that would cover all accidents.[5] Again, there is an important difference: in the O'Connell plan, on the occasion of a tort, the first-party insurer would file a claim against the injurer or his insurer. Even if these claims were expeditiously settled among insurers, the settlements would have to be reached after accidents occur, thereby reviving the same difficult individualized determinations of fault, cause, and damages that plague the current system. Moreover, whereas the O'Connell plan emphasizes private first-party insurers as the buyers of tort rights and the providers of compensation, the proposal of this essay instead foresees employers' performing those functions. Of course, employers might well call on the products and services of first-party insurers to put together and underwrite employee-benefit packages.

In one specific area, O'Connell has made a proposal that is even closer to the one advanced here. He has envisioned the preaccident transfer of work-related products-liability claims from workers to product manufacturers, in a transaction that involves employers.[6] His basic idea here is that the manufacturers can pay for the unmatured tort claims with lower prices for their products, the benefit of which can be passed on, at least in part, to the employees. O'Connell assumes that, since employers already enjoy workers' compensation protection for such accidents, many of them would be willing to make this exchange. And where existing workers' compensation was considered inadequate, the employees could bargain for stronger across-the-board, employer-provided, workers' compensation benefits. This idea is designed only to cover job-related product injuries, not personal injuries generally.

The proposal outlined here goes farther in the direction taken by O'Connell, with a correspondingly more sweeping potential to end the need for postaccident wrangling between the side of the injurer (including his insurer) and the side of the victim (including his benefit provider).

Implementation Problems

Judges who find the arguments of this essay persuasive could, acting on their own, fashion a doctrine under which adequate insurance against a loss would defeat the presumption against enforcing bargains to sell unmatured tort claims. This route, however, would be much slower than legislation. In most states the courts would have to wait for an attempted sale of tort rights before passing on the idea. The haze of legal uncertainty, however, may prevent a market for tort claims from ever getting off the ground. A clear signal from the legislature, by contrast, might induce a quick response from markets. Furthermore, legislation can specify at the outset what will constitute "adequate insurance" — or at least establish an administrative agency that would adopt regulations to that end.

One difficulty with such legislation is that courts may still, out of misplaced sympathy for accident victims, allow them to recover in spite of a previous sale of tort claims. But there is reason to hope this would not happen. A prime source of sympathy, after all, is the fear that victims will go uncompensated. Under current rules of evidence, the knowledge that a victim has access to "collateral sources" of compensation is generally kept out of the courtroom. Yet under the proposal to market tort claims, since the courts would have to decide the adequacy of insurance, evidence about collateral sources would not only be admissible but would be the focus of the trial.

Serious political problems may interfere with such a legislative initiative. The coalition of insurers and manufacturers might favor the proposal, but they would have to turn their attention away from their current agenda of simply trying to roll back victim rights. Many of them may feel sufficiently optimistic about the prospects of outright victory in that roll-back campaign to dampen their enthusiasm for a plan that would merely provide more efficient resolution of existing claims. Moreover, even if most businesses and professional groups found the proposal an improvement on the current system, some, especially those that now have poor employee benefits, might fear that the plan would put new upward pressures on their labor costs. Finally, the interests of the defense bar might not coincide with those of the firms they represent.

Potential accident victims are not well organized politically. The plaintiffs' bar, which purports to represent them, will naturally be the chief losers in the proposed market for tort claims and can be expected to attack it in any public debate.

Consumer and labor interests might be receptive to the proposal, but they would have to forsake their current coalition with the plaintiffs' bar. In all, substantial political obstacles must be overcome before legislation could be passed to facilitate the proposal outlined here.

Conclusion

The idea of an employer-mediated regulated market in unmatured tort claims is worth consideration on its own merits, but it can also shed light on what society wants its injury-compensation system to look like. Such a market, if it worked as outlined above, would come to resemble a regime of universal first-party benefits structured to replace all or part of the tort system. If a consensus were to emerge about where an efficient tort-claims market would lead, one might be able to achieve that result directly through legislative action — leaving both injured and injurers as well off substantively as they would be in an efficiently functioning market but with even more of a savings in transactions costs.[7]

NOTES

1. See, e.g., *Tunkl v. Regents of University of California*, 60 Cal. 2d 92, 32 Cal. Rptr. 33, 383 P.2d 441 (1963) and *Henrioulle v. Marin Ventures, Inc.* 20 Cal. 3d 512, 143 Cal. Rptr. 247, 573 P.2d 465 (1978).

2. A similar definition of "less serious injuries" is used, for example, in Michigan's automobile no-fault scheme. When combined with the first-party benefits under that plan, it has removed an estimated 89 percent of bodily injury claims from the tort system. See James Hammit and John Rolph, "Limiting Liability for Automobile Accidents: Are No-Fault Tort Thresholds Effective?," *Law and Policy* 7 (1985): 1, 7. That is the basis of the 90 percent and 10 percent figures in the text.

3. See, e.g., Jeffrey O'Connell, "A 'Neo No-Fault' Contract in Lieu of Tort: Preaccident Guarantees of Post Accident Settlement Offers," *California Law Review* 73 (May 1985): 898–916.

4. See, e.g., O'Connell, "Expanding No-fault Beyond Auto Insurance: Some Proposals," *Virginia Law Review* 59 (May 1973): 749–829.

5. See O'Connell, "Harnessing the Liability Lottery: Elective First-Party No-Fault Insurance Financed by Third-Party Claims," *Washington University Law Quarterly* 4 (Fall 1978): 693–712; O'Connell and Janet Beck, "Overcoming Legal Barriers to the Transfer of Third-Party Tort Claims as a Means of Financing First-Party No-Fault Insurance," *Washington University Law Quarterly* 58: 1 (1979): 55–83; and O'Connell and Craig Brown, "A Canadian Proposal for No-Fault Benefits Financed by Assignment of Tort Rights," *University of Toronto Law Journal* 33 (1983): 434–59. See also O'Connell, "Transferring Injured Victims' Tort Rights to No-Fault Insurers: New Sole Remedy Approaches to Cure Liability Insurance Ills," *University of Illinois Law Forum* 3 (1977): 749–809.

6. See O'Connell, "Bargaining for Waivers of Third-Party Tort Claims: An Answer to Product Liability Woes for Employers and the Employees and Suppliers," *Insurance Law Journal* no. 644 (September 1976): 530–55; idem., "Transferring Injured Victims' Tort Rights to No-Fault Insurers: New Sole Remedy Approaches to Cure Liability Insurance Ills," *University of Illinois Law Forum* 3 (1977): 749–809; and idem., "The Interlocking Death and Rebirth of Contract and Tort," *Michigan Law Review* 75 (March 1977): 659–85. See also Clark Havighurst, "Private Reform of Tort-Law Dogma: Market Opportunities and Legal Obstacles," *Law and Contemporary Problems* 49 (Spring 1986): 143–72.

7. For a proposed legislative reform of tort law that would leave accident victims in largely the same position they would be in if the market proposed in this essay were really in operation, see Stephen D. Sugarman, "Serious Tort Law Reform," *San Diego Law Review* 24 (1987): 795–849; and "Taking Advantage of the Tort Law Crisis," *Ohio State Law Journal* 48 (1987): 329–63.

Neo-No-Fault: A Fair-Exchange Proposal for Tort Reform

The current tort-liability system in the United States cries out for reform. Its laborious and uncertain workings inflict a great deal of personal trauma on both injured parties and defendants. Its excessive legal costs and undue delays are largely responsible for the skyrocketing of liability-insurance rates. It is increasingly viewed by the very people whose behavior it is supposed to regulate as a game of chance in which factors other than the law and the evidence influence the outcome of cases, a perception that compromises the integrity of the system's role in punishing fault and deterring unreasonably hazardous behavior.

More important, the system's haphazard manner of making decisions has undercut its ability to provide fair compensation to the injured. Some victims recover far more than their economic losses, while others who are similarly injured recover nothing at all. This problem is intensified by the awarding of "noneconomic" damages for pain and suffering or grief. The irrationality of fixing a monetary value for nonmonetary losses encourages claimants to play on juries' sympathies, thus further removing the controversy from the issues of fault and accurate compensation.

That only a small fraction of claims actually go to trial in no way lessens the severity of these problems. Both claimants and defendants assess settlement prospects in light of the likely outcome of litigation. As a result, both sides incur the same types of costs and delays in evaluating claims whether or not the claims ever reach court. While a model system of insurance would provide for settlement of typical claims by prompt, periodic payment of actual economic losses, the unpredictable and intensely adversarial nature of tort-liability suits makes such settlements the exception rather than the rule.

The author is grateful for the expert research assistance of Edmund D. Graff, University of Virginia Law School, class of 1989.

Inadequate Reforms

The obvious question is: What shape should tort reform take? The insurance industry and its institutional clients — businesses, health-care providers, and state and local governments — urge new laws that would curtail what they perceive as the excesses of the present tort system. All fifty states have considered such reforms, and more than a third of the states have enacted some form of limitation on liability. Specifically, these reforms either make it harder to sue or pay injured parties less when they win. In the first category are laws that:

1. Raise the standard of liability by requiring claimants, for example, to prove the defendant's fault by a higher standard of proof ("clear and convincing evidence").
2. Cap claimants' lawyers' contingency fees on a sliding scale of, say, 40 percent of the first $50,000, declining to 10 percent of any recovery above $200,000.
3. Revise the doctrine of "joint and several liability," under which if two or more defendants contributed to an injury either can be held fully liable for all the claimant's damages, even if its contribution was marginal. (This often occurs when the principal culprit in the injury is underinsured and "judgment-proof.") Under the most common revision, a defendant's share of noneconomic damages is limited to its share of blame.
4. Shorten the time permitted to file a claim under the statute of limitations.
5. Punish those who file "frivolous" or wholly unfounded claims.

In the second category are laws that:

1. Cap pain and suffering awards at, for example, $100,000, $250,000, or $500,000.
2. Eliminate or severely curb the amount of punitive damages.
3. Deduct from the award against the defendant the amount already payable to the claimant from "collateral sources," such as health or disability insurance.

While these reforms might temporarily alleviate the most visible symptoms of the present crisis, the high prices and unavailability of liability insurance, they do not address the system's underlying problems. To all but the insurance industry and the institutions it insures, the least appealing way to reform the tort system is to make it even harder for injury victims to be paid. Even if the number of tort cases stopped rising and liability insurance became readily available, the tort system would still require fundamental change from the point of view of injured persons.

The costs and delays of tort litigation are a burden not only to injury victims but to everyone else. Every consumer of goods and services pays the costs of litigation in the form of higher prices, and every citizen pays the cost of government-liability litigation in higher taxes.

Since a large share of these funds go directly into the pockets of trial lawyers, it is not hard to understand why that group defends the present system. But equally clear is the folly of many consumer groups in aligning themselves with this position. Consumer advocates ought to oppose changes that simply make it harder for injured parties to gain compensation, but they ought not to support a system that already makes it much too hard for the injured to collect insurance dollars. Even trial lawyers must concede this difficulty by way of justifying their practice of charging a third or more of a cash award to help get it.

In support of their position, trial lawyers argue that it is logical to require providers of defective goods or services to pay for the injuries they cause. Even aside from the question whether producers really pay (since they pass the cost of insurance along to consumers), the underlying problem is that most injuries arise in complex circumstances. Unraveling the cause-and-effect relationship between the design of a malfunctioning product and the injury it allegedly causes, or between a medical procedure and the deterioration of a patient who was already ill, can be extremely difficult if not impossible. Even much simpler events, like automobile accidents, are often too ambiguous in their circumstances for the law to determine who is "at fault." The increasing use of competing "experts" in malpractice and product cases has added to the already high cost of litigation without in any way guaranteeing the accuracy of the resulting determinations.

Further compounding the complexity of the average case is the practice of allowing injured parties to recover for not only medical expenses and wage losses but also noneconomic losses, such as pain and suffering. Lawyers prepare and present elaborate evidence of the claimant's hardship beyond the evidence already produced to establish fault. But no rational economic value can be assigned to physical pain. There is no market value for a jury to go on. So claimants' lawyers do their utmost to win juries' sympathies, thereby further distorting the issue of fault and increasing the uncertainties, and therefore the costs, of litigation.

It is easy to see why the liability-insurance system is so costly, cumbersome, and unstable, compared with the systems of health, life, and fire insurance. Its outlays depend on the mysterious and even indeterminate answers to a complex series of questions: Was the client at fault? Would the injury have happened anyway? What price tag should be put on anguish? While the liability crisis has brought the issue of tort reform to the center of the public forum, the case for a fundamental restructuring of the system goes far beyond the need to make insurance momentarily affordable or available. Any reform that fails to deal with the fundamental uncertainties of measuring fault and pain is doomed to failure.

No-Fault Reforms:
Workers' Compensation and Automobile-Accident Models

Problems similar to those in tort liability today led to the enactment of a form of no-fault insurance for workplace accidents in Germany in the 1880s, in Great Britain in the 1890s, and in the United States between about 1910 and 1920. Workers' compensation pays a worker injured on the job without requiring him to go to court to prove the employer's fault or his own lack of fault. In place of lengthy litigation, the worker automatically gets reimbursed for all medical costs and a substantial share of lost wages, generally a half to two-thirds in blue-collar cases. As a trade-off, the system makes no payment for pain and suffering or other noneconomic losses. Thus the system does away with the two issues that plague tort liability—fault and the value of pain and suffering. The result, though possibly less appealing to a feeling of rough justice than forcing malefactors to compensate victims for their suffering, amounts to a viable insurance system.

Of course, there are problems with workers' compensation. Like any reform, it does not work as well as the reformers had hoped. For example, there has been much litigation over the scope of the provision limiting eligible accidents to those on the job or "arising out of and in the course of employment." Even so, workers' compensation has worked far better than the tort system in doing what an insurance system is ultimately supposed to do—compensating victims promptly and without undue fuss.

Many reformers have worked to extend the system of no-fault compensation to the area of automobile accidents. The example of New York State, which combines the no-fault and traditional tort systems, startlingly illustrates the superiority of no-fault in securing high coverage at low cost. According to a U.S. Department of Transportation study, consumers paid an average annual premium of $46 in 1983 under New York's no-fault system. These premiums paid for all medical expenses and wage losses up to a combined total of $50,000 per case. New York also allows claims based on fault in the much smaller number of cases where a victim dies, is disabled for at least ninety days, or suffers some other serious injury. By state law, motorists must carry tort-liability insurance against such lawsuits, providing coverage of at least $10,000 a person and $20,000 for each accident. In 1983, the average premium for such liability coverage was $118.[1] In other words, tort-liability insurance, often with low limits and disputed payments, can cost about twice as much as no-fault insurance with high limits and automatic payments. Similar data could be cited from other no-fault states.[2]

The relative success of no-fault insurance in compensating the victims of workplace and automobile accidents makes it a promising solution to the problems of other forms of tort liability. Unfortunately, there are real difficulties in extending no-fault principles to other types of accidents. For example, if someone is in good physical and mental health before an automobile accident and comes out of it with a concussion or brain damage the cause of the injury is apparent. But suppose someone vacationing at the beach trips on the boardwalk and hits his head on a surfboard. Under a no-fault system, who should pay for the injury? The local or state government? The contractor who built the boardwalk? The owner of the surfboard? Its manufacturer? The store that just sold the victim new boat shoes? The travel agent? Or suppose someone is rushed to the hospital for an appendectomy and returns home a few days later with an injured back. Should the hospital pay? The doctor? The ambulance driver? The manufacturer of the ambulance or hospital bed? Causation can be just as problematic as fault. Thus, in a no-fault system, it may be impossible to make a rational determination of who should bear the cost of an injury that develops from complex circumstances.

The Fair-Exchange Answer

These problems do not mean, however, that society must abandon all efforts to extend no-fault principles into more complex areas and resign itself to the ills of the tort-liability system, whether in its current form or with prodefendant reforms. The key to the effectiveness of both workers' compensation and automobile no-fault is balance. In order to gain the advantages of compensation for economic loss without the lengthy struggle of litigation, the injured party gives up the opportunity to pursue the possible recovery of noneconomic damages. At the same time, the party threatened with liability gives up its opportunity to pursue a verdict in which it would pay less than the full economic loss or even nothing at all. Each side yields something and in the exchange ultimately benefits. While a complete no-fault system for more complex accidents may not be feasible, a less sweeping proposal could embody at least some of the trade-offs that make no-fault insurance effective.

There are two criteria for successful reform of the tort system. First, it should be made easier for injured parties to be paid promptly for economic loss without litigating the fault of products, services, or persons (including themselves). Second, liability costs should be kept stable or even lowered by offsetting any increase in new claims with a reduction in the costs of litigation and payments for noneconomic loss.

Proposals being made by the insurance industry and its allies do not meet these criteria. Unilateral restrictions on pain and suffering awards, contingent fees, joint and several liability, and the like would simply cut the high cost of liability insurance by putting an even greater burden on injured victims. Proposals for a sweeping extension of no-fault principles would have the opposite drawback: they would help rectify the difficulty of receiving compensation, but, by requiring insurers to pay an indeterminate number of new claims, would worsen the problem of insurance cost and availability.

The legislation proposed here embodies both criteria for successful reform. Under the proposed law, the alleged perpetrator of a tort would have the option of offering to pay the claimant's net economic loss, in periodic payments as incurred. The offer would have to be made within 180 days of the claim (a short period, compared with the duration of a tort case).

If a defendant made this offer of prompt payment of economic loss, under the proposed law, the claimant would in most cases be forced to accept it and would be foreclosed from further pursuit of a tort claim.[3] There are two exceptions in which a plaintiff could refuse the offer and pursue the normal course of tort litigation. One would be if the defendant intentionally caused the injury. The other would be if the victim's economic losses were minimal.

The settlement offer, to be binding, would have to cover all medical expenses (including rehabilitation) and wage losses not already covered by "collateral sources" like health or disability insurance. This collateral-source offset reflects the proposal's focus not so much on punishment as on insurance; its chief aim is to compensate those who need it most rather than to penalize fault. For like reasons, the settlement offer would have to provide a reasonable hourly fee for the claimant's lawyer, including reasonable expenses and cost of obtaining legal advice about the offer itself. This provision is necessary to ensure that injured victims recoup the full amount of their out-of-pocket loss. Requiring victims to pay these costs would force them to subtract unavoidable and sometimes sizable outlays from their recovery of economic loss. Under the present tort system, attorney's fees are often paid out of noneconomic damages,[4] and juries are often thought to boost the amount of noneconomic recovery they award to cover these fees.

Such settlements would likely be less generous than successful jury verdicts, since they would exclude noneconomic damages. But they would be more generous than the benefits payable under most health-insurance policies, which are subject to coverage limits and do not generally pay rehabilitation costs. The vast majority of victims would likely view these benefits as far more favorable than the present tort system. Most people who have been seriously injured have little taste for a lottery to decide whether their medical expenses and wage loss are to be covered or a prolonged struggle that constantly reminds them of their misfortune and exposes them to an opposing counsel who may portray them, in so many words or not, as cheats or liars. Such battles may be acceptable to the lawyers who orchestrate them and make a handsome living even if only a few of their cases succeed, but their clients hate and fear the process, especially when the course of their entire life can hinge on the outcome. Given the choice between prompt payment of real losses and a gamble for possible payment of greater sums in the distant future, all but a few injury victims would probably choose the former.

The proposal, however, would not require any defendant to make such a settlement offer. Such a requirement would place unmanageable new burdens on defendants and encourage baseless suits. If no such offer were made, the current tort system, including recovery for noneconomic losses, would be available to injured victims. Some will object that this asymmetry unfairly advantages defendants: it allows them to settle for economic loss when they would be forced to pay more in a trial, but it never forces them to settle for economic loss when they would have to pay less. In practice, however, most defendants will probably be eager to settle for economic loss even in many cases where their liability is uncertain. They will take into account the huge cost of defending tort cases and the risk that a jury will surprise everyone with a large award for pain and suffering. A prominent malpractice defense lawyer has opined that if such a neo-no-fault plan were in effect, he would advise his clients to offer to pay claimants' net economic losses in 200 of the 250 cases then being handled by his office.[5]

But if both parties would indeed prefer prompt settlement for economic loss, why are such settlements uncommon today? After all, no legal obstacle precludes private agreements of this kind. There are two answers. First, as noted above, lawyers' incentives to do well for their clients often conflict with their incentives to do well for themselves. The possibility of receiving a third or more of a huge recovery for an award that includes payment for pain and suffering may be enough to tip the balance away from settlement. The costs of delay are not felt as keenly by the lawyer, who has money stored up from other cases, as by his client. And the psychological costs of going to trial weigh far heavier on the client than on the lawyer; some lawyers may welcome trial experience and the reputational boost it can provide. In addition, the nature of the settlement process is such that an offer by either party to settle early for net economic loss is viewed as a sign of weakness, leading the other party to believe that the ultimate outcome of litigation will be even more favorable. By requiring—or at least inducing—both sides to settle early, the proposed law foils the strategic behavior that precludes the optimal result for probably the majority of claimants and defendants.

When a settlement offer was accepted, a defendant would have thirty days to pay any unreimbursed losses already incurred by the plaintiff and would make similar payments for further losses as they accrued. If the parties agreed, however, a court-approved lump sum could be substituted for these continuing payments. In such cases, the court would also be empowered to prevent the plaintiff from dissipating the lump sum and being left penniless later.

Under the proposed law, as now, the parties could agree to a settlement of less than full economic loss. It would probably be impossible, even if it were desirable, to prevent people from making separate agreements. But such a lesser offer by the defendant would obviously not be binding on the claimant, and the claimant would have the right to reject it and pursue a claim in court.

The proposal further provides that any party that believes itself at risk of liability for an event could make an early offer. The party doing so could designate any third party who may also be potentially liable as a participant in the settlement. For example, a hospital seeking to avoid a malpractice suit could make a tender of economic loss to an injured patient and name as a third party the doctor who treated the patient or the company that produced a surgical instrument used in the treatment. Being named a participant in a settlement offer would in no way disadvantage the third party, who would be thereby protected from exposure to payment of noneconomic damages. Also, a third party not named could at its own initiative join in the offer. Any dispute as to respective shares of payment of economic loss would be decided in a separate proceeding to determine degrees of relative fault. It is unlikely that such proceedings would occur often. Typically the parties joined in the settlement offer will have some continuing relationship—manufacturer and retailer, doctor and hospital—that would provide an incentive to agree beforehand on such divisions and resolve any disputes expeditiously. In any case, the injured victim would receive fair and prompt compensation in exchange for giving up the right to sue the alleged culprits.

Trial lawyers and others purporting to speak for consumers may criticize the proposal, because it removes the deterrent effect of findings of fault and damages for pain and suffering. But criminologists have long maintained that to be an effective deterrent, sanctions must be certain and swift—two things tort law is clearly not. The current system often imposes liability arbitrarily and capriciously, and even when it imposes liability rightly, a long period of delay comes between the wrongful act and any sanction. Moreover, under neo-no-fault a defendant can foreclose a tort claim only by paying the victim's losses in perpetuity—an undertaking sobering enough in itself that the deterrent effect of the current tort system should be substantially preserved.

A more valid criticism of neo-no-fault is that its arguably one-sided settlement rules, though helping most defendants and injury victims, harm (or at least fail to help) two classes of victim: those who wish to settle for economic loss but are forced into litigation because no offer is forthcoming and those who wish to attempt recovery of noneconomic damages but are foreclosed from doing so. Some victims would either not be offered the advantages of the new system or would wish to reject them, and concern for the rights of these victims is not misplaced, even though it may be impossible to redesign the system's main features to their benefit without provoking an unmanageable number of new claims.

The problem of the victim who wishes to settle quickly but is not offered payment of economic loss could be alleviated by adding a provision allowing the claimant to require a speedy arbitration on the issue of fault, with payment then limited to net economic loss if fault is found. This amendment would give the claimant a backup means of trying to procure fair compensation without subjecting potential defendants to an unmanageable number of new claims or disturbing the balance achieved by the overall plan.

It would be possible to take this revision a step further by subjecting a defendant to sanctions (such as paying the claimant's legal fees) if he or she refused a claimant's offer to settle for economic losses and then lost in court. But this added step would undermine the balance of the proposal. Settling for economic losses is only marginally better than outright loss to the defendant in many cases, as when liability is very doubtful and nearly all the damage takes the form of economic losses. The decision to hold out for vindication at trial is not so clearly mistaken as to warrant the threat of later sanctions. Indeed, it is often to society's benefit that the defendant reject the offer in some instances, such as frivolous claims.

More complicated is the problem of the victim who is offered a settlement but for some reason—the relative insignificance of his economic losses, for example, or the hope of striking it rich—prefers to enter the litigation lottery. The first alternative would be to allow the claimant to reject the offer of payment for net economic losses but impose a cap on the amount of noneconomic damages he could then recover at trial. Insurers, of course, have traditionally urged across-the-board caps on noneconomic damages. But this proposal would be fairer in a crucial respect. The effect of across-the-board caps is sometimes to diminish the settlement prospects of a claimant who would be happy to accept an offer of economic losses. The cap limits his recovery and gives him nothing in return. The modified cap described here, by contrast, would affect only claimants who had been given an opportunity to recoup their economic losses.

This proposal lessens the problems associated with caps, but it does not do away with them. There would still be the danger that a severely injured victim with massive noneconomic injuries would be treated less fairly than at present. Consumer groups could thus be expected to oppose the idea vigorously.

What other ways might be found to accommodate claimants who prefer to litigate, without abandoning the basic structure of the early-offers approach? The answers all would involve placing further limits on claimants who had spurned the offer of periodic payment of net economic loss. There are several possible approaches. First, the standard of proof could be made more stringent than the usual civil standard of preponderance of the evidence. Although it is doubtful whether variations in the formal standard of proof make much difference to a jury,[6] such a change would give the trial and appellate courts a useful mechanism to control the litigation by directing or reversing verdicts. Second, the defendant could be specifically authorized to pay for the services of a second lawyer for the purpose of giving the plaintiff a second opinion on whether to turn down an early offer. The second lawyer could not have a financial interest in either side of the case. (This provision could be made even more stringent and provide that no claimant rejecting an early offer could bring a tort action at all until he had received a second opinion advising suit from a lawyer with no financial interest in the case.[7]) Third, the claimant could recover noneconomic damages only if those damages were established to be substantial enough to justify his rejection of the defendant's offer. The formula used to define "substantial" might specify, for example, that a claimant could collect noneconomic damages only if they were at least four times greater than his net economic loss. A risk of this approach, admittedly, is that juries would have an incentive to inflate their awards for noneconomic loss in order to hit the target. Fourth, if the claimant does not recover in the subsequent litigation more than the net-economic-loss sum offered by the defendant (or perhaps some higher threshold, such as the four-times-economic-loss multiple above), the claimant must pay the defendant's costs, including legal fees, incurred after rejection of the settlement, with claimant's counsel jointly and severally liable for this obligation.

In contrast to other proposals for tort reform, the early-offers approach achieves a proper balance by demanding that the defendant give something in exchange for the stronger shield against liability it receives and as a corollary that the claimant receive something in exchange for giving up the opportunity to pursue litigation. Victims who do not receive an offer of settlement that society considers adequate maintain their tort rights intact. Only victims who reject reasonably generous offers are subject to restrictions on the amount or manner of recovery.

Conclusion

The tort system as it operates today is one of "shin-kicking litigation." It vents anger, but it fails badly to further the best interests of claimants, defendants, or society as a whole.[8] Just as at the turn of the century the rancor of workplace litigation gave way to a more rational system, so today's fault-based tort system, with its fortuities, high transaction costs, and long delays, should give way to a system of prompt compensation for actual losses.

Notes

1. U. S. Department of Transportation, "Compensating Auto Accident Victims: A Follow-Up Report on No-Fault Auto Insurance Experiences" (1983), 37.

2. Ibid., 25–40.

3. See Jeffrey O'Connell, "Offers That Can't Be Refused: Foreclosure of Personal Injury Claims by Defendant's Prompt Tender of Claimant's Net Economic Losses," *Northwestern University Law Review* 77 (1982): 589–632.

4. Personal communication to author.

5. O'Connell, "A Proposal to Abolish Defendants' Payment for Pain and Suffering in Return for Payment of Claimant's Attorneys' Fees," *University of Illinois Law Review* (1981), 333, 351.

6. O'Connell, "Jury Trials in Civil Cases?," *Illinois Bar Journal* 58 (1970): 796, 807–8.

7. O'Connell, "A 'Neo-No-Fault' Contract in Lieu of Tort," *California Law Review* 73 (1985): 898,909–10.

8. "War Aftermath: $13.5 Million Award," *New York Times*, 31 Aug. 1982.

Understanding the Liability Crisis

Between late 1984 and early 1986, reports began to accumulate of remarkable developments in the world of business insurance. Some insurance customers suffered extraordinary increases in the price of liability coverage, increases of 60, 100, and even 1,500 percent. Other customers, including some day-care centers, town governments, and nurse-midwives, could not obtain coverage at any price. Where coverage remained available, insurers drastically reduced the scope of protection they offered by revising policy terms in various ways: cutting aggregate policy limits, raising deductibles and coinsurance factors, and excluding certain activities and risks from coverage altogether.

The drying up of insurance led, in turn, to drastic responses from manufacturers and service providers. Many passed along premiums to their customers in the form of higher prices. Others, especially those denied insurance coverage, were forced to curtail operations. Corporations withdrew products from the market. Cities and local authorities removed slides and swing sets from public parks and diving boards from public pools. Some even closed jails and suspended police patrols until they could arrange mutual insurance programs with other municipal authorities.

These events were widely labeled a "crisis," a term too often used to mark no more than an undesired disruption of the status quo. Here, many who invoked the crisis label failed to inquire whether the underlying trend at work (as opposed to the momentary disruptions) was beneficial or harmful. Virtually everyone conceded that the insurance changes had something to do with the steady expansion of tort liability for corporate and institutional defendants. But although generous and widely available tort compensation taxes business assets, it also increases the often depleted resources of injured plaintiffs. Increased liability may drive some products and services off the market, but all advanced societies will want to constrain the sale of risky products. Without a closer analysis, it is hard to know whether or not the extension of corporate liability has been excessive.

The crisis is indisputably genuine, however, in one central respect. Whatever the benefits or losses from business-cost increases and product withdrawals, the disappearance of insurance itself has surely harmed the country. All humane societies want to encourage the availability of insurance, especially against bodily injury. But between 1984 and 1986, the insurance capacity available to United States citizens for many types of injuries shrank dramatically. This shrinkage is obvious in the areas where coverage was refused altogether, like day care, and where specific kinds of losses, like pollution damage, were excluded from coverage. But the other changes in insurance coverage also reduce the total amount of money available for compensating injured persons. When deductibles and coinsurance factors are increased and aggregate coverage reduced, the insured customer — and, in many cases, its potential victims — will bear more of the risk of future losses. The same is true when insurers shift toward "claims-made" policies, which cut off coverage of losses that occur while a policy is in effect but do not become manifest until after it has expired. The claims-made policy shifts the risk of latent injury or disease to the insured customer and its victims.

Many commentators blamed the disruptions, at least in part, on factors specific to the insurance business. Some, chiefly consumer advocates and critics of the insurance industry, accused insurers of fixing prices or manipulating the market in order to persuade legislatures to limit tort liability. Indeed, several state attorneys general have filed antitrust actions against insurers on these grounds. Sudden premium increases are at least consistent with a price-fixing theory. But collusion cannot explain why insurers refused to offer some customers coverage at any price, however high. It is difficult to maximize profits by refusing to sell a product. Nor could collusion explain why insurers altered their basic policy provisions so drastically, since a cartel can better maximize profits by raising prices than by changing the characteristics of the product it sells. Finally, it would be odd for an insurance cartel to focus on a line like commercial liability coverage, where rates and policy terms are usually set on a customer-by-customer basis and where it would therefore be hardest for members to police a collusive agreement. By contrast, no disruptions were reported in lines like fire and life insurance, where, because coverage is more standardized, collusion would be substantially easier.

Other commentators blamed the crisis on the insurance cycle. Because insurers must invest the premiums they collect for long periods before the time comes to pay claims, insurance prices in competitive markets vary inversely with interest rates. When interest rates drop, as they did in the mid-1980s following the decline of inflation, the cost of covering a given future payout goes up. But this insurance cycle, though undeniably a factor contributing to the crisis, is not an entirely satisfactory explanation either. The actual rise in insurance premiums was far out of proportion to the magnitude of the decline in interest rates. Moreover, the insurance cycle cannot explain why insurers changed the terms of policies, why they withdrew coverage completely in some lines instead of simply raising premiums, or why the crisis did not affect other insurance lines, such as automobile, health, and life, that are subject to the same investment cycle effect.

Still other commentators blamed the crisis on noninsurance sources: most important, the expansion of legal liability. No one really doubts that corporate tort liability has expanded since the mid-1960s or that the substantial increases in claims, trials, and damage judgments have necessarily affected insurance premiums. The expansion of liability—with the crisis—has also extended to liability defendants that self-insure or could easily do so. For example, many municipalities (like New York City) reported their claims and payouts rising just as sharply as had the insurers' over the same period. In addition, of the country's 500 largest public companies—those whose size and capacity to self-insure make them least vulnerable to the vagaries of the commercial insurance market—25 percent reportedly removed products from markets for liability reasons.

But there is trouble with the tort-law explanation as well. The rise in insurance costs, especially when policy terms are taken into account, clearly outpaced recent increases in claims and judgments, just as it far outpaced interest-rate changes. Furthermore, it is not immediately obvious why an expansion of tort liability would lead to disruptions in insurance availability, as opposed to simple increases in price. The spread of liability certainly stimulates the demand for insurance coverage, but there is no obvious reason why supply could not keep up with demand, since capital can move quickly into the insurance business. The expansion of tort law nonetheless lies at the origin of the crisis. But, as will become apparent, what has devastated commercial insurance markets is not simply the increase in tort claims but one particular aspect of that increase.

The Empirical Background

Hard evidence on overall changes in tort claims, trials, and judgments is surprisingly meager. A survey of twenty states by the National Center for State Courts found only modest changes in tort actions: an increase of 14 percent from 1978 to 1981 and an actual decrease of 4 percent from 1981 to 1984. But these data are so highly aggregated that they are of little help. Tort litigation in these courts is dominated by automobile-collision cases (which in Cook County, Illinois, for example, make up 55 percent of all jury trials). There has been no crisis whatsoever in this part of the insurance market.

Some figures are available on the specific kinds of litigation most commonly linked to the crises. Table 1 shows that products-liability claims in the federal courts rose 761 percent between 1974 and 1986. Though dramatic, this figure cannot completely explain the insurance phenomenon. Filings increased substantially in 1984 (17 percent) and 1985 (26 percent), but those increases followed years of modest increases (3 percent in 1983) and even decline (a drop of 1 percent in 1982). The reported premium increase for some buyers in 1986 alone ran far ahead of the combined 761 percent increase for the entire twelve-year period.

More liability suits are filed in state courts than in federal courts, but overall state-court data are even sparser. Detailed figures are available for the courts in two large urban counties, Cook County (Chicago), Illinois, and San Francisco County, California. Table 2 shows trends in products-liability and medical-malpractice awards in those two jurisdictions since 1960. Average products-liability judgments rose dramatically between 1970 and 1975 and again between 1980 and 1985 in Cook County; in San Francisco County, sharp rises occurred in the late

TABLE 1

Federal Products-Liability Cases Filed, 1974–86

	Cases Filed	Percent Increase from Previous Year	Cumulative Percent Increase
1974	1,579		1974–79: 288
1975	2,886	83	1980–85: 75
1976	3,696	28	1974–86: 761
1977	4,077	10	
1978	4,372	7	
1979	6,132	40	
1980	7,755	26	
1981	9,071	17	
1982	8,944	– 1	
1983	9,221	3	
1984	10,745	17	
1985	13,554	26	
1986	13,595	0.3	

Source: Administrative Office of the United States Courts.
Note: 1974 was the first year that products-liability filings were reported separately.

TABLE 2

Average and Median Jury Awards, Cook County, Illinois, and San Francisco County, California, 1960–84 (in thousands of 1984 dollars)

	Products Liability			
	Cook County		San Francisco County	
	Average	Median	Average	Median
1960–64	265	103	99	27
1965–69	287	118	194	72
1970–74	578	178	145	51
1975–79	597	196	308	81
1980–84	828	187	1,105	200
	Malpractice			
	Cook County		San Francisco County	
	Average	Median	Average	Median
1960–64	52	35	125	64
1965–69	83	48	306	157
1970–74	605	127	449	124
1975–79	324	141	644	99
1980–84	1,179	121	1,162	156

Source: Mark Peterson, Civil Juries in the 1980s (Rand Corporation, Institute for Civil Justice, R-3466-ICJ [1987]), 22.

1960s and the late 1970s, followed by a massive rise between 1980 and 1985. The pattern for medical malpractice was roughly similar. For both categories of cases and in both jurisdictions, the increases between 1980 and 1985 are particularly striking. Of course, an increase in the size of the average judgment compounds the effect of an increase in the number of suits filed.

This compounding effect—more lawsuits and more money paid on the average plaintiff verdict—goes some distance toward explaining the source of the insurance difficulties. But it leaves an important question unanswered. Do the increases in tort claims and judgments over the past decade arise from an upward trend in the underlying rate of accidents or injuries? Or are the courts changing the way they treat accidents that happened all along?

Accident-rate data are thin, like data on verdicts, but highly suggestive. Virtually all accident data show that accident rates have been consistently declining over time. Table 3, for example, shows that for almost all accident categories, death rates have been decreasing progressively, though not sharply, since 1950. The death rate from medical procedures jumped noticeably in the late 1960s but has declined steadily since then. Although none of the categories corresponds exactly to product-related accidents, the only increases appear assorted and mostly transitory in the poisoning categories, the miscellaneous "all other" category, and the "motor vehicle" category. None of these increases is substantial enough to have generated the increases in claims volume observed in the federal-court data. (Although the data end in 1980, they roughly reflect the sources of lawsuits tried in the mid-1980s, since the average time from accident to trial is three to six years.)

Many liability suits arise from injuries on the job. In 1985 worker injuries accounted for 60 percent of products-liability claims where large sums were paid. Injured workers are usually barred by workers' compensation laws from suing their own employers. Instead, they frequently sue outside companies that conduct operations on the job site or manufacture or supply products involved in the injury. Table 4, however, shows that the work-related death rate has been declining steadily since the end of World War II. The rate of disabling injuries has fluctuated mildly since 1965, although it began to decline steadily after 1979. These data in no way support the notion that a rise in the underlying accident rate might account for the rise in tort claims and judgments.

The Consumer Product Safety Commission (CPSC) collects data on the annual number of consumer product-related injuries that require hospital emergency-room treatment. These data are problematic. First, they are vastly overinclusive for present purposes: only a small fraction of the product-related injuries they report might give rise to litigation. According to the CPSC reports for 1980, for example, the products most frequently linked to injuries are stairs (662,000 injuries), followed by bicycles (526,000) and baseball equipment (432,000). Even beds "cause" more injuries annually than any of the product categories reported in table 5, which shows trends in product injuries that are among the most likely to be the consequence of defective design or manufacture. Even changes in raw accident numbers, however, do not imply that products are getting more or less hazardous, since the raw injury number is not adjusted to reflect the numbers of a product in use, the numbers of people using it, or the intensity with which it is used.

Table 5 shows that for most reported products the number of injuries has grown steadily but not spectacularly since 1974, as one would expect in a growing

TABLE 3

Death Rates by Accident Type, 1950–80 (per 100,000 resident population)

	1950	1955	1960	1965	1970	1975	1980
Motor vehicle accidents	23.1	23.4	21.3	25.4	26.9	21.3	23.5
Railway accidents	1.4	.8	.6	.5	.4	.3	.3
Fires and flames	4.3	3.9	4.3	3.8	3.3	2.8	2.6
Firearms	1.4	1.3	1.3	1.2	1.2	1.1	.9
Explosive materials	. . .	. . .	. . .	. . .	.3	.2	.1
Hot substances, corrosive liquids	.6	.5	.2	.2	.1	.1	.1
Poisoning, drugs and medicines	NA	NA	NA	NA	1.2	1.5	1.1
Poisoning, gases	1.2	.7	.7	.8	.8	.7	.5
Poisoning, other substances	1.1	.9	.9	1.1	.6	.7	.3
Medical procedures	.4	.5	.6	.8	1.8	1.5	1.1
Falls	13.8	12.3	10.6	10.3	8.3	6.9	5.9
Drowning	3.2	3.1	2.9	2.8	3.1	3.1	2.7
All other accidents	4.1	3.6	5.2	3.7	4.7	4.1	4.4
Total accidents	60.6	56.9	52.3	55.7	56.4	47.8	46.7

Source: *U.S. Statistical Abstract*, 61, 78.
Note: Excludes Alaska and Hawaii before 1960.

TABLE 4

Work-Related Death and Disability Rates, 1945–83 (per 100,000 workers)

Year	Deaths	Disabling Injuries
1945	33	2,000
1950	27	1,950
1955	24	1,950
1960	21	1,950
1965	20	2,100
1970	18	2,200
1973	17	2,500
1974	16	2,300
1975	15	2,200
1976	14	2,200
1977	14	2,300
1978	14	2,200
1979	13	2,300
1980	13	2,200
1981	12	2,100
1982	12	1,900
1983	11	1,900

Source: *U.S. Statistical Abstract*, 425.

economy. Moreover, it is worth repeating that the volume of litigation will differ vastly from the volume of product-related injuries, because many injuries do not give rise to arguable claims of recovery, and because only 4 to 5 percent of all claims ever reach trial and judgment.

In 1981 the CPSC adopted a different and more precise system of product classification. Table 6 again displays some product categories heavily involved in re-

TABLE 5

U.S. Product-Related Injuries, 1974–81 (thousands)

Product	1974	1975	1976	1977	1978	1979	1980	1981
Playground equipment	140	143	158	164	151	165	162	178
Ladders	61	73	81	85	83	98	89	98
Power lawn mowers	56	63	57	61	69	74	63	71
Swimming pools	53	56	69	68	68	89	116	124
Power saws	41	58	59	60	68	71	73	79
Cleaning agents	35	36	40	35	40	38	32	38
Electric fixtures	25	22	26	28	26	34	32	41
Chain saws	23	27	28	35	48	51	62	64
Space heaters	20	7[a]	8	10	10	16	23	25
Electric power tools	13	13	16	16	14	22	25	28
Tractors	6	7	7	10	9	10	13	13

Source: *Annual Reports, Consumer Product Safety Commission.*
Note: 1981 figures for calendar year; all other years' figures for the fiscal year ending 30 Sept. After 1981, the CPSC adopted new reporting methods discontinuous with the reported 1974–81 data. Injuries defined as "injuries requiring [hospital] emergency room treatment."
[a] CPSC differentiated its previous heater category into three separate categories.

TABLE 6

Injuries by Specific Product, 1981–86 (thousands)

Product	1981	1982	1983	1984	1985	1986
Power saws	75	73	71	70	61	62
Chain saws	64	69	58	64	56	41
Power grinders	9	11	11	11	11	10
Swings	72	84	78	84	85	79
Monkey bars	42	48	46	57	56	55
Playground slides	33	36	40	40	40	42
Diving boards	12	15	17	15	11	10
Stepladders	10	11	10	10	10	12
Extension ladders	2	1	1	3	2	2
Rotary mowers	4	3	6	10	8	8
Home acids	4	2	3	5	3	4
Above-ground pools	2	*	2	2	3	*

Source: *Product Summary Reports*, National Electronic Injury Surveillance System, Consumer Product Safety Commission.
Note: Power saws include circular, bench, band, and radial arm saws. Only chain saws correspond to a category in table 5. Injuries defined as "requiring [hospital] emergency room treatment." All data for calendar years.
* Too insignificant to report.

cent liability litigation. These figures provide a closer look at the extent to which the steep rise in products-liability litigation can be attributed to an increase in the volume of injuries.

The injury trends in table 6 will not be reflected in trial data for the same years, because of the lag between injury and trial, but they presumably indicate safety trends that extend over longer periods, and they would also reveal any sudden rash of accidents that might have caused insurers to panic in 1985-86. The figures show that power-saw injuries have declined steadily since 1981, and chain-saw injuries began a steep decline in 1985. Most of the categories of tools and home equipment have shown no clear trend, except for rotary mowers, where injuries have increased.

Table 6, however, shows no great increases in injury volume in the years 1984-86 that might have generated the extraordinary insurer reactions. Indeed, for ten of the twelve reported products, the number of injuries declined or remained constant from 1984 to 1985, and the increases for the other two products were trivial (swings and above-ground pools, both up 1,000 injuries).

The most striking trend is in the categories of playground and pool equipment. Recall that in 1986 many municipalities and park services were forced to remove playground equipment from public parks for liability reasons. What is the source of the insurance-claims pressure? Although for all of the products, the number of injuries rose modestly until 1983 or 1984, injury volume from 1984 to 1985 was virtually unchanged. Similarly, in 1986 some cities were compelled to remove diving boards from public pools, though the number of diving-board injuries had declined sharply since 1983. (Of course, after 1986 we should expect further reductions in injury volume, because the liability crisis had forced product removal.)

In short, the data on deaths and injuries cast great doubt on the proposition that the liability crisis derives from an increase in the underlying accident rate. There is simply no evidence of a general increase in accidents. Of course, in recent years some individual products have been discovered to be injurious, such as the Dalkon Shield. But claims against products of this nature have not dominated recent tort litigation. A good deal of modern litigation derives from newly discovered toxic and environmental hazards. But even this litigation cannot account for the widespread extent of the liability crisis. There have been no discoveries of previously unknown toxic damage from diving boards or playground equipment.

The Courts' Changing Objectives

If the litigation increase does not derive from a rise in the underlying accident rate, it must derive from the increasing application of tort liability in situations where liability had not applied in the past. Here the evidence is quite strong. Since the mid-1960s, courts have steadily expanded corporate, institutional, and professional tort liability. They have done so on two grounds: to give producers incentives to reduce the accident rate and to provide a form of compensation insurance for the victims of accidents that occur nonetheless, funded through a premium that in effect is added to the price of the product or service.

The "deterrence," or accident-reduction, objective is an important one and will be discussed later. There is no doubt, however, that the "compensation," or risk-spreading, objective has played a crucial role in shaping courts' actions. Courts have justified the use of liability as a surrogate form of social insurance on two insurance grounds. First, corporate defendants are said to have an advantage over consumers in the costs of obtaining insurance, since they can buy a single policy that covers all of their consumers. Second, consumers are said to buy or otherwise procure less "first-party" health and disabililty insurance than they really need, either because they are careless of their future interests or because they are too poor to afford coverage. Society can furnish them with more protection by providing "third-party" liability insurance through the sale of products and services.

The first adoption of strict products liability, in California in the 1963 case of *Greenman v. Yuba Power Products, Inc.*, was justified on exactly these insurance grounds. Since then, *Greenman* has been followed by all other states. More recently, courts have invoked the insurance rationale to justify limiting the defenses of contributory negligence, assumption of risk, and consumer misuse of products; to eliminate, in actions against landowners, the defense that the victim was a trespasser; and to restrict the application of statutes of limitation. Again, on insurance grounds, courts have extended liability affirmatively through standards of retrospective liability and the concept of products that inherently pose an unreasonable danger. They have relaxed the traditional requirement that the defendant's conduct be clearly shown to have been the cause of the plaintiff's injury, again to achieve risk-spreading objectives. In addition, they have adopted the maximization of coverage as the principal interpretive standard in construing insurance policies in all contexts, reading coverage provisions as broadly and exclusions as narrowly as possible, in order to extend the scope of compensation.

The extension of liability to achieve insurance ends, then, is the most likely explanation for the tremendous growth in tort litigation. But a perplexing question remains. Why does the extension of tort law lead to a withdrawal of commercial insurance capacity, rather than to its extension? A rise in liability exposure should generally increase the demand for liability-insurance coverage from potential corporate defendants. Even large and wealthy corporations buy liability insurance on the market rather than set aside reserves, whether because it is costly to sell assets to satisfy large judgments or because insurers can provide specialized claims-adjustment and risk-monitoring services. For either reason, the expansion of tort liability should increase the corporate demand for liability insurance. Why has the commercial liability-insurance market broken down?

As described earlier, courts justified the expansion of liability to provide victim insurance on two grounds: corporations can obtain insurance more cheaply than victims; and tort law can provide compensation insurance to individuals — chiefly the poor — who may not purchase first-party injury insurance themselves. Certainly, if tort-law insurance is cheaper than victim first-party insurance, the breakdown becomes even more puzzling. But perhaps the breakdown occurred because of the extension of insurance to the poor and uninsured? Perhaps this extension excessively taxes the insurance capacity of the society?

To investigate the insurance-capacity hypothesis, one must carefully enumerate individuals who do and do not have access to insurance sources other than tort law. To the extent that injury victims already possess first-party coverage, the extension of tort-law insurance might do no more than change the name of the insurance company that signs the benefits checks. Before the expansion of tort liability, such individuals would recover from their own insurer; after the expansion they are paid by, say, a hospital's or a manufacturer's insurer. Such a change would represent no apparent increase in society's insurance burden.

When one takes into account both governmental and private insurance, however, it appears that very few in our society must rely on tort law for compensation. The large majority of citizens are protected by private first-party health and disability insurance, including employer-provided Blue Cross/Blue Shield and workers' compensation. Government sources, such as Medicare, Medicaid, veterans' benefits, and "disability" coverage through various income-maintenance programs, fill in most (though not all) remaining gaps. Some small levels of health care are added by public general assistance and private philanthropy, though the extent of this assistance is not well known.

How numerous are the remaining individuals who lack health or disability coverage of any sort? Official reports tend to count, for this purpose, these whose incomes or assets place them above the qualifying level for government coverage but who decline to purchase private coverage. But in fact the number who can rely only on tort law for medical care or income maintenance is a subset of this uninsured group. For example, many persons fail to qualify for government health assistance while healthy and employed but would qualify if, through injury or illness, their employment were to cease. Such individuals are only technically uninsured; if struck by a seriously disabling accident, they will in fact receive government assistance. Indeed, it is an entirely rational choice for people in this position not to buy private first-party insurance.

Several recent studies have attempted to calculate precisely the number of Americans who lack first-party health and disability coverage. A report by the National Center for Health Statistics in September 1987, for example, shows that 87 percent of the population have access to private health insurance, Medicare, public assistance (including Medicaid for low-income people), or veterans' medical care. This percentage is surely an underestimate, however, since the study inquired only whether low-income respondents were currently receiving Medicaid benefits, not whether they would qualify if they fell sick or were injured.

Two recent "victimization" studies provide a better picture of the true extent of coverage. They begin with samples of individuals known to have been sick or injured and then track what their sources of compensation were, if any. The studies suggest that almost everyone in the United States enjoys some degree of basic protection against health and medical expenses.

The first study, a 1982 telephone survey, found that in only 1.5 percent of families had any member been denied health care for financial reasons. Since the study surveyed familes, the actual percentage of individuals denied care is lower. The second study, by the Rand Corporation, was of victims injured in traffic accidents. The automobile victimization study is important for two reasons. First, it has long been thought that large numbers of automobile victims remain uncompensated, because the United States relies principally on tort liability in place of "no-fault" recovery systems like those found in New Zealand or Sweden. Observers have noted that many traffic injuries do not lead to tort claims and that even plaintiffs who file claims prevail (for very different reasons) no more than half of the time;

they have concluded that many victims go uncompensated. Second, automobile liability is one of the few areas of modern tort law where courts have not expanded liability on insurance grounds. Perhaps because of the infrequency of corporate defendants, negligence has remained the standard, and there have been no great changes over time in litigation volume or magnitude.

The Rand study found that, depending on the state, from 78 to 87 percent of traffic victims who suffered medical losses received compensation from tort, private insurance, or government sources. Moreover, of the fraction that did not receive compensation, most could have filed compensation claims but chose not to, because the amounts at issue were so small (the median loss for this group was $60). The study confirmed that the number of individuals denied basic health care in the United States is very small.

Disability coverage is thought to be less comprehensive than medical coverage in this country. Workers' compensation statutes ensure that virtually all workers are covered for wage losses arising from on-the-job injuries. Moreover, government income-maintenance and other assistance programs like food stamps in effect provide disability coverage for those injury victims whose loss of wages drops them into the eligible category. Again, as with health insurance, it can be a rational choice for a less affluent person not to buy disability insurance under these circumstances.

The most detailed figures on how often wage losses go uncompensated again derive from the Rand Corporation study of traffic injuries. The study found that of road-accident victims who suffered wage losses, from 63 to 76 percent received compensation. These numbers, as one might expect, are lower than the numbers of those who received compensation for medical bills (78 to 87 percent). But the study did not include as "disability" coverage the general government assistance that is made available to many of those who suffer disabling accidents. Nor did the Rand study indicate how many individuals filed no claims for lost wages, because the amount at issue was very small; in the case of medical bills, it will be recalled, almost all those who went uncompensated failed to file for this reason.

Although the figures are not as precise as one would wish, these two studies suggest that the vast majority of the American population possesses some form of basic health and disability insurance, either through direct or individual work-related coverage or through government plans. The number that fails to receive compensation of any sort, though not known precisely, is probably quite small. A 1984 Senate subcommittee staff report explained that those who neither possess health and disability insurance nor qualify for government assistance are most often occasional workers, transients, and the homeless. These, then, are the principal groups to whom tort law provides compensation insurance for the first time.

Have we discovered the source of the liability crisis? No serious commentator could argue that the liability crisis has been caused by the tort recoveries of these groups. Occasional workers, transients, and the homeless are less likely to use the products and services that cause injury. If injured, they are less likely to sue. And if they sue, they are less likely to recover large judgments, because their expected future income is low. The recent increase in multimillion-dollar judgments does not represent recoveries of transients and the homeless.

The Problem of Adverse Selection

If the source of the crisis is neither an increase in the underlying accident rate nor the extension of tort law insurance to large numbers who previously went uncompensated, what can be left? The studies cited above suggest that the principal insurance effect of the expansion of tort liability has been to shift compensation from a first-party mechanism to a third-party mechanism. Injured individuals who earlier could have recovered from their own or their workplace insurance sources are now recovering from someone else's insurer through a tort judgment.

And here lies the real source of the liability crisis. Tort-law third-party insurance differs systematically from first-party insurance in ways that work to undermine insurance markets. Third-party insurance is much more costly to administer; it provides far more and different coverage than consumers would choose to buy voluntarily; and, perhaps most important, it disrupts efforts to distinguish highrisk from low-risk customers, a distinction that makes the business of insurance possible.

The first point is probably the most widely recognized. Despite the belief that third-party tort-law insurance is more efficient than first-party coverage, because it is purchased in larger packets, experience has shown its administrative costs to be much more substantial — by a magnitude estimated at 2.75 to 5.75 times. Much of this difference derives from litigation costs, but even out-of-court settlement costs in third-party contexts are higher because of the presence of the liability issue.

Second, tort-law insurance provides much more coverage than first-party insurance — 2.34 times as much, on average, for the identical injury. Some will automatically assume that providing additional coverage is beneficial for consumers: after all, it means that they will get more money if they are injured. But this view mistakes the consumer interest in insurance. Of course, after an injury has occurred, any victim prefers a greater to a lesser award. Before an injury, however, the interest of a potential victim is in buying the right amount of insurance, neither more nor less. In the case of the tort-law insurance, insurance premiums must be reflected in the price of products and services, so that potential victims collectively pay for their insurance in advance. Compelling the purchase of tortlaw insurance is the equivalent of compelling each owner of a $100,000 house to buy $234,000 worth of insurance on it. Those whose houses in fact burn down would retrospectively profit from the imposition. But homeowners as a class would clearly lose: for almost any rational consumer, the slim prospect of a future cash windfall (over and above the cost of rebuilding the house in its entirety and paying for temporary lodgings) would be far outweighed by the loss of real cash because of the necessarily higher insurance premiums.

Tort-law insurance is excessive in precisely this way. On average, 47 percent of tort law damages represent nonpecuniary pain and suffering. No conceivable group of consumers would want to buy insurance coverage of this sort to this extent. For good reason, consumers tend to buy insurance not against tragedy in general but against tragedy that depletes their level of wealth. The reason is not that they are indifferent to nonpecuniary tragedy, but that the function of insurance is to regularize their wealth level, or, in more technical terms, to equalize the marginal value of wealth to them over varying states of the world. Parents seldom buy life insurance for their children, for example, not because they would not suffer a terrible loss if a child were to die, but because it makes little sense to sacrifice financially by paying insurance premiums while the child is alive in order to increase the family income after the child dies. Insurance for true pain and suffering makes just as little sense.

Tort awards are higher than first-party insurance benefits for several other reasons as well. Tort judgments never incorporate the deductibles and coinsurance that typify first-party insurance arrangements, under which victims bear a share of costs. Again, the automatic reaction is to assume that consumers are better off because they get more money, but again the automatic reaction is wrong. At proper levels, deductibles and coinsurance terms are actually advantageous to consumers; by giving claimants incentives to control their own contributions to risk and restrain their claim-filing activity, they reduce ultimate insurance premiums.

The analysis changes only slightly when the injury victim has never previously dealt with the tort defendant, as when a woman standing on her front lawn is injured by flying gravel from a truck on the road or a defectively designed lawn mower in a neighbor's yard. In this case the victim has not paid a direct tort insurance "premium" in product prices to cover this particular injury. But in a broader sense, all members of society are at once product and service purchasers and potential bystander victims of accidents related to products and services used by others. Solely in insurance terms, leaving aside the law's influence on the accident rate itself, all citizens share a very similar interest in a national level of insurance coverage that corresponds to the amount of coverage potential victims would choose to purchase beforehand.

The third disadvantage of using tort law as insurance may be the most important of all. The third-party tort-law insurance system is set up in a manner that makes it extremely difficult for insurers to segregate high-risk buyers of coverage from low-risk buyers. To remain in business, insurers must control adverse selection, the process where low-risk members of an insurance pool drop out because the premium is greater than the risk they bring to the pool. The business of underwriting consists of identifying separate classes of risk and setting premiums for each narrowly defined category according to the average level of risk it brings to the pool. The wider the range between high- and low-risk members in an undifferentiated pool, the greater the difference between the premium and the risks they add and the more likely it is that low-risk members will drop out of the pool and fall back on alternative means of protection.

In the sale of first-party insurance, the insurer can obtain and put to use a good deal of information about the customer. In automobile insurance, for example, the underwriter can divide applicants into groups based on age, expected mileage driven in the coming year, whether the car is used for commuting, accident experience, record of moving violations, and so forth. Together, such classifications can reveal that one driver's contribution to the risk pool is substantially higher than another's, allowing the insurer to target a discount for the safer risks to discourage that person from leaving the pool.

Now suppose that the tort system expands and that the makers of automobiles are made to pay more of the costs of traffic accidents. Automobile manufacturers, of course, must pass these greater insurance costs to customers in the price of the automobile. But a manufacturer, unlike an insurer, can implement none of the risk distinctions among drivers. A manufacturer cannot adjust the price of the car after asking how intensely the buyer plans to use it, how many accidents or moving violations the buyer has had in the past, or how old the driver is. It may be possible to implement a few crude distinctions based on model type; sports-car buyers may submit more crash claims than owners of station wagons. But otherwise, the automaker must provide insurance at the same price to all who buy its product. As a consequence, the variance of risks within tort-law "insurance" pools is likely to be much greater than that within ordinary pools. It follows that there will be more pressure for low-risk members to drop out of third-party pools, leaving higher-risk members behind.

A different kind of adverse selection operates within provider risk pools. If insurers cannot distinguish manufacturers or, say, physicians likely to be sued from those less likely, the better risks will tend to withdraw from the pool. It is not surprising that in recent years there has occurred an extraordinary expansion of self-insurance, "captive" insurance arrangements, or professional mutual-insurance arrangements, such as those adopted by many physicians within particular medical specialties.

This accelerating process of adverse selection, at its worst, leads ultimately to the total unraveling of a risk pool. In other words, the risks become uninsurable. In milder cases, it means that the price premium needed to provide tort-based insurance ends up higher than the original level of accidents and injuries would have suggested. Of course, since tort-law benefits are two and a third times higher than first-party benefits for the same injury, the premiums will be set higher still.

Here, many central puzzles of the liability crisis are resolved. Why did so many companies — 25 percent of the 500 largest in the United States — remove products or services from the market entirely, rather then just raise the price to incorporate a liability premium? Because of adverse selection: the risks associated with the product became uninsurable. As the insurance premium in the price of the product increased, low-risk marginal buyers dropped out of a consumer pool. This forced the premium even higher. At some point, there was no consumer group sufficiently large to support a pool — compelling withdrawal of the product.

The same process explains why insurers raised premiums in 1985 and 1986 by much more than the combination of greater claims, greater damages, and lower interest rates would suggest. Again, as lower-risk customers progressively dropped out of insurance pools, the average premium for the pool had to be increased.

Insurance premiums will rise proportionately to average claims increases only as long as the same set of insureds remains in the pool. The huge discrepancy between payout increases and premium increases can be explained only by adverse selection.

Other principal phenomena of the insurance crisis, in particular the changes in the terms of policies, represent insurers' efforts to control adverse selection and retain low-risk insureds. Raising deductibles and lowering aggregate policy limits culls out high-risk members and substitutes for increases in basic premiums that would tend to drive away low-risk members less likely to incur the deductible or exceed the policy limit. Similarly, the exclusion of coverage for such risks as toxic damages (in a municipal liability policy) and merger-related claims (in a directors' and officers' policy) may be aimed at averting the departure from the pool of cities never involved with toxic disposal and directors who do not expect to be involved in risky corporate deal-making.

Only when such policy amendments are unavailing must an insurer refuse to offer any coverage at all. The complete withdrawal of insurance companies from a line of insurance writing signifies that the expansion of tort liability in an area has raised the degree of risk variance in a pool above the sustainable level. An insurer's refusal to offer coverage is a confession that liability is so uncertain that it cannot identify any risk subgroups accurately enough to support a pool.

The collapse of insurance in this area is tragic because it is unnecessary. It is not an inevitable side effect of a rising accident rate or even of the humanitarian impulse to extend insurance protection to people who have lacked it in the past. It appears, instead, to be an artifact of the kind of insurance that society has chosen to provide. When judges enlisted the tort system as an additional source of insurance, they undermined rather than supplemented existing insurance markets. With the withdrawal of market insurance coverage, injured persons found fewer financial resources to draw against than before the expansion of tort law.

What is particularly tragic is that although the price hikes and the drying up of available coverage have harmed all consumers, the ones harmed most were exactly the less affluent consumers that courts had hoped most to aid, those who were thought to lack sufficient insurance. Any increase in the general price level not matched by an increase in wages will obviously impose the most hardship on those with low levels of wealth. More important, the rewards of expanded liability are distributed in a manner that is remarkably regressive in terms of income distribution. The tort "premium" in the price of a product must be set uniformly according to the average expected liability payout. But tort judgments vary greatly from claimant to claimant and tilt hugely in the direction of high-income claimants. The major components of tort damages are past and future lost income (obviously related to wealth), medical expenses (also typically wealth-related; the affluent person patronizes more expert doctors), and pain and suffering (highly correlated with lost income, since it is typically sustained job loss, rather than short though intense hospital expense, that signals disruption of the victim's life). With each damage element linked positively to income, a uniform premium will undercharge the rich and overcharge the poor for the given coverage. In effect, the system forces those with low incomes to subsidize the insurance costs of those with high incomes.

This regressive effect is glaringly inconsistent with the well-meaning objectives of the judiciary in expanding tort liability and indeed with any coherent and defensible social policy. It is the equivalent of charging all homeowners the same fire-insurance premium whether they live in a mansion or a cottage, or charging each worker the same premium for disability insurance while sending much bigger benefit checks to the highly paid than to their less affluent comrades. The judicial expansion of liability must be acknowledged as one of the great humanitarian expressions of our time. But it has drastically harmed its chief intended beneficiaries.

Conclusion

These disastrous effects of the expansion of tort liability could be reversed easily enough in principle, though it would take a good deal of judicial discipline. The key step would be to excise the insurance component of tort law and to abandon the effort to use it as a surrogate system of social compensation. Such a step, though drastic, would in no way involve the disappearance of tort law. Insurance provision is only one intended function of the modern tort law. The other major function is to influence the accident rate and establish optimal standards of care. This second function may be handled well or badly, but it plainly has enormous potential for good. By removing the compensation insurance component from tort law and concentrating attention on the goal of accident reduction, courts could at once remove the regressive liability tax from products and services and return stability to commercial insurance markets.

Index